THE ROUGH GUIDE TO

Anime

by

Simon Richmond

www.roughguides.com

Credits

The Rough Guide to Anime

Design: Link Hall
Layout: Sachin Tanwar, Matthew Milton
Picture research: Martin Richardson, Misa Imai, Matthew Milton
Proofreading: Jason Freeman
Production: Rebecca Short

Rough Guides Reference

Director: Andrew Lockett
Editors: Kate Berens, Peter Buckley, Tracy Hopkins, Matthew Milton, Joe Staines, Ruth Tidball

Publishing information

This first edition published June 2009 by
Rough Guides Ltd, 80 Strand, London WC2R 0RL
375 Hudson St, New York 10014, USA
Email: mail@roughguides.com

Distributed by the Penguin Group:
Penguin Books Ltd, 80 Strand, London WC2R 0RL
Penguin Putnam, Inc., 375 Hudson Street, New York 10014, USA
Penguin Group (Australia), 250 Camberwell Road, Camberwell, Victoria 3124, Australia
Penguin Books Canada Ltd, 90 Eglinton Avenue East, Suite 700, Toronto, Ontario, Canada M4P 2Y3
Penguin Group (New Zealand), Cnr Rosedale and Airborne Roads, Albany, Auckland, New Zealand

Printed in Singapore

300 pages; includes index

A catalogue record for this book is available from the British Library

ISBN: 978-1-85828-205-3

1 3 5 7 9 8 6 4 2

Contents

Introduction

Every minute of every day some 600 Japanese animated videos are downloaded from the Internet – the equivalent of six million copies each week. In 2007 the Japanese government appointed an anime character, **Doraemon**, as one of the nation's cultural ambassadors. To a contemporary audience of children, teens and adults the common images of anime – doe-eyed, spiky-haired youths, giant laser-blasting robots, nifty-footed ninjas and cuddly little monsters – have become as redolent of Japan as geisha and samurai have traditionally been.

Anime – a term that covers all animation made in Japan – has become as much a part of world pop culture as the iPod and Madonna (who, incidentally, screened anime as part of the stage show for her 2001 *Drowned World* tour). In 2009, mega-budget computer generated image (CGI) versions of the iconic anime series *Astro Boy* and *Gatchaman* will hit cinema screens. Also in the works are live-action remakes by Steven Spielberg and Leonardo DiCaprio of, respectively, *Ghost in the Shell* and *Akira* – two of anime's most acclaimed movies.

Anime's international success has been a long time coming: Japan has been honing its production of animated feature films since the early years of the twentieth century. A key turning point came in 1963, when **Osamu Tezuka**'s Astro Boy, with the aid of jet-powered boots, flew out of the pages of a manga (a Japanese comic) into the world of TV animation. That cartoon's success launched an industry with production lines as efficient and unstoppable as those at Toyota and Sony. Today some sixty percent of cartoons broadcast on TV around the world originate in Japan; most people have watched some anime, probably without knowing that's what it was.

Despite anime's longevity and increasingly high profile with both critics and the wider public, there remains a multitude of misconceptions about exactly what anime is and how, as an art form, it differs from animation made elsewhere. *The Rough Guide to Anime* aims to throw some light on a phenomenon that, while tricky to pin down, includes some acknowledged classics of animation, beautiful works of cinematic art and examples of imaginative, compulsive storytelling.

Since the 1980s anime has had a reputation for being violent, edgy and alternative, thanks to the breakout film *Akira* and subsequent TV and video hits, such as the perplexing giant robot saga *Neon Genesis Evangelion*. But anime is a medium, not a genre: the cute antics of *Hello Kitty* and *Pokémon*, and complex psychological thrillers such as *Perfect Blue* are all part of the anime universe. An anime can be a five-minute arty short, a TV series of anything from six to over two hundred episodes, or a straight-to-DVD release, known in anime parlance as an **OVA** or **OAV** (Original Video Anime/Anime Video). It can be made in the traditional manner with thousands of two-dimensional (2D) drawings, by computers generating life-like 3D images, or by a combination of techniques. Every so often there's a media scare about the extreme, pornographic, end of the medium – which conveniently ignores the fact that the vast majority of anime are, just as with Western cartoons, made for kids and about harmful as a mushy banana.

The vast array of anime on offer, aimed at audiences from tots to their parents, reflects a culture where manga – the source material for some sixty percent of anime – are equally diverse

Language, credits and titles

Japanese is written in a combination of three types of characters: **kanji** (Chinese ideograms) and two phonetic scripts – **hiragana**, used to transcribe Japanese words, and **katakana**, used mainly for names and words loaned from Western languages. Transliteration of Japanese in this guide uses the standard Hepburn system of romanization, called **rōmaji**, except for the katakana rendering of English words: here the original English word is used instead of direct transliteration, which can make pronunciation (and comprehension) difficult.

In Japan the family name appears first, followed by the given name. The vast majority of anime titles available outside Japan list **credits** in Western style, with the given name followed by family name. This guide follows the Western naming convention and only lists in the Japanese order names of real-life historical figures.

The bar (macron) over the o in rōmaji means the vowel sound is twice as long – hence "roe-ma-ji" not "ro-ma-ji". Most credits on English-language DVDs omit macrons and a few use alternative spellings (for example, ou for ō). The macrons used in this book indicate the correct pronunciation of a word and are only omitted in words such as Tokyo or Kyoto (correctly transliterated Tōkyō and Kyōto), which are well known in their English form.

Where an official English **title** of an anime exists, this is given first, followed in brackets by the rōmaji for the Japanese title and – in the Canon chapter only – the title in Japanese characters if that exists. A few anime only have an English title. In the Canon chapter, under an anime's title, *dir* stands for director, *scr* for screenplay and *m* for music. The year of original release in Japan is listed, as is the running time (and number of episodes if the anime is a TV series). Running times can vary for overseas releases, depending on how a title has been edited.

in topic and target demographic. Chapter four provides a succinct history of manga's rise to prominence as a mode of expression for all ages in Japan, and profiles major artists such as Osamu Tezuka and **Rumiko Takahashi**, whose work is the basis for some of the most successful anime.

The essence of what makes anime special can be found in the fifty key films and shows highlighted in Chapter two. Rather than a unified theme or look, it's the approach to characters and storytelling that is the distinguishing factor. Compared to your average Hollywood animated product, anime are far more complex, and less likely to have clear-cut heroes and villains, or to stick to absolute definitions of right and wrong – let alone feature a happy, neatly wrapped-up ending. Among the selection discussed here you'll find films you may already know, such as *Princess Mononoke, Spirited Away* and *My Neighbour Totoro*, all directed by the Oscar-winning **Hayao Miyazaki**. Alongside them are works by **Isao Takahata**, Miyazaki's Studio Ghibli colleague and long-time collaborator, whose *Grave of the Fireflies* and *Only Yesterday* rank among the cream of all Japanese cinema in the last century, animated or otherwise. Also covered are **Mamoru Oshii**'s distinctive *Ghost in the Shell*, *Patlabor* and *Urusei Yatsura*, as well as the splendidly diverse works of **Satoshi Kon**, including *Tokyo Godfathers* and *Paprika*. Titles by emerging talents such as **Makoto Shinkai** (*5 Centimeters per Second*), **Shinichirio Watanabe** (*Cowboy Bebop* and *Samurai Champloo*) and **Masaaki Yuasa** (*Mind Game*) make the grade, as do older, groundbreaking works from anime's relative infancy, like *Panda and the Magic Serpent*, *Astro Boy* and *Kimba the White Lion*. These fifty key films are supplemented throughout the book by mini-reviews of over a hundred other anime, chosen to illustrate a variety of genres and to pick out some of the top talent working in the industry, who are also profiled in Chapter three.

For many overseas fans what makes anime cool is not so much its production quality (which, frankly, is sometimes shoddy) but its otherness – that it stems from a culture different from their own. Japanese language, culture and modes of behaviour – everything from the differences in the schooling systems to what people eat for breakfast – permeate anime, adding depth and nuance. Chapter five decodes the key elements of this Japanese world and how it shapes what goes on in anime.

For all of its intimate connections with Japan, anime is not formed in a monocultural bubble. It is the product of multiple influences, including Disney films, US comic-book superheroes and the works of sci-fi and fantasy writers from around the world. Chapter six picks up on some of these cross-cultural threads, also detailing how for all its "Japaneseness", the vast majority of anime wouldn't exist without the input of animators from outside Japan.

Finally, chapter seven provides the lowdown on how to immerse yourself in anime's wider world. What may start with the viewing of a couple of **Studio Ghibli** DVDs or an episode or two of *Cowboy Bebop* on the Adult Swim cable network can lead to surfing anime websites, playing anime-derived computer games, indulging in some **cosplay** (dressing up in character) at anime conventions, and even travelling to Japan to see the locations featured in favourite shows, where there are museums and theme parks devoted to the medium and its creators. This is the reality of anime – you'll find it's dangerously addictive.

Simon Richmond
January 2009

Acknowledgements

I'd like to thank Sean Mahoney for commissioning this book and Matthew Milton for his editing. During my research I was very fortunate to be afforded the time and opinions of many anime scholars, fans and practitioners in the industry. Chief among these are Helen McCarthy, Jonathan Clements, Andrew Osmond, Ben Pollock, Jo Curzon, Ari Messer, Gilles Poitras, Brian Camp, Julie Davis, Justin Sevakis, Fred L. Schodt, Benjamin Ettinger, Angie Alexander, Roland Kelts and Ian Condry. An extra special thanks to Ada Palmer who was exceedingly generous with her knowledge and supportive of my work. Thanks also to Kylie Clark and colleagues at JNTO and finally to Tonny for his loving support and for patiently waiting for me to return from planet anime.

Rough Guides would like to thank Martin Richardson and Misa Imai for all their hard work, Gainax for their patience and generosity, FUNimation Entertainment, Evan Ma, Francesco Prandoni, Jerome Mazandarani, Link Hall, Stephen Cryan, Bandai, CoMix Wave, Studio Ghibli, Gonzo Digimation Holdings, Madhouse, Mushi Pro, Showgate, Studio 4°C, Sunrise, Tezuka Productions, and all the studios and production houses that have been so helpful in contributing to this book.

1

Anime chronicles

the story of anime

Today, most viewers take for granted the smooth-as-silk computer-generated images and effects we see in contemporary animation. But nearly a century ago it was jerky celluloid images in black and white that were causing a sensation.

Like an unstoppable transforming android, with each technical leap – from film to television, to video and now to the digital world – anime has adapted and progressed to become a multi-billion yen business accounting for well over half of all animation seen around the world.

1917–1930: an experimental infancy

Little is known for sure about the birth of anime, because so few examples of any Japanese film from the early twentieth century have survived. Quite apart from the general ravages of time, Japan suffered the double whammy of the Great Kantō Earthquake, which wiped out much of Tokyo in 1923, and also the cataclysmic air-raid fire bombings of World War II.

It's reckoned that some ninety percent of pre-World War II films have been destroyed, including what are generally agreed to be the first examples of anime. By contrast, it only takes a few clicks on a keyboard and an internet connection to view the pioneering American animations created by **Blackton and McCay** (see box opposite) at the start of the twentieth century.

In January of 1917 it's believed that **Oten Shimokawa**'s five-minute short *Mukuzo Imokawa the Doorman* (*Imokawa Mukuzo Genkanban no Maki*) was screened publicly. Over a period of six months, Shimokawa – a 26-year-old political cartoonist at *Tokyo Puck* magazine (see p.177) – made several short, experimental animated films. He used **stop-motion** techniques that essentially applied the same principle that makes static images in a flick-book appear to move if they are thumbed at speed. Shimokawa's essential method was to draw an image on a blackboard in chalk, film it for a frame or two, alter it slightly, film it again, and so on. It's possible that he also drew directly onto the film itself, a technique used on another very early anime (see box opposite).

Shimokawa was not the only anime pioneer of 1917. This is also the year given for the first short features by

Coining the word "anime"

The earliest Japanese animation studios often had the word *dōga* as part of their name, since *dōga* means "moving pictures". But generally, until well into the 1960s, animated movies and shorts were commonly referred to as *manga eiga* (cartoon movies). People in the industry used *animēshon*, the katakana rendering of the English word. A few, such as Hayao Miyazaki and the folks at **Studio Ghibli**, still do so in order to differentiate their finely honed product, created for the cinema screen, from the limited animation common on TV (see p.13).

But eventually, like many foreign words absorbed into Japanese, a more Japan-friendly version emerged when film critic **Taihei Imamura** coined the word *anime* in his book *Manga Eigaron* (*On Animated Movies*) in 1948. To the Japanese, anime covers all animation regardless of provenance; outside of Japan, it has come to mean animation made in Japan, squeezing out of fashion the odd-sounding "Japanimation" concocted by US fans in the 1970s.

The advent of animation

In the late nineteenth century, before Japan had even the most primitive of anime (or live-action films, for that matter), it had magic lantern light shows. This form of entertainment, known as *utsushi-e*, involved the use of a lantern to back-project still images onto a screen – some of which were moved around by hand to give an approximation of animation.

In 1906, the British-born, US-based film pioneer James Stuart Blackton improved on the magic lantern with his revolutionary *Humorous Phases of Funny Faces*, generally acknowledged as the world's first animated film. Just three minutes long, the short film mixed live action and animated effects which had involved the drawing of faces and figures in chalk on a blackboard – a technique that Oten Shimokawa, one of Japan's proto-animators, is also said to have used. Closer in style to the animated cartoons we are familiar with today is Winsor McCay's *Gertie the Trained Dinosaur*, a smash hit from 1914 for which the artist personally drew ten thousand images by hand. It's likely that McCay's work was among the 21 foreign animations screened in Japan in 1915.

However, in late July 2005 several Japanese newspapers reported the discovery of a small piece of aged film stock in a private residence in Kyoto by Ōsaka University instructor Natsuki Matsumoto. Just fifty frames long, accounting for little more than three seconds of screen time, the 35mm film shows a boy in a sailor uniform drawing the characters for a moving picture on a blackboard. Matsumoto didn't know who had drawn the anime, exactly when, or even whether it had ever been screened, but given the technique by which the images had been drawn directly onto the film he speculated that the fragment could be up to ten years older than the anime of 1917, previously believed to be Japan's first.

If it does indeed date from around 1907, it would almost certainly mean that its existence was entirely independent of animation in the West, the first examples of which were not screened in Japan until 1915. In the *Anime Encyclopedia*, Jonathan Clements and Helen McCarthy note the discovery but also point out that no further evidence has been produced to support Matsumoto's theory. For them, the jury is still out on whether the Kyoto film strip could be the world's first animation.

Shimokawa's *Tokyo Puck* colleague **Junichi Kōchi** and by the artist **Seitarō Kitayama**, whose earliest works, *The Monkey and the Crab* (*Saru Kani Kassen*) and *Momotarō*, were based on traditional folk tales (see

Mukuzo Imokawa the Doorman (1917): one of the oldest anime in existence

p.206). Kitayama saw the potential of the new medium, producing animated commercials and short educational films as well as setting up Japan's first animation studio. His *Momotarō* was also screened in France, making it the first anime export.

Among the oldest anime that can be viewed today are *The Mountain Where Old Women are Abandoned* (*Obasuteyama*) and *The Tortoise and the Hare* (*Usagi to Kame*), both created in 1924 by **Sanae Yamamoto**, one of Kitayama's most promising apprentices. When originally screened, these silent anime would have been accompanied by live music (just like silent live-action movies) and a spoken commentary by a *benshi* (narrator) who would explain the story, which was not always that easy to follow from the disjointed images on screen. Yamamoto went on to work on propaganda anime during World War II and he set up the forerunner of the **Tōei Dōga** animation studio in 1947 (see p.143).

In 1927, *The Whale* (*Kujira*), the first anime to feature sound, was created by **Noburō Ōfuji**. It was only a simple silhouette, animated to move in time to the *William Tell Overture* but it sealed Ōfuji's reputation as one of anime's pioneers. A year after Ōfuji's death in 1962, the daily newspaper *Mainichi Shimbun* inaugurated an award for animation in his name as part of their annual film awards ceremony. As the Roaring Twenties drew to

The Tortoise and the Hare (1924)

a close, Ōfuji continued to experiment with the still-fledgling medium, creating both *Black Cat* (*Kuro Nyago*), a ninety-second anime featuring a couple of jazz-dancing felines, and *Golden Flower* (*Ogon no Hana*), the first colour anime, in 1929.

Japanese animation classic collection

Digital Meme, 2007, 326m

Anyone interested in anime's origins will want to add this four-DVD box-set of 55 short anime features, produced between 1928 and 1950, to their collection. Some of the films have newly recorded music and commentaries by *benshi* (narrators). The collection includes the *Norakuro* and *Momotarō* shorts of the 1930s and early works by award-winning pioneer animator Noburō Ōfuji, creator of *The Whale*, and Kenzo Masaoka who went on to make the critically praised *The Spider* and *the Tulip* and *Cherry Blossom – Spring Fantasy*. Enlightening notes by film critic Tadao Satō, translated into English, accompany each disc. It's available through Digital Meme (www.digital-meme.com).

1930–1945: an aggressive adolescence

The World of Women and Power (*Chikara to Onna no Yononaka*), made by **Kenzo Masaoka** in 1932 and screened the following year, is credited as Japan's first fully synchronized "talking" anime. In 1934 Masaoka chalked up another innovation with *Dance of the Teapots* (*Chagama Ondo*), the first anime wholly made with transparent cels, as opposed to the translucent papers that had been used previously in Japan.

As with animation of this period elsewhere in the world, anime's flat two-dimensional style and subject matter reflected its primary source material – newspaper and magazine comic strips otherwise known as **manga**. Early US cartoon shorts such as *Felix the Cat* and *Betty Boop* were also influential. A popular manga of this time was **Suiho Tagawa**'s *Norakuro*, the tale of an orphan mutt who joins a doggie army, rising up through the ranks from private to captain. Norakuro made his screen debut in 1933's *Private Second Class Norakuro* (*Norakuro Nitohei: Kyoren no Maki*) and appeared in at least two subsequent screen adventures, his military career mirroring Japan's turbulent times as the country

Let slip the dog of war: Suiho Tagawa's Norakuro featured in several anime shorts of the 1930s

became an aggressive colonial power in Asia.

The militaristic government saw the propaganda potential of anime for spreading its bellicose message to the population. Public funding and national distribution became available to animators for the first time, resulting in the production of far more ambitious and technically accomplished work. In 1931, **Yasuji Murata**, the animator of Norakuro, made *Aerial Momotarō* (*Sora no Momotarō*) in which the peach-born boy hero Momotarō flies down to an island near the South Pole; en route he fights off the enemy Wild Eagle and on arrival breaks up a war between penguins and albatrosses. The parallel with Japan's invasion in the same year of the Manchurian region of China is pretty clear.

More explicit anti-foreigner anime of the time includes **Takao Nakano**'s *Black Cat Banzai* (*Kuroneko Banzai*) from 1933, in which flying bat bombers piloted by Mickey Mouse lookalikes attack a parade of toys, and Ōfuji's *Aerial Ace* (*Sora no Arawashi*) from 1938, featuring a plucky Japanese fighter plane up against mighty clouds in the unmistakable shapes of Popeye and Stalin. **Kenzo Masaoka**'s *The Spider and The Tulip* (*Kumo to Churippu*) is a beautifully realized sixteen-minute short released in 1943, in which a spider with a blacked-up face, that recalls Al Jolson's turn as a minstrel in *The Jazz Singer*, attempts to lure a ladybird into his web. The ladybird finds shelter in the petals of a tulip while the spider is swept away by the wind – an allegory, perhaps, for Japan protecting Asia from the US.

The Film Law passed in 1939 brought Japan's media under even stricter central government control and in 1942, a year after Japan entered World War II, **Kajiro Yamamoto** made *The War at Sea from Hawaii to Malaya* (*Hawaii Mareioki Kaisen*) featuring an anime re-creation of Pearl Harbor. In 1943 Momotarō was back doing his bit for Japan's war effort in **Mitsuyo Seo**'s *Momotarō's Sea Warriors* (*Momotarō no Umiwashi*). Commissioned by the imperial navy, this movie sees the peach-boy and an army of animal buddies (representing fellow Asian nations) taking on the devils of Onigashima (representing the Americans and British). It ran for an unprecedented 37 minutes and was such a box-office hit that an even longer follow-up, *Momotarō's Divine Sea Warriors* (*Momotarō Umi no Shinpei*) was authorized. The scale and pacing of Japan's first full-length anime was inspired by the Chinese animation *Princess Iron Fan* (*Tie shan gong zhu*). Asia's first feature-length animation, it was made by the Wan brothers in Japanese-occupied Shanghai and released in 1941.

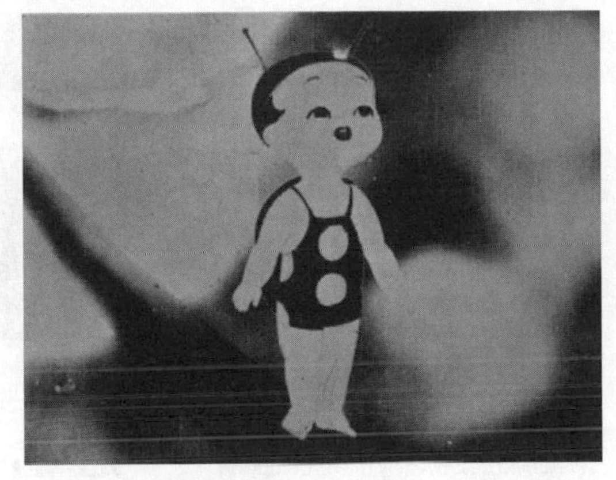

The ladybird heroine of *The Spider and the Tulip* (1943), one of Japan's wartime anime; below is her arachnoid nemesis

Momotarō's Divine Sea Warriors might have been the pinnacle of anime to date but its theme of a victorious, virtuous Japan was about to crash into reality. Released on 12 April 1945, the movie was eclipsed four months later by events that have had dramatic resonance in Japan – and anime – ever since: the dropping of the **atomic bombs** on Hiroshima and Nagasaki. These devastating explosions put an apocalyptic full stop to World War II. For anime, however, they have been the inspiration for everything from *Astro Boy* to *Akira*, not to mention the source material for *Barefoot Gen* (see Canon), one of the most powerful anti-war anime.

Momotarō's Divine Sea Warriors

Momotarō Umi no Shinpei

dir Mitsuyo Seo, 1945, 74m

In Japan's first feature-length anime, Momotarō and an army of Japanese animals come to the aid of an exotic assortment of fellow creatures on a southeast Asian island that is under the colonial thumb of the British. Separate teams worked on different sections of the film, resulting in varying quality and styles. The propaganda – from the wide-eyed island animals being taught the Japanese language, to the depiction of the British vacillating over surrender – is predictably heavy. Presumed destroyed by the US occupying forces after the end of World War II, a negative of the film was discovered in 1984 and subsequently released on video along with the 1943 short *The Spider and the Tulip*.

Momotarō's Divine Sea Warriors: anime from the close of World War II

1945–1960: the rise of Tōei Dōga

Anime was low on the list of priorities for the defeated nation. However, the US forces occupying Japan after the surrender recognized the value of such films in shaping hearts and minds to Western-style values. *The Magic Pen* (*Maho no Pen*) by **Masao Kumagawa** was a fantasy from 1946 (a time when many people had nothing), about an orphan boy in Tokyo who finds an English-speaking doll that uses its magic pen to create food and shelter – the latter taking the shape of a modern Western-style house rather than a traditional Japanese home. **Taiji Yabushita**'s *Animal Great Baseball Match* (*Dobutsu Daiyakyu-sen*) in 1949 was another short that embraced a

Stars and Stripes-emulating future for Japan – although baseball had been popular with the Japanese ever since its introduction into the country in the 1870s.

Drawing on traditional but uncontroversial Japanese culture and images was *Cherry Blossom – Spring Fantasy* (*Sakura – Haru no Gensō*), directed by **Kenzo Masaoka** and released in 1946. Possibly inspired by Disney's *Fantasia,* it features a series of poetic vignettes of cute creatures and kimonoed geisha frolicking in the falling cherry blossom, all set to the classical score of Karl Maria von Weber's *Invitation to Dance*.

By 1956 the Japanese economy had recovered sufficiently for the formation of **Tōei Dōga** (renamed in 1998 Tōei Animation). Tōei's aim was ambitious: to take on Walt Disney, the world champion of animation. Post-World War II the Japanese developed an ongoing love affair with Disney, with films such as *Bambi, Pinocchio* and *Peter Pan* influencing the legendary manga artist **Osamu Tezuka** (see p.165) among others. The 1950s also saw the Japanese appetite for action-orientated animation piqued by the programming of US cartoons such as *Superman* and *Popeye* on television (although TV as a true mass medium in Japan wouldn't happen until the early 1960s).

Tōei's premier production, *Hakujaden* (better known overseas as *Panda and the Magic Serpent*; see Canon), was the first Japanese feature made in colour, and was based on a Chinese fairy tale. The Disney influence is reflected in the depiction of cute animal characters with a tendency to break into song and dance. Unlike the made-for-TV anime to follow (see box on p.13) the quality of the animation was high.

Panda and the Magic Serpent won a Grand Prix prize at the Venice Children's Film Festival in 1959. It was released (with an English soundtrack and a seven-minute cut in its original running time) in the US a couple of years later, along with two

A smiling geisha in Kenzo Masaoka's *Cherry Blossom – Spring Fantasy* provided distraction for an impoverished, post-war Japanese audience

other Tōei productions: *Magic Boy* (*Shōnen Sarutobi Sasuke*), Japan's first CinemaScope (widescreen) anime, and *Alakazam the Great* (*Saiyūki*), adapted from a Tezuka manga which in turn was based on the Chinese tale *Journey to the West* (see p.203). All these films provided hands-on experience for future artists and directors including Shigeyuki Hayashi (better known by his *nom de plume* Rintarō), Gisaburo Sugii and Isao Takahata, one of the founders of Studio Ghibli.

Tōei's success cemented the idea that forming anime studios was the way forward. But it didn't quite kill off **independent animation**. Ōfuji, one of anime's founding fathers, was again pushing the creative boundaries by remaking *The Whale* in 1952 using coloured cellophane silhouettes – it scored second prize at that year's Cannes Film Festival and garnered the praise of Pablo Picasso and Jean Cocteau. His short *Flower and Butterfly* (*Hana to Cho*) in 1954 was made in colour, while *Ghost Ship* (*Yūreisen*) bagged a gong at the Venice Film Festival of 1956.

Magic Boy
Shōnen Sarutobi Sasuke

dir Akira Daikuhara & Taiji Yabushita, 1959, 83m

The Disney influence continues in Tōei's sophomore feature (also known as *The Adventures of Little Samurai* and *Young Sarutobi Sasuke*) about feisty youngster Sasuke, who learns ninja skills and magic – both of which come in handy in his fights with the sharp-featured evil princess Yasha-hime. The scene in which a faun watches as its protective mother is killed by a lake monster recalls *Bambi*. Released in the US in June 1961, it is thought to be the first anime to be screened theatrically there.

Alakazam the Great
Saiyūki

dir Daisaku Shirakawa & Taiji Yabushita, 1960, 88m

In its US release many of the original Chinese and religious roots of the characters and plot were Westernized, thus explaining the incongruous appearances, in the dubbed version, of Merlin the magician and Hercules alongside the lead character Alakazam – an arrogant young monkey king who learns various lessons on his journeys before becoming the true hero he always promised to be. Frankie Avalon provided the singing voice of Alakazam, and Sterling Holloway did the narration.

1960s: the TV revolution

Tōei credited **Osamu Tezuka** as a director and screenwriter of *Alakazam the Great*, and the great manga artist would go on to collaborate with the studio on two more feature-length anime: 1962's *Arabian Nights: The Adventures of Sinbad* and 1963's *Doggie March* (*Wan Wan Chushingura*). This latter anime is the first production on which a young **Hayao Miyazaki** got his break into animation (see p.158). Tezuka later disclaimed much of his involvement in *Alakazam the Great*, other than having allowed his manga *Boku no Son-goku!* (*My Songoku!*) to be the basis for its plot.

Osamu Tezuka's beautiful modernist classic *Tale of a Street Corner*, from 1962

The experience of working with Tōei, however, inspired Tezuka to form his own animation studio **Mushi Productions** (a.k.a Mushi Pro) in 1961. The studio's initial project, a 38-minute feature entitled *Tale of a Street Corner* (*Aru Machikado no Monogatari*) was a radically different kind of animation from Tōei's Disney-emulating works. Drawn in modernistic style, it had a story told solely through pictures and music, with an anti-war theme. The short snapped up the first **Ōfuji Sho** prize in 1962.

Tezuka continued to dabble in experimental animation throughout his career but it was towards **television** that he and his studio employees directed their most serious efforts. Colour broadcasting began in 1960 and as the country geared up for the 1964 Olympics in Tokyo, TVs became common in Japanese households. In 1961 animation was used for one minute of the three-minute-long TV series *Instant History* (*Otogi Manga Calendar*) covering key historical events and occasions. The time was ripe for an anime adaptation of one of Tezuka's popular manga series and the obvious choice was *Tetsuwan Atom* (*Mighty Atom*), which had already been made into a live-action TV show.

On 1 January 1963 *Tetsuwan Atom* premiered on Fuji TV. It was an immediate hit, attracting overseas interest within days, according to Tezuka. A few months later a deal was struck with the NBC network for syndication and by September of the same year, the series, retitled *Astro Boy* by its American producer **Fred Ladd** (see box on p.157), was the first anime to be broadcast in the US. A tsunami of *Astro Boy* merchandising made the series the *Pokémon* of its day and its cute little boy robot star became the first international icon of anime.

Astro Boy's success, however, was not achieved without a great deal of sacrifice. In order to clinch the initial deal with Fuji TV, Tezuka had agreed to an unrealistically low production budget and a super-tight schedule. This resulted in Tezuka's team not only being poorly paid but also being pushed to their physical limits to create the series on time. Artists later recalled how their fingers blistered and bled from constant work and how they slept under their desks rather than returning home. The end result was the technically limited form of animation used in *Astro Boy* and many more anime to come.

Astro Boy's US success opened the way for other anime to make the leap across the Pacific. *Tetsujin 28-go*, featuring a giant radio-controlled robot, took the trip in 1965 and, like *Astro Boy*, found itself with a new name (*Gigantor*) and theme

Anime the limited way

The budget-busting production techniques used by Tezuka's team at Mushi Pro on *Astro Boy* got the job done so effectively that they fast became the industry default. They are still used today even though modern technology can compensate for many of the labour-intensive processes that once required corners to be cut if an anime was to be made on time and budget. The key techniques are:

- **Filming fewer pictures per second** For motion on film to appear fluid and lifelike it's necessary to draw at least 12 different sequential illustrations for the 24 frames of film that run through a projector per second. Limited animation relies on fewer images (sometimes as few as eight per second) and so is more jerky, and sometimes even static.

- **Extra use of still shots** For a close-up on a character's face or a particular detail or scene, just one drawing could be used for several seconds.

- **Using the camera to zoom in** and pan across single images to create the illusion of movement.

- **Creating an animation loop** to show repetitive movements, such as characters running.

- **Characters are drawn before the voice track is recorded**, with just three mouth positions when speaking – open, half-open and shut. The voice track is added later and the lines are spoken to coordinate as best as possible to the images, rather than the other way round. Characters speaking are also drawn with their backs to the camera, or at a distance, to cut down on the times a mouth needs to be animated.

- **Creation of a bank of common images** that could be reused later.

- **Higher image count** (hence more expensive) animation is only used in one or two key scenes, to give the veneer of quality.

tune, with plot and character details tweaked for the US market. In 1965, Mushi Pro followed up *Astro Boy* with *Kimba the White Lion* (*Jungle Taitei*; see Canon), the first full-colour TV anime, made specifically with US audiences in mind.

While *Astro Boy* and *Kimba* were entrancing US audiences, the US comedy show *Bewitched* had become so popular in Japan that in 1966 it inspired *Little Witch Sally* (*Mahō Tsukai Sally*), based on a manga by **Mitsuteru Yokoyama**. This story of a cute alien girl with witch powers was the first in what has come to be known as the **"magical girl"** genre (see p.208). *Princess Knight* (*Ribon no Kishi*) was also appealing to the younger female audience. This series, made in 1967 and based on a popular genre-defining manga of Tezuka's from the 1950s, introduced a gutsy female heroine with a penchant for cross-dressing, an archetype since aped in a host of other anime.

Boys were courted with 1965's more action-orientated *Marine Boy*, featuring the Oxygum-chewing diving boy Marine, his pet dolphin Whitey (Splasher in the dubbed English version) and the slinky mermaid Neptina. Although it had a chequered history of production and screenings in Japan (going through three different title changes), *Marine Boy* was a hit in Australia, the UK and the US, despite the series being slammed there for its excessive **violence** – a charge that has haunted anime in general ever since. Episodes were cut and amendments often made to these early exports. For example, when the bad guys were caught in *Mach Go Go Go* (screened as *Speed Racer* in the US in 1967) they appear merely dazed and confused, while in the original version they would generally have been killed.

Despite the rise in cheaply produced TV anime, a handful of full-animation **cinema releases** were still being made by Tōei. Among their best works were *The Littlest Warrior* (*Anju to Zushiōmaru*), a gorgeously conceived film based on a classic Japanese folk story; *Little Norse Prince (Taiyo no Ko Hols no Daibōken*; see Canon), the feature debut of Isao Takahata as a director; and the joyful romp *Puss 'n Boots* (see p.112).

Ever the innovator, Tezuka chanced *Arabian Nights* and *Cleopatra*, a couple of films for adults or, as he dubbed them, **animerama**, a combination of anime and drama. Both included experimental styles of animation and faux erotic scenes that would have brought a blush to *Astro Boy*'s cheeks.

The Littlest Warrior

Anju to Zushiōmaru

dir Yugo Serikawa & Taiji Yabushita, 1961, 83m

Based on the novel *Sansho Dayu* (*Sansho the Bailiff*) by Ogai Mori, this beautifully produced feature has a design that reflects traditional Japanese art. Even though its cast includes a bevy of cute talking animals, friends to the anime's human heroes, the plot, which revolves around the trials of a brother and sister separated from their parents and sold into slavery, is closer to Dickens than Disney.

Speed Racer
Mach Go Go Go

dir Tatsuo Yoshida et al, 1967–68, 52 x 30m

Much beloved by baby-boomers, few of whom were aware of its original Japanese roots. Go (rechristened Speed in the US version) is one of three racing car driver sons in the Mifune family. He drives the super pimped-up Mach Five (Mach Go in Japanese, clueing you into the punning original title) in races around the world, giving the animators great scope to depict exotic locations as backdrops for the onscreen action. The 1993 remake *The New Adventures of Speed Racer* is a wholly American-made cartoon series; a live-action version by the Wachowski Brothers of *The Matrix* fame was released in 2008.

Arabian Nights
Senya Ichiya Monogatari

dir Osamu Tezuka & Eiichi Yamamoto, 1969, 128m

Also known as *A Thousand and One Nights*, Tezuka's first foray into adult-orientated anime territory sees him spin a convoluted yarn that is remarkably faithful to Scheherazade's classic tale, and packed with experimentation and visual gags. The fantastic adventures of hero Aladdin (modelled, apparently, on French movie star Jean-Paul Belmondo) include numerous sexual assignations – all very tame compared to what's seen in some hentai anime today. The music score is by Isao Tomita, who also composed the lush symphonies of *Kimba the White Lion*, and the animation was contributed to by future stars of the medium including Gisaburo Sugii and Osamu Dezaki.

Cleopatra

dir Osamu Tezuka & Eiichi Yamamoto, 1970, 112m

Despite the financial success of *Arabian Nights*, Tezuka's second animerama feature was made in a desperate attempt to save his nearly bankrupt Mushi Pro studio. It received an X rating on its US release, but the titillation element is far closer to a *Carry On* comedy than a Linda Lovelace porn film. There are plenty of arthouse flourishes: the presenting of Caesar's murder as a scene from a *kabuki* play; a Roman parade that parodies art by Bosch, Chagal, Modigliani, Miro and Picasso (among many others); and the bookending of the film with *Star Trek*-like live-action scenes, only with the actors' faces replaced by animated ones. They are all interesting but they ultimately can't save a mess of anachronism and silly gags.

1970s: the age of space sagas

The early 1970s were not promising for anime, nor for Japanese cinema in general. Following years of poor financial management, Mushi Pro finally declared bankruptcy, shutting up shop in 1973. Tōei also eased out of expensive cinema animation to focus on the growing market for cheaper TV shows. Isao Takahata and Hayao Miyazaki both left Tōei

courtesy of FUNimation Entertainment

The daredevil criminal Lupin III has proved to be one of anime's most enduring creations, shown here during the adventure *Farewell to Nostradamus*

to work on *Heidi* (*Alps no Shōjo Heidi*), a TV serialization of Johanna Spyri's much-loved children's book. Its success led to the long-running anime series **World Masterpiece Theater**.

In 1971, the suave master thief Lupin III, based on a manga by **Monkey Punch**, made his debut on Japanese TV. By the end of the decade he was entertaining fans on the big screen in the classic *Lupin III: The Castle of Cagliostro* (see Canon), directed by Hayao Miyazaki. Crime capers were not to be the leitmotif of 1970s anime, however. This was the era of science fiction and in particular the ongoing development of robot-fixated, **mecha**-obsessed, anime.

Leading the way was **Go Nagai** (see p.159) whose *Mazinger Z*, adapted by Tōei into a TV series in 1972, introduced the now common concept of a pilot-driven giant robot, the pilot preferably being a teenage boy. In the same year Nagai's *Science Ninja Team Gatchaman* (*Kagaku Ninjatai Gatchaman*), usually shortened to just *Gatchaman*, spruced up the formula for a team of anime superheroes in space. A heavily edited version of *Gatchaman* would morph, at the end of the decade, into the US series *Battle of the Planets*, while in France and Spain Nagai's other giant robot series *Grandizer*, retitled *Goldorak*, became required tea-time

A tale of two cats

On a par with *Astro Boy* and the *Pokémon* brigade as anime royalty are a pair of cats: **Doraemon** and **Hello Kitty**. Of the two, *Doraemon* is the least well known to Western anime fans, although he's as popular across Asia as he is in Japan. This is likely to change as the Japanese government in 2008 drafted the blue robot cat into public service as the official anime ambassador for the country.

Doraemon was created by Hiroshi Fujimoto, one half of the famous manga duo Fujiko Fujio (the other being Motoo Abiko). He first appeared in a manga published in December 1969 along with his ten-year-old pal Nobita (his name means "falling down"), who he's always helping out of scrapes. This usually involves producing some fantastic gadget, such as a helicopter hat to help them fly around, or the *doko-demo* door, a portal to anywhere in the world. When *Doraemon* made its anime debut in 1973, in a series that ran for 26 episodes, it was not a ratings success, leading to its hiatus from TV until 1979. But the following year, the first in what has become an annual series of feature-length movies was released. A couple of these have won the Grand Prize in the Mainichi Awards.

As practically the entire world knows – thanks to her cute visage gracing a gazillion and one products – *Hello Kitty* is a white kitten with a jaunty red hair ribbon. According to the official biography, concocted by parent company Sanrio, Kitty was born in 1974 in London, UK, where she lives with her parents and twin sister Mimi. Like a J-pop idol being groomed for stardom, Hello Kitty made cameo appearances in the anime of other Sanrio characters from 1977 to the late 1980s – the big surprise was that although she has no mouth she could still talk. Kitty graduated to her own series in 1987 with *Hello Kitty's Furry Tale Theater* in which she appeared in versions of fairy tales and children's books, including Cinderella, Snow White and Alice in Wonderland. With the world at her paws, the kitten recently starred in the 2006 clay animation series *Hello Kitty's Stump Village*. She's also considered to be the inspiration for Maromi – the devilish pink puppy in Satoshi Kon's *Paranoia Agent*. The truly devoted will want to plan a trip to the Hello Kitty theme park **Sanrio Puroland** (www.puroland.co.jp/english/welcome.html), in the suburbs of Tokyo.

Dressed to kill – literally – in *Mobile Suit Gundam*

viewing. Both series formed a strong foundation for anime's growing international appeal.

It was into outer space again in 1974 for the epic *Space Battleship Yamato* (*Uchu Senkan Yamato,* see Canon). With its single continuing storyline and dramatic structure based on traditional war movies, the series set a precedent. When, later in the decade, it resurfaced overseas under the title *Star Blazers*, it caught the imaginations of a new and, crucially, slightly older demographic. One of the creators of *Space Battleship Yamato* was **Leiji Matsumoto** who became to the 1970s what Tezuka was to the 1960s, his stylish manga the source material for a string of other hits including *Space Pirate Captain Harlock* (*Uchu Kaizoku Captain Harlock*), *Galaxy Express 999* (*Ginga Tetsdō 999*) and *Queen Millennia* (*Shin Taketori Monogatari Sennen Jō-ō*).

Another pivotal science-fiction series of the 1970s was *Mobile Suit Gundam* (*Kidō Senshi Gundam*, see Canon), which, like *Space Battleship Yamato,* refreshed the giant robot genre by overlaying it with a serious, sprawling saga peopled with fully fleshed-out characters.

Gundam's popularity was boosted by a juggernaut of a merchandising campaign focusing on the series' multiple mecha creations, providing a blueprint for the similar cross-promotional success of series such as *Transformers* and *Pokémon* in subsequent decades.

In a completely different vein, Riyoko Ikeda's bestselling manga *Rose of Versailles* (*Versailles no Bara*) was adapted for TV in 1979. Its cross-dressing star, Oscar François de Jarjayes, may have referenced Tezuka's *Princess Knight*, but *Rose*'s incorporation of historical figures, such as Marie Antoinette, and the events of the French Revolution into the plot was practically an anime first. The anime's enduring influence can be seen in other popular series such as *Revolutionary Girl Utena* (see Canon) and *Le Chevalier d'Eon* in 2006.

Mazinger Z

Majing Zetto

dir Tomoharu Katsumata, Yugo Serikawa et al, 1972, 92 x 30m

It's been done countless times since, but this was the original anime to feature a teenager piloting a giant robot-style machine. Spiky-haired Koji is the pilot and his mechanized plaything is Mazinger Z. Together they battle, episode after episode, with the imaginatively conceived machine beasts of Dr Hell and his freakish accomplices. Action-packed scenes and a spunky hero give this series a rough charm. Other *Mazinger Z* series followed, as well as a couple of movies: 1973's *Mazinger Z vs Devilman* featured characters from Go Nagai's *Devilman*.

Gatchaman

Kagaku ninja tai Gatchaman

dir Hisayuki Toriumi, 1972, 105 x 30m

There are shades of *Thunderbirds* in this classic series, which pits the five-strong Science Ninja Team against the evil Galactor army that's threatening Earth with a variety of fiendish giant robots. Despite the team's jokey bird costumes, it's serious in tone and most of the characters and their weaponry have a more realistic look than had previously been the case in anime. It's better known in the West as *Battle of the Planets*, a heavily edited version of the show. The clunking holes in the plot, left after much of the violence was cut and other details changed, are smoothed over by 7-Zark-7, a comical R2D2-like robot, introduced to cash in on *Star Wars*' popularity.

Galaxy Express 999

dir Nobutaku Nishizawa, 1978–81, 114 x 30m

There's a fairy-tale quality to this science-fiction series from a manga by Leiji Matsumoto, featuring a steam train chugging through outer space. Onboard is the orphan boy Tetsuro and his companion Maetel, an enigmatic blonde who's along for the ride to far-flung Andromeda, where Tetsuro plans to exchange his mortal human body for an eternal mechanical one. The underlying theme, about the dangers of technology, would echo through many anime to come.

Son Goku and his pals kung-fu kick their way through *Dragon Ball* and *Dragon Ball Z*, one of anime's most successful franchises
courtesy of FUNimation Entertainment

Rintarō directed the movie of the same name in 1979 and *Adieu Galaxy Express 999* in 1981. The series was given a glossy remake in 2003 under the title *The Galaxy Railways*.

1980s: the golden age

The 1980s are generally referred to as anime's golden age and it's easy to see why. This was the era that not only saw the birth of Studio Ghibli and Gainax, two of the major studios working in Japanese animation today, but also the rise of auteurs such as **Mamoru Oshii** and **Katsuhiro Ōtomo**: for more details on all of these see chapter three.

Highly popular manga were adapted for TV, including **Rumiko Takahashi**'s *Urusei Yatsura*, directed by Oshii in 1981. In 1986, Takahashi's touching domestic drama *Maison Ikkoku* premiered on TV, while in 1989 it was the turn of her gender-swapping comedy *Ranma 1/2*. In 1986 *Dragon Ball* would leap from the page with a karate kick to become one of the longest running anime franchises, finally signing off in 1997.

The medium's increasing prevalence, not to mention mountains of associated-character merchandise, fed an emerging **otaku** subculture – that of the obsessive devotee – which found expression in Japan in fan conventions and anime magazines such as *Animage*, first published in 1978, and *Newtype* which kicked off in 1985. The overseas fanbase was also growing, as US shows such as *Robotech* (spliced together from three separate anime including *Macross*, see Canon) and, across the Atlantic, Japanese-French co-productions such as *Ulysses 31* and *Mysterious Cities of Gold* primed audiences for more visually ravishing and densely structured anime to come.

In 1983, *Golgo 13: The Professional* (see p.194) was the first anime to

Death by a thousand cuts?

When *Nauiscaä of the Valley of the Wind* made its US debut in 1986, it was in a poorly dubbed version entitled *Warriors of the Wind* that had over thirty minutes hacked from its running time. Many of its key details, including its heroine's name, were altered, watered down or deleted entirely. Miyazaki was horrified. It would be another decade before Studio Ghibli felt confident enough in the integrity of their partners to engage in a deal to distribute their movies in the US again.

Nauiscaä's experience was not uncommon for anime making the perilous journey from Japan to overseas markets. From the early days of Tōei's features, character names had been routinely Westernized and films edited to make the plots more acceptable and understandable to a non-Japanese audience. On American, European and Australian TV the violent scenes in anime screened for children had always been a problem but so too had been religious references and dodgy cultural stereotypes. Often episodes would be dropped entirely while others would be changed almost beyond recognition. For example, when *Gatchaman* surfaced on US TV as *Battle of the Planets*, not only were some twenty episodes missing but within the much-edited remaining episodes appeared a funny robot character (7-Zark-7) who'd never even been in the original.

Anime fans familiar with the originals bemoaned what were often barbaric alterations. But to a generation who knew of nothing else there was still much to admire in the chopped and changed versions – and certainly sufficient difference with US and European animation to feed a desire to see more, thus sparking the overseas anime boom of today.

experiment with the use of **computer-generated images** (CGI). The short sequence, involving a helicopter attack on a skyscraper, is embarrassingly crude compared to what's possible today, but it was the start of a process in which computers would play an increasingly large role in anime production, eventually supplanting traditional cel animation.

The success of *Nausicaä of the Valley of the Wind* (*Kaze no Tani no Nausicaä*, see Canon), directed by Hayao Miyazaki and produced by Isao Takahata, enabled the duo to team up with Toshio Suzuki of *Animage*'s publishing company in 1985 to form **Studio Ghibli**. Before the decade was done, Studio Ghibli would have created some of the most accomplished and best-loved animated films of all time, among them the classics *Castle in the Sky* (*Tenku no Shiro Laputa*, see Canon),

A still from one of Gainax's much-admired animations for the Daikon fan conventions of 1981 and 83

My Neighbour Totoro (*Tonari no Totoro*, see Canon) and *Kiki's Delivery Service* (*Majo no Takkyubin*, see Canon).

Gainax, formed in 1982 by a group of Ōsaka-based anime enthusiasts including **Hideaki Anno** (see p.150), kicked off its screen career by creating wildly inventive shorts for the fan convention Daikon in 1981 and 1983. In 1988 the studio delivered a memorable double whammy: the ambitious cinema feature *Wings of Honneamise* (*Oneamisu no Tsubasa*) and the straight-to-video classic *Gunbuster* (*Top o Nerae! GunBuster*), the directorial debut of Hideaki Anno and a dry run for his psychologically more complex *Neon Genesis Evangelion* (see Canon for more about all three).

Helping to push anime's popularity to the next level was the rise of the video cassette format. Mamoru Oshii's sci-fi effort *Dallos*, in 1983, is notable solely for being the first anime made for **straight-to-video** release. Termed OVAs or OAVs (Original Video Anime or Original Anime Video) by the industry, the format revolutionized anime distribution. No longer did producers have to go to the trouble and expense of securing a cinema release or TV slot for their work, opening up the way for short-run series such as fan favourite *Bubblegum Crisis* (one of the first unmistakeably Japanese series made available in the West), more experimental, niche works like the anthology *Robot Carnival*, and – inevitably – an explosion of porn titles (see p.227).

The decade was rounded off by two key events in anime history: the arrival of Katsuhiro Ōtomo's *Akira* (see Canon), and the **death of Osamu Tezuka**. Adult in its themes and incredibly dynamic in its presentation, *Akira* was rightly acknowledged as a seminal work and did no end of good for anime's international reputation. In contrast, Tezuka's passing away hardly registered outside of Japan. But within the country, the premature demise at the age of sixty of the father of modern manga and anime easily eclipsed the death of Emperor Hirohito only a few weeks earlier. It truly was the end of an era.

Dragon Ball
Dragon Ball Z

dir Daisuke Nishio, 1986–96: *Dragon Ball* 153 x 30m; *Dragon Ball Z* 291 x 30m

If you can get past the interminable martial arts battles, there are a few things to admire in this kung-fu-fantasy-sci-fi flip-out. Based on the manga by Akira Toriyama (who in turn used elements from the ancient Chinese fable *Journey to the West*), the epic saga follows the adventures of monkey-tailed alien Son Goku, raised by a kung fu master on Earth and constantly striving to improve his fighting skills well into old age. Along the way he gains allies and battles foes while searching for the seven dragon balls of the title. The two series spawned seventeen movies and three TV specials between them. The much inferior series *Dragon Ball GT*, a sequel to *Dragon Ball Z*, is not based on Toriyama's original manga.

Neo-Tokyo

Meikyū Monogatari

dir Yoshiaki Kawajiri, Katsuhiro Ōtomo, Rintarō, 1986, 50m

This trio of shorts based on the stories of Taku Maruyama includes the directing debut of *Akira*'s Ōtomo. His *The Order to Stop Construction*, in which a bucktooth salaryman (looking like Mickey Rooney in *Breakfast at Tiffany's*) doggedly battles out-of-control robots working on a construction project in the Amazon, is the most fun of the three. The film is bookended by Rintarō's surreal *Labyrinth*, in which a young girl and her cat slip through a portal in a grandfather clock into a bizarre alternative world, while Kawajiri's *Running Man* tells the noirish horror story of a high-speed racing driver's final drive to destruction.

Robot Carnival

various directors, 1987, 90m

One for lovers of mecha. Nine different directors, including Katsuhiro Ōtomo, contributed to this anthology of shorts, all with robotic or mechanical themes. Mainly set to music (some of it composed by frequent Studio Ghibli collaborator Joe Hisaishi), it's like an anime version of *Fantasia*, the superb visuals ranging from slapstick to serious and framed by the last gasps of the clapped-out robotic carnival attraction of the title (a reference to one of the initial *Astro Boy* episodes). The best piece is Yasuomi Umetsu's *Presence*, about a decades-long affair between a robot and her creator.

The Tale of Genji

Genji Monogatari

dir Gisaburo Sugii, 1987, 110m

The *Asahi Shimbun* wanted a classic Japanese subject for the anime it commissioned to mark the newspaper's centenary. In Murasaki Shikibu's tenth-century *Tale of Genji* – considered the world's first novel – it found the ideal material. At a thousand pages long Sugii had to chop much of the novel's epic sweep, focusing on a few episodes in the hero Genji's complicated love life and struggle for power. The anime's sluggish pace allows plenty of time to admire the ravishing visuals, inspired by traditional Japanese art, and the computerized effects that Sugii includes such as falling cherry blossom.

1990s: anime goes global

As US fans began organizing their first large-scale conventions in places such as Dallas and San Jose, it was becoming clear how financially important overseas markets now were for anime. The internet was helping to connect fans and spread news and debate faster and wider than had been previously possible, through websites such as Anime Web Turnpike. Hit series such as *Sailor Moon* (see p.210), the latest incarnation of the magical girl genre, also extended anime's popularity by tapping into the teenage female audience in the US and elsewhere.

The early 1990s also saw the rise of fantasy as an anime genre, spurred on by the global craze for role-playing games such as Dungeons and Dragons. The results varied widely, from the serious quest tale *Record of Lodoss War* (*Lodoss to Senki*) in 1990 to the ditzy comedy *Dragon Half* in 1993. Samurai swordplay also got a look in, with Yoshiaki Kawajiri's *Ninja Scroll* (*Jūbei Ninpocho*, see Canon).

Anime was far from done with science fiction, however. Mamoru Oshii leapfrogged from the *Patlabor* series in the late 1980s into a couple of *Patlabor* movies (see Canon) in the early 1990s, landing with the international sensation *Ghost in the Shell* (see Canon) in 1995. The studio responsible for realizing most of Oshii's work was **Production I.G**, a pioneer in the growing field of computer and digital animation. In 1999 they would create the eerily beautiful *Jin-Roh* (see Canon) based on a script by Oshii, using traditional cel animation before switching entirely to digital animation.

For all its importance elsewhere in turning on a new generation of anime addicts, *Ghost in the Shell* was all but ignored in Japan where fans instead went gaga over *Neon Genesis Evangelion*. Hideaki Anno's reinvention of the mecha/robot series as an existential meditation for an anime-savvy audience was the mega-hit of 1995, spawning two follow-up movies and, in 2007, a state-of-the-art reboot in the form of the first of an all-new quartet of features based on the original series.

Studio Ghibli continued to build on its reputation for the finest quality animation with beautifully conceived features including *Only Yesterday* (see

Animation with dimension

The principal difference between **2D** and **3D animation** is that the latter has depth and doesn't appear as "flat" as the former. Sometimes 3D animation is conflated with computer-generated animation even though computers are integral to both forms of animation today. While 2D essentially involved drawing movement on a flat surface, 3D is about "modelling" an object within a virtual environment that also has three dimensions. In the past, before computers reached their current level of sophistication, 3D animation was achieved by *claymation* – the stop-motion photographing of clay models, such as in the *Wallace & Gromit* movies or Ray Harryhausen's classic *Jason and the Argonauts*. Now such effects can be achieved within a computer and result in such anime as *Appleseed* and its sequel *Appleseed Ex Machina*.

Canon), *Porco Rosso* (see Canon), *Pom Poko* and *Whisper of the Heart* (see Canon). Some of the company's younger staff also made a foray into made-for-TV animation with *Ocean Waves* in 1993. The studio's biggest hit of the 1990s would be *Princess Mononoke* (see Canon), which was also the first of their films to be given a theatrical release in the US, under a distribution deal agreed with Disney in 1996.

Meanwhile, the "pocket monsters" of a Nintendo video game were on the brink of world domination via *Pokémon* (see p.205). This was not the first anime based on a video game – that honour goes, by a whisper, to Nintendo's *Super Mario Brothers* from 1986. There was also *Street Fighter II* in 1994, directed by anime veteran Gisaburo Sugii. However, neither of these had *Pokémon*'s universal appeal, enabling a multitude of cross-promotional possibilities. In its wake, much to the chagrin of cash-strapped parents, followed the likes of *Card Captor Sakura*, *Digimon* and *Yu-Gi-Oh!*.

Adult fans were not completely forsaken. In 1997 Satoshi Kon (see p.154) made a dazzling directorial debut with *Perfect Blue* (see Canon). The sophisticated plots and themes of series such as *Revolutionary Girl Utena* (see Canon), *Cowboy Bebop* (see Canon) and *Serial Experiments Lain* (see Canon) also spoke to a more mature audience. *His and Her Circumstances*, Hideaki Anno's follow-up to *Evangelion*, might have been set in a Japanese high school, but it was no less experimental and stylized in its execution.

Ocean Waves

Umi ga kikoeru

dir Tomomi Mochizuki, 1993, 72m

The disruptive impact of a transfer student into a high-school class is a hoary anime theme. But Studio Ghibli's first (and so far only) animation series for TV breathes fresh life into it by tapping into the same realistic approach adopted in *Only Yesterday* to tell a touchingly romantic, leisurely paced story of a love triangle between Taku, Matsuno and Rikako. The series has an arthouse movie feel to it and the main setting of the sun-kissed southwestern city of Kōchi contrasts nicely with other scenes in Tokyo.

Pom Poko

Heisei Tanuki Gassen Ponpoko

dir Isao Takahata, 1994, 120m

As all Japanese know, the *tanuki* – raccoon-like creatures – have big balls. Some of the funniest scenes in this overlooked Ghibli gem are when the shape-shifting tanuki heroes use their ample scrotums in an unorthodox manner. Although an awareness of Japanese culture will certainly increase your enjoyment of this surprisingly touching movie about the tanuki's attempts to save their forest habitat from human development, everyone will get the broader environmental message.

Digimon

dir Hiroyuki Kakudo, Yukio Kaizawa, 1999-2003, 205 x 30m

Debuting in the wake of the worldwide success of Pikachu and his buddies, it was inevitable that this "kids and their pet monsters" series would be compared to *Pokémon*. However, *Digimon* distinguished itself over four seasons and seven movies, by allowing the kids to grow older, live in real-world settings and become involved in more complex adventures and challenging plots. The fifth season, *Digimon Savers,* was on Japanese TV in 2006.

2000s: the digital present

Early in the new millennium the **DVD**, which debuted as a delivery method for anime around 1997, had consigned videos to the dump-bin. The new format exponentially broadened anime's appeal by allowing viewers to easily toggle between original Japanese soundtracks and English subtitles or dubs in English or other languages. Better sales led to English-language distributors significantly improving the quality of their dubs, both in terms of translation and voice acting.

New technology also changed the way anime was made. Computer graphics had reached a level of sophistication and affordability that made them ubiquitous throughout the industry. The results, however, were not always impressive: witness *Final Fantasy: The Spirits Within,* which, for all the effort and money pumped into it, still came off as wooden and sterile.

Shinji Aramaki's remake of *Appleseed*, which also used cutting-edge digital and motion-capture technology to blend live action with animation, was more successful. However, despite former Studio { president **Toshio Suzuki**'s speculation that this movie's production methods would revolutionize the animation business, most anime, made on miniscule budgets compared to the fat-wallet production of Hollywood, adheres to the cheaper 2D style.

Money isn't everything, however, as computer games graphic designer **Makoto Shinkai** (see p.162) proved in 2002 with the highly impressive *Voices of a Distant Star*, which he created alone on a home computer. Five years later, the first part of Shinkai's latest project *5 Centimeters Per Second* (see Canon) was premiered on Yahoo! Japan as streaming video, confirmation that online digital delivery is where anime is heading.

DIY anime wizardry: the astonishing *Voices of a Distant Star*

Future challenges

In switching from computer games to anime, Shinkai is swimming against the tide. Historically low wages and increased outsourcing of work to Asia is leading to what several see as a dangerous hollowing-out of talent in Japanese animation, as potential Miyazakis and Tezukas opt for the more lucrative pay and creative challenges of other content industries. Anime producers and licensors are also finding it more difficult to turn a profit in the face of tumbling DVD sales – mainly a result of fans easily being able to download practically any anime from the internet, illegally, for free. Such developments provoked wails from the industry and commentators in 2008 that "anime is dead".

The savviest producers are branching out into other areas where animation does make money, such as TV commercials, promotional video clips for music and ads, as well as computer games. Titles such as *.hack//SIGN*, which taps into the online gaming phenomena, have become games, while studios such as

The return of the short anime

Animation in Japan started with experimental shorts and it's this format that has become the one to watch again for the most creative work from new talents. There's likely to be a lot more of this kind of anime in the future as producers commission shorts for screening on mobile phones and other portable media devices.

The Oscar win in 2003 for Hayao Miyazaki's *Spirited Away* overshadows the fact that in the same year there was also a nomination in the short animation award category for anime prodigy Koji Yamamura's *Mt. Head*. This film went on to win awards in all the major international animation festivals including Annecy, Zagreb and Hiroshima. Yamamura's 21-minute-long *Franz Kafka's A Country Doctor* won the 2007 Ōfuji prize as well as a slew of other gongs. Yamamura was born in 1964 and made his first animated film at the age of thirteen; he's one of a handful of animators working in Japan today who is constantly trying out different styles, expanding his range. Find out more about him at his website www.yamamura-animation.jp.

Another up-and-coming animator working in the short medium is Kunio Kato (kiteretsu.robot.co.jp/kunio/index.html) who's part of the animation company Robot (www.robot.co.jp/charanim_en/index.html). Kato's twelve-minute-long *The House of Toy Building Blocks*, a surreal, dialogue-free work about an old man reflecting on his life, bagged the top prize at 2008's Annecy festival. You can watch *The Apple Incident*, another of his distinctive pieces at www.viddler.com/explore/Ms_Valerie/videos/367.

In 2007 Japan's public broadcaster NHK started screening a series of one-minute shorts by some of the nation's top animators in its *Ani-Kuri 15* series. Ani-Kuri is the Japanese contraction for "anime creators" and among the fifteen talents contributing pieces to the series have been established directors of the calibre of Satoshi Kon, Makoto Shinkai and Mamoru Oshii. All the shorts can be viewed online at www.nhk.or.jp/ani-kuri.

Championing the short film form has been Studio 4°C, with their ambitious two-part cinema release of *Genius Party* in 2007 and *Genius Party Beyond* in 2008. The project involves fourteen "geniuses" in the anime field, from veteran directors and animators such as Masaaki Yuasa to manga artists like Yoji Fukuama, who are making their directorial debut. Also in 2008 the studio's fifteen-minute *Wolfie the Pianist* was chosen as an Official Selection in the Cannes Film Festival's Short Film Corner.

© Studio 4°C

A moment from the summit meeting of anime's finest minds, *Genius Party*

Production I.G have created games based on their anime hits, including *Ghost in the Shell* and *Blood: The Last Vampire*.

Studio 4°C, whose surreal *Mind Game* (see Canon) and *Tekkon Kinkreet* (see Canon) are some of the most visually exciting anime of recent years, has also worked on computer games as part of its wide portfolio of projects, including a *Second Life*-style game called *Tokyo Zero Ward*.

Sticking to what it does best is **Studio Ghibli**. Miyazaki's Oscar win in 2003 for *Spirited Away* gave Japanese animation an international respectability and profile to match its growing financial clout. Ghibli has become a more trusted brand in Japan than Sony or Toyota – which partly explains why the studio's *Tales from Earthsea*, the directorial debut of Miyazaki's son Gorō, was the fourth biggest money earner at the local box office in 2006, despite being a lacklustre movie in comparison to other Ghibli offerings.

Well into his sixties, and having already announced his intention to retire, Miyazaki senior's latest production *Gake no Ue no Ponyo*, may be his last. Miyazaki is Japanese animation's living national treasure but, as he prepares to step out of the picture, it is far from clear who will succeed him, and Miyazaki has himself been openly critical about the dearth of creative talent in the industry. **Shinji Higuchi**, a founding member of Gainax, in reviewing the submissions for the 2007 **Japan Media Arts Festival** expressed "a sense of stagnation" at anime producers getting too wound up in their stories and skimping on finding interesting and new visual frameworks with which to engage their audience.

New directions

Such doom and gloom doesn't entirely reflect the facts. In 2006, Production I.G developed a technique they called "superlivemation" for **Mamoru Oshii**'s satirical fantasy documentary *Tachigui: The Amazing Lives of the Fast Food Grifters*. Superlivemation, which combines animation, photography and paper puppetry, consists of digitally processing, then animating, flat paper puppet theatre-style characters and locations based on real photographs. For the movie over thirty thousand photographs were processed to produce the final images to be animated. It's not anime as many may see it but has a clear connection with the paper cutout animations made by Ofuji and his contemporaries earlier in the century.

Combining different media in animation is nothing new – Tezuka dabbled in it back in the late 1960s in his *Cleopatra* and *Arabian Nights*. Masaaki Yuasa has more recently mashed up live-action film and animation in his *Mind Game* (see Canon). It's also a feature of the 2008 magic-girl series *Mahōtsukai ni Taisetsu na Koto: Natsu no Sora* directed by Osamu Kobayashi in which real photos are used as the background to the animation.

© Studio 4°C

The geniuses had so much fun the first time, they decided to throw another one in 2008: *Genius Party Beyond*

Flash animation and other computer technologies are also inspiring a new generation of animators to get their films out there, an example being *URDA: Third Reich* (see below) directed by Romanov Higa (www.romanov.x0.com), and animators, such as Shinkai and others, who appear happy to produce short features (see box opposite) rather than unrealistically extend their ideas into feature films or series.

Amid this variety there's still room for the traditional approach as epitomized in new feature-length movies in 2008 by both Miyazaki and Oshii. With Japan's government and some of its leading trading companies scrambling to support the medium as a pop cultural ambassador and investment growth opportunity for the nation, the final chapter in anime's history is clearly a long way off yet.

URDA: Third Reich

dir Romanov Higa, 2003, 5 x 5m

Indicative of one of the future directions of anime is this sci-fi meets World War II spy entertainment cobbled together from five-minute episodes made using flash animation and originally available for free download over the internet. Shoehorned into the compact running time is a complex tale involving a spaceship from 2112 that has somehow crash-landed in Germany in 1943. Battling over its technology is Erna Kurtz, a genetically engineered killing machine fighting for the Allies and the one-eyed Nazi commander Glimhild Kurtz with whom she shares a past.

Tales from Earthsea

Gedo Senki

dir Gorō Miyazaki, 2006, 115m

As to be expected from Studio Ghibli, there's a quality look to *Tales from Earthsea*. However, the patricide that kicks off the plot echoes one aspect of the anime's stormy production, in which first-time director Gorō struggled to prove himself to his illustrious father. The behind-the-scenes machinations are, unfortunately, more fascinating than this tedious tale of troubled youth Prince Arran and his battle against evil nemesis Cob. It's all loosely based on Ursula Le Guin's *Earthsea* series of fantasy novels. She wasn't very happy with the result either.

The Girl Who Leapt Through Time

Toki o Kakeru Shōjo

dir Mamoru Hosada, 2006, 98m

A high-school romance with a fantasy twist, *Toki Kake*, as it's been dubbed in Japan, is a charming movie about Makoto, a skittish baseball-loving tomboy who discovers she has the ability to jump (quite literally) back in time. The fun results of this new skill soon prove to be more complicated, particularly where it concerns two of her classmates. Director Hosada is a Studio Ghibli alumnus, as are several other key members of the crew, and their training shows in the movie's assured pacing, quality of characterization and beautifully detailed animation, with some scenes edging towards photorealism. The film's lyrical mood is enhanced by a delicate piano score by Kiyoshi Yoshida.

The Sky Crawlerss

dir Mamoru Oshii, 2008, 121m

Oshii makes a triumphant return to anime with this movie based on a five-part sci-fi novel by Hiroshi Mori, a tale of daredevil teenage pilots pitted against each other in deadly aerial dogfights as entertainment for the masses: think *Porco Rosso* (see Canon) mixed with *Top Gun* and infused with a retro World War II look. The plot revolves around Yuichi Kannami, a pilot with amnesia, his stern female commander Suito Kusanagi (voiced by Oscar-nominated actress Rinko Kikuchi) and their flying ace nemesis Teacher. The air battles, complete with stomach-churning ascents, plummets and rolls, are awesome.

Gake no ue no Ponyo

dir Hayao Miyazaki, 2008

For his tenth animated movie as a director, the master jumps back into the mind of a child, as he did so successfully in *My Neighbour Totoro*. He also returns to basics to craft a beautiful film of distinctive visuals all drawn by hand and embellished with minimal computer effects. Elements of Hans Christian Andersen's *The Little Mermaid* peek through in the plot about Ponyo, a little girl – part fish, part human – who longs to see what lies above water. Her wish comes true when she gets stuck in a glass jar and is washed ashore to be rescued by the boy Sosuke, who lives with his mum and dad, who's a fisherman. Ponyo loves it on dry land, but her parents want her to return to their underwater world and set out to get her back.

The Top Ten

1. Akira (1988)

Dynamic action sequences drive forward this nihilistic sci-fi fantasy about biker gangs, terrorists, government plots and a telekinetic teenager mutating in Tokyo, 2019.

2. Astro Boy (1963)

Osamu Tezuka's robot boy with a soul may have become a cute international icon, but the anime series reveals his complex, sometimes tragic history.

3. Ghost in the Shell (1995)

A sophisticated sci-fi thriller that's among director Mamoru Oshii's finest works, alongside his visually dazzling sequel *Innocence*.

4. Jin-Roh (1999)

Darkly atmospheric film noir-style remix of the Red Riding Hood fable set in an imaginary Japan of the 1950s and about a doomed love affair between the wolf and his quarry.

5. Only Yesterday (1991)

Isao Takahata's beautifully realized movie follows a woman, on a life-changing vacation in the countryside, recalling episodes from her childhood.

6. My Neighbour Totoro (1988)

Hayao Miyazaki's charming kid's story, set in a pastoral Japan of the 1950s introduces one of Japanese animation's greatest characters – the giant grinning fur ball of the title.

7. Neon Genesis Evangelion (1995)

The otaku's ultimate anime is an ambitious, densely plotted sci-fi conundrum examining the psychological implications of being the teenage pilot of a supreme weapon of destruction.

8. Mind Game (2004)

Take a brain-boggling trip into this visually dazzling, surreal and highly original cocktail involving an aspiring manga artist, the Yakuza and a giant whale.

9. Wings of Honneamise (1987)

A richly imagined sci-fi about the fantasy land of Honneamise, curiously like our own world (but not), and its Royal Space Force's efforts to launch a man into orbit.

10. Tokyo Godfathers (2003)

Satoshi Kon's heartwarming Christmas fairy tale of redemption for three tramps and the baby they discover in the trash is pure anime magic.

the canon

fifty must-see anime

Of course, this whole book is testimony to the fact that there are thousands of anime that more than repay several viewings. On the opposite page, you'll notice the author's entirely personal top ten favourites – which will no doubt divide opinion among this book's readers.

But the rest of this chapter focuses, in alphabetical order, upon the fifty anime that you really owe it to yourself to watch: they are the ones that are most likely to stand the test of time.

Akira

アキラ

dir Katsuhiro Ōtomo, 1988, 124m

scr Katsuhiro Ōtomo *m* Shoji Yamashiro *cast* Mitsuo Iwata/Johnny Yong Bosch: Shotarō Kaneda; Nozomu Sasaki/Joshua Seth: Tetsuo Shima; Mami Koyama/Wendee Lee: Kei; Tesshō Genda/Robert Wicks: Ryūsaku; Tarō Ishida/James Lyon: Colonel Shikishima (*English cast refers to the 2001 Pioneer version*)

Official Bandai site www.bandaivisual.co.jp/akira

Just as the bubble of Japan's economy of the 1980s was about to burst, a bomb of a more positive nature detonated, with the premiere of *Akira*. The nuclear-style explosion that wipes out Tokyo at the start of the movie is an appropriate metaphor for the shattering effect *Akira* would have on the world's perception of anime. As Hiroshima was to warfare, so was *Akira* to the film industry: after *Akira*, no one would ever look at Japanese animation in quite the same way again.

Using state-of-the-art technology, *Akira* had impeccable production values that racked up costs reputedly in excess of $10 million. It was an unheard-of budget for an anime up to that point, and the movie took the combined efforts of eight different companies to bring it to the screen. In Japan the film flopped and took years to recoup its backers' investment. To the rest of the world, however, it was nothing short of a revelation. Two decades after its initial release, *Akira*'s power to dazzle and provoke remains undiminished, even if its state-of-the-art look might have been eclipsed by technically more accomplished works. *Akira*'s revved-up energy barely flags for a second as it unfolds its tale of sinister establishment plots and dark, doom-laden menace.

Rather than the titular character, who remains an enigmatic presence, *Akira* focuses on juvenile delinquents Kaneda and Tetsuo, members of a motorbike gang who tear up the streets of Neo-Tokyo, battling rival gang the Clowns. The movie's brutal violence and social critique of a corrupt society on the brink of collapse recalls Anthony Burgess's novel *A Clockwork Orange* and the scene in which Kaori, Tetsuo's girlfriend, is assaulted is an echo of a similar one in the classic Stanley Kubrick movie adaptation.

Tetsuo is kidnapped by shady government forces and begins to discover hitherto unsuspected

Akira: the manga connection

Katsuhiro Ōtomo's manga *Akira* was first serialized in *Young* magazine in 1982 and finished in July 1990, two years after the movie's release. Published in six *tankōbon* volumes, it's a sprawling saga with a total of over two thousand pages, additional subplots and a completely different ending from the movie. Akira is a major character in the manga, who ends up joining forces with Tetsuo.

Observant anime and manga fans will have already noted the coincidence in certain character details between *Akira* and *Gigantor*. Mitsuteru Yokoyama's original manga *Tetsujin 28-go*, on which *Gigantor* was based, is one of Ōtomo's favourites, so he paid homage to it by copying the names of its key characters Kaneda, Tetsuo, Ryūsaku and Shikishima (a professor in *Gigantor*, a colonel in *Akira*). Just as Gigantor is the 28th robot of its ilk, Akira is number 28 of the mutant psychic children bred by the government.

telekinetic powers within himself. Kaneda, attracted to a proto-revolutionary girl called Kei, joins a terrorist cell to help free his friend. The climactic showdown comes at the half-built Olympic stadium, beneath which the remains of the mysterious Akira are buried. Here the monstrous nature of Tetsuo's power is revealed as he transforms into a terrifying force of nature.

Akira imagines a future Tokyo of 2019, but it takes its inspiration from the appearance of the city in the 1980s, and the student protests against the Vietnam War that rocked the capital back in the 1960s. Despite the violence it is also a sympathetic, multifaceted portrait of teenage rebellion and anarchy. One glimpse at the brutal world of the reform school the gang is sent to, or behind the door of the corrupt government running the city, is enough to convince you that Tetsuo, Kaneda and company are much better off toughing it out on their own.

So imaginative and otherworldly were the images created for *Akira* that it was once said that it could never have been a live-action movie. Times change, and technology moves on. Now plans are afoot for a live-action treatment of *Akira*, courtesy of Leonardo DiCaprio's production company and Warner Bros. Whatever the outcome, *Akira* remains essential viewing, not just for its cinematic merits but also because it was a crucial step in anime's evolution as a globally popular art form.

Astro Boy

Tetsuwan Atomu; 鉄腕アトム

Series 1: 1963–66, 193 x 30m

dir Osamu Tezuka *scr* Osamu Tezuka and others *m* Tatsuo Takai *cast* Mari Shimizu/Kazue Tagami ep. 97–106/Billie Lou Watt: Atom; Hisashi Katsuta/Ray Owens: Dr Ochanomizu/Dr Elefun; Hisashi Yokomori: Dr Tenma/Dr Boynton

Series 2: 1980–81, 52 x 30m

dir Satoshi Dezaki, *scr* Osamu Tezuka and others *m* Nariaki Saegusa *cast* Mari Shimizu/Billie Lou Watt: Atom; Hasashi Katsuta: Dr Ochanomizu/Dr Elefun; Yoko Mizugaki: Uran; Kazuo Kumakura: Higeoyaji

Series 3: 2003–04, 50 x 30m

dir Kazuya Konaka *scr* Keiichi Hasegawa, Chiaki Konaka, Sadayuki Mura, Ai Ota *m* Takashi Yoshimatsu *cast* Makoto Tsumura/Candi Milo; Atom; Hisashi Katsuta/Wally Wingert: Dr Ochanomizu/Dr O'Shay; Shinya Owada/Darien Harewood: Dr Tenma

Astro Boy official site astroboy.jp
Tezuka Osamu World page en.tezuka.co.jp/anime/sakuhin/ts/ts002.html
Astro Boy Online www.astroboy-online.com
Manga site astroboy.manga.com
Astro Boy Episode Guide astroboy.tv
Astro Boy Encyclopedia Project tezukainenglish.com/?q=node/70

If anime has a Mickey Mouse, it is **Astro Boy**. The iconic character broke ground for the medium not just in Japan, where the series based on **Osamu Tezuka**'s original manga, was one of the first animated TV programmes, but also in the US, where it was the first anime to be translated for TV syndication. A ratings smash on both sides of the Pacific, the cute robot boy with Betty Boop eyes and Superman-like powers fast became a cherished mascot for the baby-boomer generation and its children.

In an action-packed first episode Astro was created then rejected by Dr Tenma (Dr Boynton in the English dubbed version), a scientist driven mad by the death of his young son Tobio/Aster, in whose image Astro is designed. The story of Pinocchio looms large as Astro is sold to the robot circus, from which he is soon rescued by Dr Ochanomizu (Dr Elefun). In subsequent episodes the kindly doctor fashions a robot family for Astro, including a sister called Uran. Programmed to always think of others, Astro proceeds to save

One of Japan's national treasures, Astro Boy is possibly the most iconic of all characters in the anime universe

humanity from multiple disasters – even though much of the world remains suspicious, if not downright hostile, to him and his fellow robots.

Made in black and white on a miniscule budget, *Astro Boy* rises above its creaky, limited animation to weave an enchanting spell through a combination of strong characterization, inventive visuals (including the puns and slapstick so beloved by Tezuka) and thought-provoking plots embracing topics not typically broached with its target audience of children. There are clear parallels with racism and prejudice in the real world in the discriminatory treatment of robots throughout the series. And, in the original series' final episode ("The Greatest Adventure on Earth"), Astro flies directly into the sun to save the Earth from catastrophic global warming, becoming anime's first environmental martyr.

Origins of Astro Boy

In the story, Astro Boy's date of "birth" is 7 April 2003; that year saw massed celebrations for the boy robot throughout Japan, including a new series and many promotional events, including the unveiling of a jewel-encrusted model of Astro, valued at over $1 million. The character's public debut was of course some fifty years before that, in a manga series drawn by Osamu Tezuka and published in *Shōnen* magazine in 1951. Entitled *Atomu Taishi* – "Ambassador Atom" – it introduced the cute mechanical boy who would indeed become an emissary between humans and robots.

A year later Astro Boy graduated to star in his own series *Tetsuwan Atomu* (*Mighty Atom*), but it wouldn't be until the original TV series was sold for syndication in the US in 1963 that Astro gained his English name. Although Tezuka had a complex relationship with his most famous creation, killing him off once on screen and three times in print, he kept on producing new stories featuring Astro up until 1981. For the definitive biographical details about Astro Boy and his creator read Fred L. Schodt's insightful *The Astro Boy Essays*. Schodt is also the translator of the 23 volumes in the *Astro Boy* manga series published by Dark Horse Comics.

Although it looked like sayonara for Astro, the robot boy had become far too popular to be killed off for good. Resurrected in a manga barely a month later, Astro returned to the screen for a blink or you'll miss it cameo in Tezuka's *Arabian Nights* movie, followed by a longer role in the 1969 TV special *Star of the Giants vs the Mighty Atom* in which characters from *Astro Boy* take on the baseball team the Yomuri Giants.

The financial collapse of Tezuka's animation company Mushi Pro in 1973 kept his most famous creation in limbo for a decade until his return to the screen in a new colour series in 1980, which Tezuka supervised. This series followed more faithfully the original storylines of the manga, and the result was a more sombre *Astro Boy* that, in an environment now awash with anime robots, failed to capture the public's imagination in quite the same way.

The 2003 edition of the series was a great improvement. This was Astro rebooted for an anime-literate audience, with not only an intriguing non-linear storyline packed with foreboding menace, but also with its star dubbed with the voice of a young teenager rather than that of the little boy he had always been in the past. The high-quality animation was light years removed from both previous versions yet the muted colour palate and retro design stayed true to the spirit of the original.

As this book goes to press, a new generation is about to discover the magic of *Astro Boy* when a long-awaited movie version is released in late 2009, produced by the Hong Kong based Imagi Animation Studios, the same CG production studio behind the *Tokyo Mutant Ninja Turtles* and *Gatchaman* movies (see p.244). Purists might freak at a CG version of their beloved hero, but as Tezuka Productions are a partner with Imagi on the movie, it's fairly certain that this will essentially be the same old Astro Boy, a lovable, fallible, brave innocent in a frequently venal world, standing for justice and harmony. In short, he's the robot many humans wished they could be.

Barefoot Gen

Hadashi no Gen; はだしのゲン

dir Mori Masaki, 1983, 85m

scr Keiji Nakazawa *m* Kentaro Haneda *cast* Issei Miyazaki: Gen; Masaki Kōda: Ryuta & Shinji; Seiko Nakano: Eiko; Takao Inoue: Daikichi Nakaoka & Father; Junji Nishimura: Mr Pak; Kae Shimamura: Kimie & Mother; Katsuji Mori: Seiji Yoshida

Madhouse www.madhouse.co.jp/works/1986-1983/works_movie_hadashi.html

Toyofumi Ogura is of a generation that can recall the moment that Little Boy (as the atomic bomb dropped on Hiroshima was nicknamed) exploded. "I saw, or rather felt, an enormous bluish white flash of light, as when a photographer lights a dish of magnesium," he writes in *Letters from the End of the World*. Gen Nakaoka, the Gen of the title, is also a little boy, and it's through his eyes that we witness this shattering split-second and its apocalyptic aftermath in *Barefoot Gen*. Horrific images show people melting like candles, their clothes blown to shreds, and their eyeballs popping and dangling from exposed skulls. Buildings crumble, orange flames curl into an acid yellow sky, a burning horse gallops through the street, and a purple mushroom cloud rises.

This hellish, Bosch-like scene marks the start of the traumas that Gen must endure in this intensely moving anime, based on the autobiographical manga of Keiji Nakazawa who, like his heroic

The family of plucky and stoical young Gen

six-year-old title character, lost most of his family in the Hiroshima blast. It's a tragic tale but, largely because of brave Gen's indefatigable nature, a life-affirming one, too. Gen and Ryuta, another of this anime's plucky little survivors, are drawn as robust, expressive, cartoon boys – in contrast to the far more realistic depiction of the other characters.

The anime starts a few days before the blast by introducing Gen's family – his father who hates the war and those in Japan who support it, his heavily pregnant mother, his dutiful older sister Eiko and younger brother Shinji who faithfully follows Gen everywhere. Food is rationed and everyone is hungry. Kimie, Gen's mother, is so weak she collapses. A neighbour tells Gen that she should eat carp to get strong, so he heads to the temple pond and with Shinji's help catches a fish. In the process, the temple priest finds the boys and angrily wallops Gen. Uncowed, Gen explains how the fish is for his stricken mother and the priest relents. This episode shows how resourceful, determined and unselfish Gen can be – all attributes that will help him get through the nightmares to come.

Amid Hiroshima's charred ruins, surrounded by the dead and dying, Gen continues to support his mother and baby sister, whom he delivers shortly after the blast in which the rest of his family have perished. He finds them food and builds a shelter into which they take the orphan boy Ryuta, who reminds them both of Shinji. Gen's hair starts to drop out through radiation sickness (or *pika* as it's known in Japan) but he doesn't give up. The anime ends on a note of hope with wheat sprouting in the fields just as the hair on Gen's head begins to regrow.

Toshio Hirata's 1986 sequel *Barefoot Gen 2* takes up the story three years later as Gen, Ryuta and the increasingly sick Kimie struggle to rebuild their lives in a still shattered Hiroshima. Brimming with tear-jerking scenes of human brutality and tragedy, it's worth watching for an insight into the conditions that survivors like Gen endured for years after the blast. The trauma of Hiroshima haunts many anime, but only in these movies do you really see what it was like at ground zero.

Castle in the Sky

Tenkū no Shiro Laputa; 天空の城ラピュタ

dir Hayao Miyazaki, 1986, 124m

scr Hayao Miyazaki *m* Joe Hisaishi *cast* Mayumi Tanaka/James Van Der Beek: Pazu; Keiko Yokozawa/Anna Paquin: Sheeta; Kotoe Hatsui/Cloris Leachman: Dola; Minori Terada/Mark Hamill: Muska

Set in the late nineteenth century in an alternative world that looks a lot like Earth but isn't, and which has technology out of sync with its time, *Castle in the Sky* is the first movie made by **Hayao Miyazaki** and **Isao Takahata** after they formed Studio Ghibli. A lively Indiana Jones-style fantasy, packed with endearing and memorable Miyazaki characters, creations and ideas, it is partly inspired by a passage in Jonathan Swift's *Gulliver's Travels* about an ancient civilization that created flying cities.

Pazu, a poor but indefatigable orphan boy who works in a coal mine, cherishes a photo taken by his late father of the floating citadel known as Laputa. Even though nobody else in his village believes such a place exists, Pazu is determined to find it. Then, quite literally, a young girl called Sheeta drifts down from the sky and into his life, a mysterious blue stone pendant glowing around her neck. They instantly form a bond but have little time to relax as pursuing Sheeta are both the sinister Colonel Muska, who had previously kidnapped her, and Dola, a fearsome Ma Baker-type figure who leads a comic bunch of sky pirates, some of whom are her sons. Everyone is after Sheeta's pendant.

Muska succeeds in recapturing Sheeta, who is incarcerated in a fortress where the dormant remains of a huge robot, believed to have

Pazu and Sheeta first make each other's acquaintance in *Castle in the Sky*

fallen from Laputa, also lie. Pazu teams up with Dola's brigade and they launch an aerial attack on the castle to rescue Sheeta. In the meantime, the robot comes back to life and seeks to protect Sheeta but is destroyed by Muska's military airship, which having discovered the location of Laputa heads off in its direction. Pazu and Sheeta–now onboard Dola's airship–follow, leading to a spectacular showdown on the floating city.

As with *Nausicaä* and his future films, Miyazaki's concern for environmental balance and respect for nature is a central theme of *Castle in the Sky*. So too is his love of flight and flying machines, which appear here in many guises from the dragonfly-like "flapter" planes of the pirates to the Tower of Babel-inspired Laputa. The opening credit images give a succinct history of how the technology to make such flying castles developed. *Castle in the Sky* is also lovely to look at, with better quality animation than in *Nausicaä*. Miyazaki drew on a host of references apart from Swift for the film's visuals. Pazu's village is inspired by a visit Miyazaki made to mining villages in Wales in 1984 where he was impressed by the tenacity of the striking miners who fought to protect their jobs. His design of the giant robot is in homage to one of the **Fleisher Brothers**' Superman cartoons from 1941. A life-size replica of the Laputa robot stands on the roof of the Ghibli Museum (see p.278).

Cowboy Bebop

Kaubi bibappu; カウボーイビバップ

dir Shinichirō Watanabe, 1998–99, 26 x 25m

scr Keiko Nobumoto *m* Yokō Kanno *cast* Kōichi Yamadera/Steven Jay Blum: Spike Spiegel; Unshō Ishizuka/John Billingslea: Jet Black; Megumi Hayashibara/Wendee Lee: Faye Valentine; Aoi Tada/Melissa Charles: Ed

Bandai Channel site www.b-ch.com/cgi-bin/contents/ttl/det.cgi?ttl_c=130

Adult Swim site www.adultswim.com/shows/cowboybebop/index.html

Cowboy Bebop The Movie www.sonypictures.com/cthe/cowboybebop

Featuring an unlikely team of bounty hunters chasing down their quarry across the solar system in 2071, *Cowboy Bebop* is a dish made from leftovers that, on paper, ought not to work, but in practice tastes delicious. As the title and the bounty-hunting theme suggest, this is archetypal Western territory overlaid by the science-fiction setting of the near future. Other influences, among its many, include kung fu (hero Spike is pretty nifty with his feet and hands), and yakuza flicks. Throw in a set of mysterious but gradually revealed back stories and it starts to become clear why the highly entertaining *Cowboy Bebop* is such a fan favourite.

The *Bebop* of the title is the running-on-the-smell-of-an-oily-rag spaceship of Spike Spiegel and Jet Black, the proverbial tough guy with a soft heart to Spike's laid-back coolster. Within the first few episodes this duo pretty much by accident acquire a motley crew of three: the confidence trickster and gambling addict Faye Valentine, who dresses like a cheap hooker (a blatant concession to one audience constituency); a Welsh corgi "data dog" Ein, whom nobody seems to notice is a supercomputer in disguise; and a teenage girl called Ed, a rubber-limbed ace hacker who talks weird gibberish.

The show's sci-fi trappings are fancy but not too fancy – there are no giant robots, aliens or planet-destroying space stations to deal with. Instead, this is a world that looks very familiar, right down to the multi-racial cast of bit players and extras – a rarity in anime. Director **Shinichirō Watanabe** takes the bold move of just assuming that the audience will figure out the background to the action, namely that Earth has largely been laid to waste by rock showers from a shattered moon and that humans now live on colonies on the other planets and moons of the solar system.

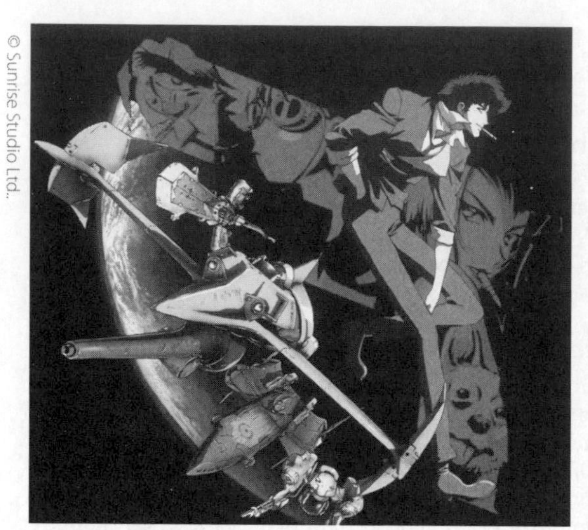

If the future is this cool, sign us up: Spike Spiegel and the gang in *Cowboy Bebop*

Intriguing details about the lead characters are dished out as the series progresses. Flighty Faye regains her blanked-out memory of traumatic childhood events, becoming a far more nuanced character than the two-dimensional sex-bomb she at first appears. The same goes for the other three leads (you never really learn much about Ein). Gangster turned good-guy Spike was burned by a past love affair with Julia, a classic *femme fatale*. When she resurfaces in the final episodes, *Cowboy Bebop*'s comedy evaporates to be replaced by bloody violence and tragedy.

For a series in which the lead characters are chasing ghosts of their past, it's apt that the story for *Cowboy Bebop* is credited to one of the most infamous of anime phantoms: **Hajime Yatate**. This fictitious "writer" is often used by Studio Sunrise (part of the Bandai Group) to ensure they retain the copyright to their projects.

Cowboy Bebop's conclusion made follow-ups tricky. When the polished movie version was made in 2001, it was designed to fit into the timeframe between episodes 22 and 23 of the series, just before the Bebop's crew splinters. Like the series, the film has a killer soundtrack. It's the work of Yokō Kanno and her band The Seatbelts – a brilliant pastiche of jazz, blues and rock tunes and an essential element in setting *Cowboy Bebop*'s retro atmosphere and hip credibility.

5 Centimeters per Second

Byōsoku Go Centimeter; 秒速５センチメートル

dir Makoto Shinkai, 2007, 63m

scr Makoto Shinkai *m* Tenmon *cast* Kenji Mizuhashi/David Mantraga: Takaki Tono; Yoshimi Kondo/Hilary Haag: Akari Shinohara; Satomi Hanamura/Serena Varghese: Kanae Sumida

Official Japanese site 5cm.yahoo.co.jp

A sense of the fleeting nature of beauty is something intrinsic to Japanese aesthetics. It is encapsulated in Japan's appreciation of cherry blossom, or *sakura*. As a frothy pink tide of blooms ripples across the archipelago each spring, parties are held beneath the gently falling petals, which are said to drift to the ground at the speed of 5cm per second. Which is where the anime wunderkind **Makoto Shinkai** derived the title of his third major production, a trio of interlinked shorts in which *sakura* flurries are a motif.

Like the cherry blossoms, Shinkai's movies are gorgeous to look at. Audiences and critics alike adored his second short film *Voices of a Distant Star* and he further cemented his reputation as a precocious talent with his full-length feature *The Place Promised in our Earlier Days* (for both see p.162). *5cm* is his best effort yet. It is set in the real world rather than in a science-fiction concept, but its themes are ones he's essayed in the past: enforced separation, unrequited love and learning how to move on.

Photorealistic images, precise in their detail and composition, are Shinkai's forte. His lighting effects are amazing – street lamps casting luminous circles in the snow on a dark night, a fluorescent light reflecting off the handrails of a swaying commuter train, the flickering green reflection of a cellphone screen in the pupil of an eye, the scurrying shadows of clouds passing over verdant fields, the golden glow of a setting sun – it's all captured beautifully.

In the first, and most poignant, segment a pair of elementary school sweethearts, Takaki and Akari, are thwarted in their plan to attend junior high school together in Tokyo when their families move to opposite ends of the country. The devoted couple remain in contact by letter (this is the pre-texting, pre-email age) and, just before his move south, Takaki makes a lonely journey north by train in a snowstorm for a brief reunion with Akari.

Snowy landscapes are exchanged for tropical sunlight on sugar cane

© Makoto Shinkai/
CoMix Wave films

Makoto Shinkai shows his painterly touch in his masterful depictions of Japanese cherry blossom in *5 centimeters per Second*

fields in the middle segment, entitled *Cosmonaut*. Set on the island of Tanegashima, base for Japan's space programme (which allows Shinkai a brief sci-fi-esque flourish when a rocket blasts off at a crucial moment), the main character this time is Kanae, an aimless high school student and surfer, who struggles to voice her love for Takaki, who in turn is still obsessing about Akari. The shortest episode, capping off the film, shows the adult Takaki working back in Tokyo as a computer programmer; he still thinks of Akari, who is seen heading to the capital to join her fiancé.

In the final moments Takaki and Akari perhaps pass each other at a railway crossing they played around when they were kids, igniting a montage of fleeting images accompanied by the theme song "One More Time, One More Chance", sung by **Masayoshi Yamazaki**. This is one of the director's favourite songs – the lyrics inspired parts of his script while the melody is picked up by composer Tenmon in his score, which does as fantastic a job in setting the anime's mood as did his music in Shinkai's previous movies.

Fullmetal Alchemist

Hagane no Renkinjutsushi; 鋼の錬金術師

dir Seiji Mizushima, TV series 2003–04, 51 x 30m; movie 2005, 105m

scr Akatsuki Yamatoya, Aya Yoshinaga, Jun Ishikawa, Katsuhiko Takayama, Natsuko Takahashi, Shō Aikawa, Toshiki Inoue *m* Michiru Ōshima *cast* Romi Paku/Vic Mignogna: Edward Elric; Rie Kugimiya/Aaron Dismuke: Alphonse Elric; Tōrū Ōkawa/Travis Willingham: Roy Mustang; Megumi Toyoguchi/Caitlin Glass: Winry Rockbell; Masashi Ebara/Scott McNeil: Hoenheim Elric; Yumi Kakazu/Monica Rial: Dante; Junich Suwabe/Chris Patton: Greed

Adult Swim site www.adultswim.com/shows/fullmetal

Funimation site www.FullMetalAlchemist.com/season2_2

Appropriately for an anime with the pseudo-science of alchemy at its heart, *Fullmetal Alchemist* (*FMA*) has proved to be a golden property. Based on an ongoing manga by female *mangaka* **Hiromu Arakawa** (in its 21st volume as of December 2008), *FMA* is a modern blockbuster, and has transmuted into an award-winning anime series and movie (*Fullmetal Alchemist The Movie: Conqueror of Shamballa*), toys, video games and novels. The reasons for its success are simple: it has one of the most engrossing plots of recent anime and great characters, particularly its central heroes, the brothers Edward and Alphonse Elric, and the fascinating *homunculi* – creatures created through alchemy and named after the cardinal sins.

In *FMA*'s fantasy world of Amestris, alchemy is not just some hocus pocus about turning base metal into gold but a fully fledged science involving analysis, deconstruction and reconstruction (all in a clap of the hands!) of practically anything into anything else. The only thing that is forbidden – because it has dire results, if attempted – is to use alchemy to bring back the dead. Such an ill-fated use of the science by the brothers Elric to resurrect their mother is what kicks off this epic tale, leaving elder brother Ed without an arm and a leg, and younger brother Al little more than a talking soul encased in a suit of medieval-looking armour.

From this point on the brothers start a quest for the philosopher's stone, a fabled substance that is reputed to have the power to overcome the "law of equivalent exchange" – that to obtain something, another thing of equal value has to be lost. Ed, who is the youngest State Alchemist in Amestris (and holds the title of Fullmetal Alchemist), knows this law only too well as he was forced

courtesy of FUNimation Entertainment

He ain't heavy, he's my brother: Ed (right) not Al (left) is the *Fullmetal Alchemist*

to sacrifice one of his limbs to save Al's soul. The brothers hope that the stone will enable them to replace their missing body parts.

As the story progresses, Ed and Al are increasingly forced to question alchemic law. Sometimes people do seem to get something for nothing, and hard work and goodness are not always rewarded. Such contradictions and paradoxes are satisfying food for thought for those who prefer their anime served with a seasoning of moral quandaries. Politics is also thrown into the mix. The series has a sub-plot about the suppression of the Ishbalans – a religious people living in the desert who are clear stand-ins for Islamic Arabs. The movie, partly set in Munich in the 1920s and about the separated brothers attempts to be reunited, has the rise of fascism in Nazi Germany as its background.

All of this may make it seem like *FMA* is heavy going – which it can be at times. There are lighthearted moments, however, particularly when the hot-headed Ed loses his rag each time characters pass comment on his diminutive size or mistake the tall, armour-clad Al as not only the Fullmetal Alchemist of the title but as the older sibling.

In a series with not particularly distinguished animation, one of the most accomplished elements is how Ed, Al and their childhood friend Winry, who helps design and maintain Ed's prosthetic limbs, appear at different ages. Over the course of the series and movie you watch them grow up, which is uncannily similar – and similarly affecting – to witnessing the maturing of the child actors in the *Harry Potter* films.

Gankutsuō

The Count of Monte Cristo; 巌窟王
dir Mahiro Maeda, 2004–05, 24 x 25m

scr Natsuko Takahashi, Tomohiro Yamashita *m* Jean-Jacques Burnel, Koji Kasamatsu, Reiji Kitazato *cast* Jōji Nakata/Taylor Henry: Count of Monte Cristo/Edmond Dan Dantès; Jun Fukuyama/Johnny Yong Bosch: Albert de Morcerf; Daisuke Hirakawa/Ethan Murray: Franz d'Epinay; Akiko Yajima/Jennifer Sekiguchi: Haydée; Mai Nakahara/Carrie Savage: Peppo; Kikuko Inoue/Mia Bradley: Mercédès de Morcerf; Jūrōta Kosugi/Francis C. Cole: Fernand de Morcerf

Official Japanese site www.gankutsuou.com

Official US site www.montecristodvd.com

Do not adjust your screen! *Gankutsuō* is a gorgeous visual firework that takes anime in a radically different artistic direction. It's as if the high priests of "superflat" (see p.246) had soaked up the sumptuous gilded art of Gustav Klimt: this sci-fi refraction of Dumas' classic tale of revenge largely ditches the traditional painting and shading of characters and sets in favour of slabs of rich textile designs and textures, and metallic and natural surface treatments, over which the outlines of images glide.

Even though it is achieved by computer, this painterly *tour de force* is the antithesis of the hyper-realistic yet curiously alienating CGI trappings of countless other contemporary movies and immersive video games. *Gankutsuō*'s design is not just superficial or a gimmick. The multi-layered look, as if all the characters are hiding behind opulent Venetian screens, is a visual metaphor for the deceptions, corruption and scheming that lie at the heart of this complex morality tale.

We're millennia away from nineteenth century France at the show's start, when young aristocrats Albert and Franz swing by the appropriately named lunar city of Luna in search of fun and adventure at its carnival. The characters' clothing (which includes a few costume designs by the real-life fashion designer **Anna Sui**) and Luna's European ambiance, however, purposefully allude to the novel's post-Napoleonic setting. So does the social structure with its class system, arranged marriages and entertainments such as grand balls and opera. It is at the opera that the boys first encounter the mysterious **Count of Monte Cristo**, who tends to stand out in a crowd thanks to his ice-blue skin, pointed ears and different-coloured eyes – one red, one green.

Combining the flamboyance of Byron with the menace of Dracula, the charismatic Count quickly has the naïve, trusting Albert enthralled, but the more suspicious Franz on his guard. When the Count rescues Albert from bandits, the pieces fall into place for the Count's return to Paris, where he puts into motion his carefully laid plan of revenge on the three men and their families who robbed him of his life and true love many years previously.

Gankutsuō may be eye candy but the true pleasure of the series is in the strength of its character development and the tantalizingly slow revelation of the story, with flashbacks used to fill in crucial details. Many of Dumas' original plot elements are skilfully incorporated into their fantastic new clothes, but there are some changes. Albert, a minor character in the novel, takes centre stage and the audience see most of the action unfold through his innocent wide eyes. There are homoerotic tensions between Albert, Franz and the Count. And, despite the wrongs done to him, the Count is not such a sympathetic victim.

The conclusion is also radically different from the novel, which in Japanese is known as *Gankutsuō* (meaning *King of the Cave*). If you can handle subtitles over the busy visuals, it's worth watching the series with its original Japanese soundtrack – the voice acting is generally better and the French narration from the Count, at the start of each show, is a classy touch missing in the English dub.

Ghost in the Shell

Ghost in the Shell/Kōkaku Kidōtai; 攻殻機動隊

dir Mamoru Oshii, 1995, 83m

scr Kazunori Itō *m* Kenji Kawai *cast* Akio Ōtsuka/Richard George: Batou; Atsuko Tanaka/Mimi Woods: Major Motoko Kusanagi; Iemasa Kayumi/Abe Lasser: The Puppet Master; Kōichi Yamadera/Christopher Joyce: Togusa; Tamio Ōki/William Fredrick: Aramaki

Production I.G site www.productionig.com/contents/works/02_/000037.html

Ghost in the Shell: Stand Alone Complex official Japanese site www.kokaku-s.com

Ghost in the Shell: Stand Alone Complex official English site www.ghostintheshell.tv

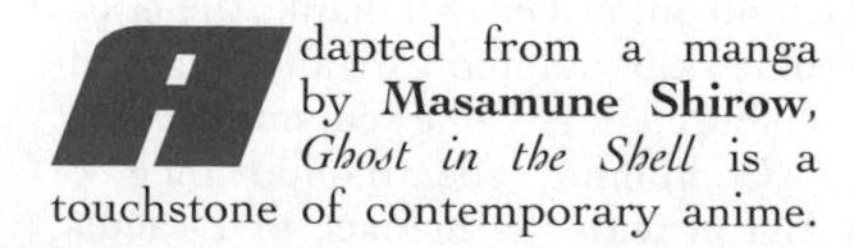

Adapted from a manga by **Masamune Shirow**, *Ghost in the Shell* is a touchstone of contemporary anime. Famed for its full-throttle action scenes, worthy of any Hollywood blockbuster, and its kick-ass cyborg babe heroine, Major Motoko

Kusanagi, it has a distinctive visual style that makes creative and appropriate use of computer graphics. More than vacuous eyecandy, the film poses several philosophical questions about the interaction of man and technology and what it means to be human.

It's 2029 in a city resembling Hong Kong – a cacophonous mass of brightly coloured Chinese calligraphy, crowded street markets and soaring skyscrapers. Technology has evolved to the point that most people have some kind of cybernetic augmentation to their bodies. Possibly the only thing that remains truly human is the "ghost" (i.e. soul). Kusanagi has a ghost floating around inside her titanium-clad shell, but she's in the midst of an identity crisis. Might that soul also be an artificial program, no more real than the rest of her? And if so, does it really matter?

Kusanagi and her colleagues Batou and Togusa work for Public Security Section 9 (S9), a covert police unit dedicated to investigating cyber crimes. They're assigned to track down a criminal hacker known as the Puppet Master. Gradually it becomes clear that the elusive Puppet Master is not a human but an artificial intelligence born independently from an illegal government program. It now wants political asylum, but the government department that created the programme wants the Puppet Master shut down – permanently. With Kusanagi and S9 caught in the middle, it comes down to an all-guns-blazing climax in which Kusanagi and the Puppet Master finally connect in an unexpected way.

Ghost in the Shell was made as a co-production between UK and US anime distributor Manga Entertainment and Production I.G in an attempt to replicate the overseas success of *Akira*. Director Oshii, whose earlier *Patlabor* movies had similar themes, proved to be the ideal man for the job, infusing Shirow's manga with more intellectual depth, and the look and feel of Ridley Scott's *Blade Runner*. Kenji Kiwai's ethereal music score, incorporating chants in ancient Japanese, is one of the most distinctive and memorable in anime.

The movie has been the creative inspiration for projects as diverse as *The Matrix* and a Britney Spears video ("Break the Ice"), as well as forming the foundation of a franchise of equally accomplished spin-offs, including the movie sequel *Innocence* and several TV series. In 2008 **Steven Spielberg**'s Dreamworks studio announced plans to make Shirow's manga into a live-action movie. To steal three words from its immortal concluding lines, *Ghost in the Shell*'s appeal remains as "vast and infinite" today as it was in 1995.

Ghost in the Shell 2: Innocence

Innocence; イノセンス

dir Mamoru Oshii, 2004, 99m

scr Mamoru Oshii *m* Kenji Kawai *cast* Akio Ōtsuka: Batou; Kōichi Yamadera: Togusa; Atsuko Tanaka: Major Motoko Kusanagi; Naoto Takenaka: Kim; Tamio Ōki: Aramaki; Yoshiko Sakakibara: Harraway

Production I.G site www.productionig.com/contents/works/02_/000002.html

Go Fish Pictures site www.gofishpictures.com/GITS2

Ghost in the Shell was the first anime to top the US DVD sales charts, but it would take Production I.G and Oshii almost a decade to get around to making a sequel. The impetus for this was the success of the 2002 *GITS* TV series, using Shirow's characters but set in an entirely different place and time frame (see box). The result, *Innocence*, is a darkly seductive *film noir* that makes lavish use of the advances in computerized animation since the first movie, and which packs in even more dense philosophical musings about interactions between man and technology.

One of the many expressions of Japanese culture's desire to improve on nature is its embrace of robotics and dolls (see p.200). *Innocence* is in effect an Oshii essay about dolls and what their creation tells us about the human condition. Particularly influential to the design of the film's robots were the erotic doll sculptures of the German artist Hans Bellmer (1902–75). The credits, which mimic those of the first movie in showing how such a doll-robot might be created, are wonderful.

Three years have passed since Major Motoko Kusanagi's "ghost" left her cybergenic shell and disappeared into the Net. She's pined after by bolt-eyed cyborg Batou, her former colleague in covert security agency S9, who wonders when, or if, she might return. Along with Togusa – he of the mullet haircut, human body and synthetic brain – Batou is assigned to a murder investigation involving doll-like robots. A model of "gynoid", made by the shady corporation Locus Solus and specifically engineered as sex toys, has been running amok then committing suicide.

It's an intriguing setup, but the ponderous musings that are a leitmotif

More Ghost in the Shell

In 2002 Kenji Kamiyama helmed a 26-episode TV series called *Ghost in the Shell: Stand Alone Complex*. A Production I.G alumnus who had worked on *Jin-Roh* and *Blood: The Last Vampire*, he had also directed the hilarious *MiniPato* parody of *Mobile Police Patlabor*.

The *Ghost in the Shell* series, set in Japan in 2030, has a separate storyline from the first movie, focusing on Major Motoko Kusanagi and her colleagues at S9 as they pursue a hacker involved in the blackmail of top-level businesspeople and politicians.

Mixing up self-contained "stand alone" episodes with those that further its "complex" story arc – there's a very odd logic behind the bizarre English title – the series strikes a good balance between brainy plotting and visceral action. It's laden with pop cultural references to everything from *The Catcher in the Rye* to *One Flew Over the Cuckoo's Nest* and has a classy score by Yoko Kanno. The "complex" episodes were extracted and edited together to form the feature-length movie *Stand Alone Complex: The Laughing Man*.

In 2004 another 26-episode series *Ghost in the Shell: Stand Alone Complex 2nd Gig* continued the first season's themes, but this time with some story input from Mamoru Oshii. Details about the two world wars that were alluded to in the previous series are revealed. It too was edited into a 160-minute movie – *Stand Alone Complex 2nd Gig: Individual Eleven* – with some new material added.

Sticking with a convention of ridiculously long titles, Production I.G's latest instalment in the *GITS* franchise is 2006's *Ghost in the Shell: Stand Alone Complex – Solid State Society*, which premiered on Japanese satellite TV and was later released on DVD. Kusanagi has left S9 and Togusa is the team leader. Batou is still on the case and still watching Kusanagi's back in a cyber thriller that poses the question: could the Major be the über-hacker Puppeteer?

of the franchise – stacked with quotes by everyone from Buddha to Max Weber – kicks in soon after. An overly long scene involving the chain-smoking forensic scientist Harraway threatens to sink the movie. Thankfully, Oshii is a savvy enough director not to allow this to happen and *Innocence* remains afloat, powered along by its convoluted mystery plot, an atmospheric music score that incorporates the choral chants of the original *Ghost in the Shell*, and astonishing visual design.

Often when traditional 2D animation is blended with 3D computer-generated visuals there's a disconnect that the eye catches. There's none of that in *Innocence*, where meticulous care has been taken to seamlessly blend the two, with CGI used to create incredibly detailed "sets" to which complex lighting design and camera work can be applied. Standout scenes include a dreamlike sequence in a convenience store where the rendering is so uncanny you almost feel you could take one of the drink cans out of the fridges or a box of dog food off the shelves. The spectacular Chinatown parade, complete with a huge mechanical elephant float, took over a year to perfect. Best of all is the lifelike animation of Batou's pet basset hound Gabriel – modelled after the director's own dog and something of a trademark in Oshii films.

Grave of the Fireflies

Hotaru no Haka; 火垂の墓

dir Isao Takahata, 1988, 88m

scr Isao Takahata *m* Michio Mamiya *cast* Tsutomo Tatsumi: Seita; Ayano Shiraishi: Setsuko; Yoshiko Shinohara: Aunt; Akemi Yamaguchi: Mother

Central Park Media site www.centralparkmedia.com/gotf

The tragic human consequences of war drive this five-handkerchief weepie, based on a semi-autobiographical novel by Akiyuki Nosaka. Focusing on a couple of orphaned siblings, fourteen-year-old Seita and his four-year-old sister Setsuko, and their struggle to survive in the final months of World War II, this beautifully produced film builds to one of the most heartbreaking climaxes in cinema.

Nosaka's one-year-old sister died of malnutrition during the war and his novel was partly an attempt to expurgate the guilt he felt over her death. He remembers chewing rice and trying to pass the cud directly to her mouth, but being so hungry himself that he swallowed each time. The book's publisher Shinchosha hired Studio Ghibli to do the animation and it was originally screened in Japan in a double bill with *My Neighbour*

Totoro, partly to provide light relief after *Grave*'s unblinking glimpse at life's cruel realities. Every August in Japan the movie is screened on TV as part of the memorials connected to the dropping of the atom bomb on Hiroshima.

Grave of the Fireflies' unhappy ending is revealed right at the start, when an emaciated Seita collapses on a train platform, his body stepped over by uncaring passers-by. "September 21, 1945. That was the night I died," says the voiceover. The rest of the film is relayed in flashback, from the moment Seita and Setsuko are separated from their mother during the firebombing of Kōbe, a major port on Japan's main island of Honshū. With their mother dead, the homeless siblings move in with their aunt, a hard-hearted woman who makes it clear that the pair are not welcome.

The overly proud Seita decides that he and his sister will be better off living on their own in a country-side bomb shelter housed in a cave beside a lake. It is in this seemingly idyllic spot that the youngsters take delight from the fireflies that illuminate their cave at night. By dawn the fireflies have expired and, in one of anime's saddest scenes, we see Setsuko dig them a tiny grave, wondering if this was how her mother was also buried. As Setsuko grows increasingly weak from hunger and Seita is forced to steal to survive, the desperate nature of their situation becomes clear.

The movie sees Takahata working at the top of his game. The images evoke the detailed beauty of Japanese prints while the characters are all very true to life – Setsuko in particular. Her childlike deliberate movements and expressions are entirely convincing – and all created without the benefit of motion-capture computer technology. You smile at Setsuko's wide-eyed delight at the fireflies and wince at the sight of her malnourished body, its skin smothered in a painful-looking rash.

Like falling cherry blossom, fireflies are a poetic symbol of impermanence in Japanese culture. Their brief but bright lives are mirrored by those of Seita and Setsuko. Despite the horrors of war and the meanness of fellow humans, they still take delight from simple, beautiful things such as a trip to the seaside, playing with bubbles in the bath and, of course, the glowing fireflies.

Gunbuster

Top o Nerae! GunBuster; トップをねらい!GunBuster

dir Hideaki Anno, 1988, 6 x 30m

scr Hideaki Anno, Toshio Okada, Kazuya Tsurumaki *m* Kōhei Tanaka *cast* Noriko Hidaka: Noriko Takaya; Rei Sakuma: Kazumi Amano; Norio Wakamoto: Koichiro "Coach" Ōta; Maria Kawamura: Jung Freud; Kazuki Yao: Smith Toren

Bandai Visual US www.bandaivisual.us/gunbuster

Gunbuster Index www.toponeraegunbuster.com

With battalions of space monsters out to destroy the world, the fate of humanity hangs in the balance (once again). Our last hope is the monolithic machine-robot Gunbuster piloted by plucky teenager Noriko Takaya and her "big sister" Kazumi Amano. The premise sounds hackneyed – and it is – but under the wry, inventive direction of **Hideaki Anno** and his similarly minded colleagues at Gainax, this straight-to-video parody of the giant robot genre emerges as a classic late 1980s anime and a trial run for their later success *Neon Genesis Evangelion*.

Noriko is an orphan, but in all other respects she's an average sixteen-year-old girl at high school in Okinawa in 2023. She dreams of becoming a space pilot to honour the memory of her father Admiral Yuzo Takaya, who died six years earlier fighting the space monsters. The only problem is that Noriko is a klutz in the driving seat of the huge training mecha. However with the encouragement of elder classmate Kazumi and stern Coach Ōta (who inspires her with his rather unimaginative mantra for success – "hard work and guts"), Noriko's innate piloting skills begin to emerge.

So far, so standard. Yet in subsequent episodes, as Noriko and company are launched into space to fight the enemy, the more complex underlying themes of the series emerge. The phenomenon known as time dilation is explored: while only a few months may have passed in space, years have fled by on earth. There's a poignancy as Noriko returns to Earth to graduate with Kazumi only to realize that the rest of her class did so a decade earlier, and that her best friend Kimiko is now married with a three-year-old child of her own.

The jokes and parody finally give way to a dramatic conclusion, filmed in stark monochromatic tones as a homage to **Kihachi Okamoto**'s live-action war film from 1971, *Battle of Okinawa*. When one of the characters calls humans "bacteria" and "garbage" compared to the organic and weirdly beautiful-looking space monsters there's an inference that in rooting for mankind we may in fact be on the side of the real enemy.

No matter how serious it gets, *Gunbuster* remains fun and irreverent. Laughs are guaranteed by the codas to each episode, in which the caricatured **super deformed** versions of Noriko, Kazumi and Coach teach a lesson on one of the scientific principles (both real and imagined) seen in the series – super deformed being one of anime's favourite stock bits of horseplay. The infamous "Gainax bounce" – the authentic-looking but entirely gratuitous jiggling motion of anime breasts – was perfected for this project, too. The movie's so-called "fan service" is brazen, with utterly superfluous shots of skimpily clothed girls in training, on the beach, or naked in showers and baths. Indeed Noriko's precocious breasts often have a hard time remaining covered, one being bared – like France's national heroine Marianne – during the ultimate confrontation with the enemy.

The original Japanese title is a reference not only to *Top Gun* (which the series parodies) but also the tennis-themed manga and anime *Ace wo Nerae!* (*Aim for the Ace!*). In 2004 Gainax produced the six-episode follow-up *Diebuster*, which takes place several millennia after the events of the first series. Both series were edited into two 95-minute features for the 2006 DVD release, the cumbersomely titled *Gunbuster vs Diebuster: Aim for the Top! The GATTAI!! Movie*.

Like pilotable mecha? You probably like *Gunbuster*

Howl's Moving Castle

Hauru no Ugoku Shiro; ハウルの動く城

dir Hayao Miyazaki, 2004, 119m

scr Hayao Miyazaki *m* Joe Hisaishi *cast* Takuya Kimura/Christian Bale: Howl; Chieko Baisho/Emily Mortimer & Jean Simmons: Sophie; Tatsuya Gashuin/Billy Crystal: Calcifer; Ryunosuke Kamiki/Josh Hutcherson: Markl; Akihiro Miwa/Lauren Bacall: Witch of the Waste; Haruko Kato/Blythe Danner: Madam Suliman

Disney official site disney.go.com/disneypictures/castle

Official UK site www.howlsmovingcastlemovie.co.uk

They seek him here, they seek him there, but who exactly is Howl? In the seaside town of Porthaven, he's the wizard Jenkins. In the royal seat of Kingsbury he's the equally magical Pendragon. In other places, including the Germanic turn-of-the-twenteith-century town in which Sophie lives, he's feared as a dandified sorcerer who eats pretty maidens' hearts for breakfast. Later we see him as a monstrous black-feathered bird. Just to confuse matters, he's voiced in the original by one of Japan's top pop stars.

When a gallant Howl rescues Sophie from the unwanted attentions of two soldiers, she realizes that the rumours about him can't all be true. However, that chance encounter incurs the wrath of the Witch of the Waste, an obese *grand dame* who casts a spell over the dutiful, dowdy young milliner, causing her to age by about seventy years. After initial bewilderment, Sophie quickly adjusts to her advanced years, balancing the cons (arthritic bones) against the pros, notably having the wisdom and worldliness to do and say things that her younger self would never have imagined.

The basic plot of *Howl's Moving Castle* comes from the novel by **Diana Wynne Jones**, in which Sophie, seeking to reverse the spell, climbs aboard the wizard's mobile home. Miyazaki's animated vision of this fantastic fortress is a highlight of this follow-up to *Spirited Away*. Lumbering out of the mist on giant, spindly chicken legs across an alpine meadow, the castle is a Heath Robinsonesque contraption – equal parts bloated albatross and patched-up battleship. It is powered from a boiler-room-cum-living-room by a fire demon called Calcifer, who is bound up with Howl in a mysterious pact that he asks Sophie to find a way of breaking.

Essentially a love story, the movie also offers pungent political comment through the ominous backdrop of a senseless war – a major departure from Diana Wynne Jones' original story. Talk of magic being used to shield palaces while innocent villages are bombed clues viewers into the deliberate parallels being drawn with the Gulf War of 2003, a conflict that enraged the pacifist Miyazaki during this movie's production.

Miyazaki came out of supposed retirement to make *Howl*, so it's perhaps not so surprising that he would also be drawn to a story with more aged than youthful characters. Sophie is not the only one to be transformed: the Witch of the Waste is reduced to a slobbering, enfeebled figure later in the movie, by which time a wheezing old dog has also joined the unlikely family aboard the equally creaky castle.

If there's one criticism, it's that the overly neat happy ending feels like a cheat after the previous seriousness of the war strand of the story, during which a mother betrays her daughter – an event that in some ways

If W. Heath Robinson had been an architect, he might have come up with something like Howl's moving castle

Allegories of war

Allusions to real-life conflicts, as in *Howl's Moving Castle*, are common in Japanese animation. Many shows, such as *Space Battleship Yamato* and *Gunbuster*, have re-trodden the ground of World War II from the safe distance of a sci-fi setting. In *Zipang* (see p.218) Japan effectively gets to replay World War II with the benefit of both hindsight and futuristic firepower.

Parallels with the war in Vietnam arise in *Votoms* (*dir* Ryōsuke Takahashi, 1983, 52 x 25m), while *Gasaraki* (*dir* Ryōsuke Takahashi, 1997, 25 x 25m) uses actual events and tweaked news reports from the first Gulf War, and features a dictator character who bears more than a passing resemblance to Saddam Hussein, in a Middle Eastern rework of *Evangelion*.

The setup of *Flag* (*dir* Ryōsuke Takahashi; 2006–07; 13 x 24m) pitches a terrorist against UN troops – a conflict that could also have been ripped directly from the headlines of either Iraq or Afghanistan. This handsome series further enhances its CNN-like look by depicting everything as if shot via a hand-held video camera.

is more shocking than the copious bombs that fall. Yet *Howl* remains a complex, rewarding movie graced with the acutely observed, colourful and imaginative artwork that is the hallmark of Japan's greatest living national treasure of animation.

Jin-Roh: The Wolf Brigade

Jin Rô; 人狼

dir Hiroyuki Okiura, 1999, 98m

scr Mamoru Oshii *m* Hajime Mizoguchi *cast* Sumi Motō/Moneca Stori: Kei Amemiya; Yoshikatsu Fujiki/Michael Dobson: Kazuki Fuse; Hiroyuki Kinoshita/Colin Murdock: Atsushi Henmi; Yoshisada Sakaguchi/Doug Abrahams: Hachirō Tōbe

Production I.G site www.productionig.com/contents/works_sp/15_/index.html

Within his first few moments of screen time, *Jin-Roh*'s enigmatic hero Kazuki Fuse is faced with an existential crisis. A member of the crack anti-terrorist unit Panzer Corp, Fuse (pronounced "fu-say") has been trained to act mercilessly, like the monstrous three-headed dog Kerberos of Greek mythology, whose image is the Corp's mascot. His quarry – a "Red Riding Hood", or courier of bombs for the terrorist group the Sect orchestrating violent riots against the authorities in Tokyo – is pinned down at point-blank range with no way of escape. The blood-red eyes of his night- vision helmet are fixed on the terrified but determined girl. But Fuse finds himself unable to shoot, instead asking her the one-word question: "Why?".

By letting his humanity get the better of him, Fuse seals his fate in this haunting, adult anime that marries elements of the famous Grimm's fairy tale to an alternative history of Japan in the 1950s. Pay close attention as the movie starts and you'll catch that in this fantasy replay the occupying force of Japan after their defeat in **World War II** is not the United States but Germany. It's an intriguing premise that adds to the movie's brooding atmosphere.

Jin-Roh, meaning "human wolf", is based on a story by **Mamoru Oshii** which started life as a radio drama. The tense action is ably helmed by Ōkiura, an animator who had previously worked with Oshii on *Patlabor 2* and who is known for his attention to detail – which shows not only in the impressively realistic characterization (this is one of those rare anime in which Japanese characters actually look Japanese) but also in the evocative details such as the fashions, the trams and retro buses that were so much a part of Tokyo fifty years ago.

Apart from the opening montage the movie's alternative historical context is barely spelled out. Instead it raises it's head subtly in minor details, such as when the girl terror-

A futuristic re-telling of the Little Red Riding Hood story: *Jin-Roh*

ist's sister gives Fuse a Red Riding Hood book – its title is in German. This is the final **Production I.G** film to be made using traditional cel rather than computer animation, which makes its fluid, detailed visuals even more amazing. Lyrical scenes of characters riding trams, lingering in deserted playgrounds or wandering the rain-lashed streets, alternate with claustrophobic chases set in gothic sewers beneath Tokyo,

The Kerberos Saga

The alternate history that underlies *Jin-Roh* is the basis of Mamoru Oshii's magnum opus, a multimedia series of works that together have become known as the *Kerberos Saga*. Starting with the 1987 radio drama *Akai Megane Omachi Tsutsu* (*While Waiting for the Red Spectacles*), the saga proceeded with the live-action film *Akai Megane* (*Red Spectacles*) and the manga *Kerberos Panzer Cop* (1988–90). *Jin-Roh* is based on the first volume of this manga.

Kazuki Fuse, *Jin-Roh's* lead character, is a member of the crack anti-terrorism unit known as Kerberos. Their uniform and firearms, copies of those used by the German army, are imagery typical of Oshii's alternative history – a "what if?" scenario in which a victorious Germany occupies Japan immediately after World War II, instead of the Americans, who did so in reality.

The *tachiguishi* pop up throughout the *Kerberos Saga*, a set of characters who first made their appearance in an Oshii-directed episode of *Urusei Yatsura* (see Canon). These maverick freeloaders of the stand-up dining scene are also the stars of the experimental animation *Tachigui: The Amazing Lives of the Fast Food Grifters* (see p.160).

recalling **Carol Reed**'s *The Third Man*. As with that classic thriller, several key characters in *Jin-Roh*, including Fuse and Kei Amemiya (a girl he falls for) are not whom they seem. Repeat viewings are necessary to fully pick up on the intricacies of the complex plot, a maze of cross and double-cross involving rival security agencies.

Working out the nuances of exactly what's going on will certainly improve your appreciation of *Jin-Roh*, but the main enjoyment – if that's the right word for such an ultimately tragic tale – is more in the melancholy tone and the larger, more philosophical questions posed, such as what it means to be human and how different really are men and beasts?

Kiki's Delivery Service

Majo no Takkyûbin; 魔女の宅急便
dir Hayao Miyazaki, 1989, 102m

scr Hayao Miyazaki *m* Joe Hisaishi *cast* Minami Takayama/Kirsten Dunst: Kiki; Rei Sakuma/Phil Hartman: Jiji; Kappei Yamaguchi/Matthew Lawrence: Tombo; Minami Takayama/Janeane Garofalo: Ursula; Keiko Toda/Tress MacNeille: Osono

Cute teenagers with magic powers have been a staple of Japanese animation ever since *Little Witch Sally* in the 1960s (see p.208). Few, however, have been as charming and true to life as Kiki, the star of Miyazaki's fifth directorial outing and the fourth theatrical release for **Studio Ghibli**. Developed specifically to appeal to teenage girls, *Kiki's Delivery Service* is partly based on a popular novel by Japanese writer **Eiko Kadono**, which follows the adventures of the thirteen-year-old apprentice as she earns her witch's stripes by spending a year living apart from her family in a foreign town.

In transferring Kadono's episodic coming-of-age story to the screen, Miyazaki added his own twists to emphasize the challenges that Kiki faces in her new life. About two thirds of the way in, Kiki loses her ability to fly her broomstick. This witch's power has been the means by which she has earned her living – by offering a parcel delivery service. On top of this she also stops being able to communicate directly with her faithful companion, a black cat called Jiji, whose miaows are a lot less impressive than the feline's previous advice and wisecracks. The dramatic finale involves a runaway airship that puts the life of Kiki's besotted boyfriend Tombo in danger. Will Kiki be able to regain her confidence to fly and save her friend?

As is always the case with Miyazaki, what saves the film from becoming saccharine is his ability to reflect authentic emotions and experience through his characters. Kiki might be a witch but she's also a typical teenager, dealing with a host of conflicting emotions and fumbling her way to adulthood through minor crises as humdrum as catching a cold or worrying about her budget.

The animation is fantastic, particularly the scenes of Kiki on her broom soaring through the skies – reminiscent of Miyazaki's earlier heroine Nausicaä (see p.88). One notable scene is dominated by a dazzling painting, reminiscent of Chagal. In the movie it is the work of Ursula, a free-spirited artist whom Kiki befriends and to whom she turns during her crisis of confidence. The artwork was in fact painted by pupils from a school for the physically and mentally challenged. The seaside town that Kiki settles in is a sun-drenched dreamscape straight from 1950s Europe, with hilly cobbled streets, Hanseatic spires and cupolas, trundling trams and vintage Peugeot cars. The inspiration was mainly Stockholm, a city that Miyazaki first visited back in the 1970s when he was attempting to secure the rights to make *Pippi Longstocking* into an anime, and to which he returned with his key staff in the early production stages of *Kiki*.

The Japanese title of *Kiki's Delivery Service* uses the word *takkyūbin* – the brand name for the service offered by the Yamato Transport Company. (As with Hoover and Biro in English, Yamato have been so successful that *takkyūbin* has supplanted *takuhaibin*, the generic word for home delivery service, in Japanese.) Yamato was one of the movie's sponsors and there's certainly a resemblance between the black cat in the company's striking logo and Kiki's pet Jiji.

Broomstick is the only way to fly for Kiki the teenage witch and Jiji the cat

Kimba the White Lion

Jungle Taitei; ジャングル大帝

dir Eiichi Yamamoto *et al*, 1965

Series 1: 52 x 25m

Series 2: 26 x 25m

Series 3: 52 x 25m

cast Yoshiko Ōta/Billy Lou Watts: Kimba/Leo; Asao Koike/Ray Owens: Panja/Caesar; Noriko Shindo/Billy Lou Watts: Eliza/Snowene; Hisashi Katsuta/Ray Owens: Mandy/Dan'l Baboon

Kimba W. Lion's Corner of the Web www.kimbawlion.com

55 Years of Kimba www.50yearsofkimba.com

Based on the **Osamu Tezuka** manga *Jungle Taitei* (*Jungle Emperor*), *Kimba the White Lion* is a milestone anime on several levels. Not only was it the first colour animated TV series made in Japan, it was also specifically tailored with an overseas audience in mind.

Partly funded by the US network NBC in the wake of *Astro Boy*'s success (see p.38), it tells the story of a charming white lion cub called Kimba (Leo in the English-dub version) who, despite being orphaned as a child, pursues his father Panja/Caesar's dream of uniting the animal kingdom, rising to become king of the jungle. If that plot sounds familiar, then it's probably because you've seen **Disney**'s *The Lion King*. Accusations of plagiarism were bandied about when the Disney movie came out, but there are differences between the two works. For instance, in the Tezuka show, Kimba gains the unique ability to talk with humans, some of whom become his friends.

Kimba might have rather simple animation – it is after all a series that is now over forty years old – but it is memorable for its distinctive artwork with vividly painted, stylized jungle scenes that give the anime an often surreal look. The cartoon cuteness of cub Kimba is contrasted against the much more realistic appearance of his fellow animals. Offering up weighty topics such as slavery and discrimination that are hardly typical of your average children's TV show, *Kimba* nonetheless remains fun family entertainment. The 1966 feature-length special, *Jungle Emperor* (basically an edit of the first series),

Kimba and friends: he may look cute, but he's not afraid to get his claws out

won the Silver Lion Award (appropriately enough) at the **Venice International Film Festival** in 1967.

The second series, from 1966, features a grown-up Kimba married with two cubs of his own. Produced without US input, it retains much of the graphic violence from the original manga that was never permitted in the first series. However, contrary to some accounts (including the official one), the plot of the second series is significantly different from Tezuka's original manga – the focus being on the development of Kimba's son Rune. The 1989 series remake,

Kimba versus Simba: Disney and anime

The heated debate over the uncanny coincidences between Tezuka's *Kimba the White Lion* and Disney's *The Lion King* is very revealing of the severe antipathy some anime fans have to Disney. Tezuka Productions has always politely acknowledged the differences between the two works, while Disney's official line remains that *The Lion King* is an original story inspired, if anything, by their earlier work *Bambi*.

However, Disney did itself no favours by its categorical denial of *any* link between their movie and *Kimba*, a stance that noted manga and Tezuka expert Frederik L. Schodt called "preposterous". Tezuka always openly acknowledged the huge influence Disney's work had on his creations and clearly had some of its animal characters in mind when he developed the original Kimba manga. Many Japanese felt that Disney were being disrespectful to Tezuka, an artist frequently described as Japan's very own Walt Disney, in refusing to acknowledge Simba's debt of honour to Kimba.

In 2001 another controversy began to bubble up among anime fans about similarities between Disney's *Atlantis: The Lost Empire* and Gainax's series *Nadia: The Secret of Blue Water* (*Fushigi no Umi no Nadia*), which was screened on NHK, Japan's public TV channel between 1990 and 1991. Both works had been inspired by Jules Verne's *20,000 Leagues Under the Sea*. This time Disney had learnt its lesson and issued no formal statement in response to the criticism.

partly directed by Tezuka before his untimely death the same year, was even darker in tone and incited the wrath of fans who had grown up loving the sugar-coated 1960s version, neutered of the more brutal realities of life both in and out of the jungle. In one of the harshest episodes an atomic-powered satellite crashes into the jungle causing many deaths including that of a mother gorilla and her baby, who dies of radiation sickness.

In much the same vein is the movie *Jungle Emperor Leo* (*dir* Yoshio Takeuchi, 1997, 99m) in which Kimba is the grown-up Leo and his son Rune takes the role of the cute cub. The movie's high-quality animation brings the jungle to lush and verdant life and, in terms of plot, it is the most faithful of all the Kimba anime to Tezuka's original manga, and to its philosophy that the only constants of life are birth, death and ceaseless renewal.

Little Norse Prince

Taiyô no Ôji Horusu no Daibôken; 太陽の王子ホルスの大冒険

dir Isao Takahata, 1968, 82m

scr Kazuo Fukuzawa *m* Michio Mamiya *cast* Hisako Ōkata: Hols; Etsuko Ichihara: Hilda; Mikijirō Hira: Grunwald; Yukari Asai: Coro, the bear cub

Nausicca.net www.nausicaa.net/miyazaki/otherfilms/#hols

Toei Animation corp.toei-anim.co.jp/english/film/the_little_north_prince_valian.php

History doesn't record what Isao Takahata thought of the trailer for his directorial debut, which boasted of *Little Norse Prince*'s three-year production schedule, its 150,000 plus drawings and its cast of thousands. In an era when anime's default position was solidifying into cheap, hastily churned out TV fodder, here was a quality film, drawn on an epic scale to the highest of production values. Its story was about a courageous Scandinavian boy in days of yore, battling nature and a dastardly villain, and it tackled mature themes such as treachery and bereavement.

And yet *Little Norse Prince*'s achievement was in spite of, rather than because of, Tōei Animation's support of its talented young director. The production house had forced Takahata to alter his original vision – a story based on a legend from the Ainu, the aboriginal people indigenous to the Japanese island of Hokkaidō and the Russian islands of Kuril and Sakhalin. The top-of-the-line animation took far more time and money than Tōei was willing to spend, so over half an hour of the movie's planned running time was ditched and a couple of key scenes reduced to a montage of stills.

None of this seriously compromises *Little Norse Prince*, which remains an outstanding animation, perhaps the single best feature of the 1960s. Although it was a financial flop on release it gathered critical praise and a devoted following among Japanese college students who, in an era of protest politics, harkened to the movie's underlying message about the importance of united action.

The movie is a forerunner of the quality-first approach that Takahata would adopt at Studio Ghibli alongside Hayao Miyazaki, who was among the many talented young animators the director gathered for his team. Together they helped create a distinctly non-Disney style of animation, despite the inclusion in the cast of a couple of talking animal friends. It's impossible to imagine a

Disney animation commencing as violently as *Little Norse Prince* does – with Hols expertly wielding a hatchet on a string to keep a ravenous pack of wolves at bay. Death is also commonplace, starting with Hols' father and swiftly followed by a victim of the giant pike that Hols later catches in one of the movie's most thrillingly animated sequences.

The film is full of imaginative characters, such as Moug the Rock Giant (from whom Hols, in an Arthurian parallel, pulls the Sword of the Sun), and such vividly drawn creations as the enormous mammoth made of ice that Grunwald rides into the village at the climax. Most memorable of all is Hilda, the movie's complex *femme fatale*. This sweet-faced girl seduces Hols and the villagers with her mournful songs. However, Hilda is the sister of Hols' nemesis, the ice demon Grunwald, and is bound to her sibling by a pendant that grants her eternal life. The conflict that Hilda faces between doing her brother's bidding to help destroy the village and her growing affection for Hols and the village children drives forward the movie's second half.

Lupin III: Castle of Cagliostro

Rupan Sansei: Cagliostro no Shiro; ルパン三世カリオストロの城

dir Hayao Miyazaki, 1979, 100m

scr Hayao Miyazaki, Haruya Yamazaki *m* Yuji Ōno *cast* Yasuo Yamada/Sean Barker: Arsene Lupin III; Eiko Masuyama/Dorothy Melendrez: Fujiko Mine; Goro Naya/Dougary Grant: Inspector Zenigata; Kiyoshi Kobayashi/Ivan Buckley: Jigen Daisuke; Makio Inoue/Richard Epcar: Goemon Ishikawa XVII; Sumi Shimamoto/Ruby Marlowe: Lady Clarisse; Tarō Ishida/Sparky Thornton: Count Cagliostro

Lupin III network lupin-3rd.net

Manga site www.manga.com/titles/castle_of_cagliostro

As the pronunciation of his name indicates – "Loo-pan" – there's a French heritage to this lovable rogue of an anime character. His adventures – which have featured in over 200 TV episodes, 6 theatrical-release movies and, at the latest count, 17 feature-length TV specials – are partly based on the manga by **Monkey Punch** (the pen name of Kazuhiko Katō), whose larrikin hero borrowed heavily from Maurice LeBlanc's gentleman thief Arsene Lupin. A little too heavily for the LeBlanc estate's liking – which caused some problems initially with the naming of Lupin in overseas releases.

Lupin III, the grandson of the original French Lupin, is joined in his crime capers by his two trusty sidekicks: the laconic Jigen Daisuke and Goemon Ishikawa XVII, an anachronistic samurai whose skill with a sword is as good as Jigen's is with all kinds of firearms. Often assisting them, but sometimes also the gang's competition, is Fujiko Mine, a quick-witted, resourceful babe who is more than a match for Lupin – which is why he's infatuated with her. Always several steps behind the gang is the bumbling but indefatigable Inspector Zenigata.

In the anime canon, it's Lupin's second cinema outing that grabs the attention because it was also Hayao Miyazaki's debut as a feature-film director (he'd already earned his directorial stripes on TV with the series *Future Boy Conan* as well as episodes of the initial *Lupin III* series). Many typical Miyazaki trademarks are in place including exciting flying sequences and a heroine in peril who proves to be tougher than she looks. As with all Lupin capers, there's a fair amount of slapstick humour and our hero always seems to have some handy device up his sleeve or cunning plan in place to get him out of impossible situations.

Miyazaki dives into the action with a pre-credits sequence that sees Lupin and Jigen fleeing the Monaco Casino with sacks full of loot. Careful pre-planning ensures their pursuers don't get very far, but the laugh is on Lupin when he discovers his haul is all counterfeit. With a pretty good idea of where the dud bills were printed, he and Jigen steer their Fiat Uno in the direction of the alpine principality of Cagliostro.

A flat tyre delays the duo's progress, but as soon as it's mended a winsome bride in a Citroën CV speeds by with a gang of thugs in hot pursuit. Lupin and Jigen come to her rescue in a standout car chase of the kind that's only possible in animation. The girl is the orphan Clarisse, fresh from a convent and set to marry, against her will, the venal Count Cagliostro. Lupin and co mount a gallant rescue of Clarisse from the Count's seemingly impregnable castle, which is also the headquarters of the international counterfeiting operation. Naturally, Fujiko has already beaten him inside the fortress and soon both Goemon and Zenigata have also turned up.

Miyazaki tones down Lupin's usual lascivious and mercenary interests for this adventure, but he seldom lets the action flag. It's a shame therefore that the otherwise well-performed English dub amps up the strong language – so you may want to switch to the original Japanese if you're watching it with the kids.

Macross

Chô Jikû Yôsai Macross; 超時空要塞マクロス

dir Noburo Ishiguro, 1982–83, 36 x 25m

scr Kenichi Matsuzaki & others *m* Kentarō Haneda & Yokō Kanno

Super Dimension Fortress Macross cast Arihiro Hase/Vic Mignogna: Hikaru Ichijo; Mari Iijima: Lin Minmei; Mika Doi/Monica Rial: Misa Hayase; Akira Kamiya/Brett Weaver: Roy Focker

Macross Plus cast Mako Hyōdō: Sharon Apple; Rica Fukami: Myung Fang Lone; Takumi Yamazaki: Isamu Alva Dyson; Unshō Ishizuka: Guld Goa Bowman

Official Japanese site www.macross.co.jp

Macross World www.macrossworld.com

Macross Compendium macross.anime.net

According to Shōji Kawamori, the creator of the *Macross* franchise, the original idea for his humans-versus-aliens saga was to depict "a small love triangle against the backdrop of great battles". But it's far from being a one-note soap opera. *Macross* can also thank its transforming mecha, winning pop songs and the complex nature of its larger themes for its success.

The series debuted under the title *Super Dimension Fortress Macross* – a bit of a mouthful that was quickly shortened by fans to just *Macross*. It came to the attention of overseas audiences as the first 36 episodes of the series *Robotech* (see box opposite) and has, over the years and in various permutations, cemented itself as one of the sacred cows of sci-fi anime.

A decade after an enormous alien spaceship (the Fortress of the title) crashed into an island on Earth, humans have figured out its advanced technology and adapted it to new planes called Valkyries that can transform into pilotable robots. They have also managed to resurrect the spaceship itself, now dubbed SDF-1. But on the day of the SDF-1's relaunch, the Zentradi – a race of giant warmongering aliens – strike. In the ensuing chaos, a warp mechanism is accidentally activated sending the SDF-1, the island, its surrounding sea and population way into outer space. Among the fifty-eight thousand castaways is the young pilot Hikaru Ichijo, who initially bonds with wannabe singer Lin Minmei, but ends up in love with Misa Hayase, one of the SDF-1's officers.

Any romantic regrets Lin may have are swept aside as she becomes the pop idol of the SDF-1. In the meantime the Zentradi, who are the creation of a long forgotten "Protoculture" (the universe's first advanced civilization), are hellbent on stopping the SDF-1 returning to Earth. However, exposure to the virtues of human culture such as love and friendship, as well as the beguiling sweetness of Lin's love songs, eventually stop them in their tracks.

Eleven years on from the original series and a couple of follow-up movies, came the distinguished *Macross Plus*, co-directed by Shoji Kawamori and Shinichirō Watanabe of *Cowboy Bebop* fame. Set mainly on the lush colony world of Eden (looking suspiciously like parts of San Francisco), it sticks to the love triangle. This time it is between former school friends Myung Fan Lone, the producer of holographic pop diva Sharon Apple, and two rival aircraft test-pilots Isamu Dyson and Guld Bowman.

This technically impressive anime, which is possible to follow without having watched the earlier series, is the gem in the *Macross* universe

The Robotech chronicles

In 1985 *Super Dimension Fortress Macross* was combined with the unrelated *Super Dimension Cavalry Southern Cross* and *Genesis Climber Mospeada* series to create the 85-episode-long English-language series *Robotech*. Produced by Harmony Gold USA in partnership with Tatsunoko, *Robotech* broke ground in the US for being broadcast largely intact, thus winning over a new generation of anime fans who were fascinated by the adult complexity of its plot.

The reason the three separate series had to be sculpted into a coherent storyline was to fill out a weekday syndication deal requiring a minimum of 65 episodes. Within its combined narrative Robotech refers to the advanced technology humans glean from the crashed alien spaceship on Macross island.

Robotech's success prompted Harmony Gold to produce several other *Robotech* series and movies over the years, but none have really hit the spot in quite the way of the original. The latest addition to the franchise is *Robotech: The Shadow Chronicles*, directed in 2006 by Korean American comic-book author Tommy Yune. A second Yune-helmed title, *Robotech: Shadow Rising*, is in production and there's talk of a live-action version produced by and possibly starring Tobey Maguire of *Spiderman* fame. The "official headquarters of the Robotech universe" on the web is Robotech.com (www.robotech.com).

"Scott" and "Ariel" – renamed heroes from the *Macross*-adapted *Robotech* chronicles

and can be viewed either in its original four-part straight-to-video version or as a 115-minutes feature that edits some of the extended *Top Gun*-style aerial ballets in favour of a nude scene, a sex scene and a more grizzly death scene. Such titillation aside, both versions benefit from the ethereal music of Yōko Kanno (see p.173) who wrote the eclectic, dramatic score and performs some of Ms Apple's songs.

Metropolis

メトロポリス

dir Rintarō, 2001, 107m

scr Katsuhiro Ōtomo *m* Toshiyuki Honda *cast* Kei Kobayashi/Brianne Siddall: Kenichi; Yuka Imoto/Rebecca Forstadt: Tima; Junpei Takiguchi/Simon Prescott: Dr Laughton; Kōki Okada/Michael Reisz: Rock; Kōsei Tomita/Tony Pope: Shunsaku Ban; Tarō Ishida/Jamieson Price: Duke Red

Sony Pictures site www.sonypictures.com/cthv/metropolis

Bandai Visual site www.bandaivisual.co.jp/metropolis

Early in his career as a manga-ka, **Osamu Tezuka** drew a sci-fi trilogy which included *Metropolis* (1949), about the creation of an androgynous robot who is made of mainly biological parts and can be used as a weapon, and *Nextworld* (1951) which parodies the Cold War nuclear posturings of the US and USSR in a sci-fi tale about an approaching apocalypse and the efforts of a superhuman race to escape Earth. Half a century later, elements from both these stories were combined to form the plot of the visually splendid and thought-provoking movie fashioned by Rintarō, one of Tezuka's protégés.

Japanese detective Shunsaku Ban arrives in Metropolis with his nephew Kenichi to arrest Dr Laughton for illegally trading in human organs. Celebrations are in full swing for the completion of the Ziggurat, a monolithic skyscraper built by the scheming industrial magnate Duke Red. It is Duke who has secretly commissioned Laughton to create Tima – the definitive robot – in the shape of his deceased daughter. Tima has also been designed to be the key by which the Ziggurat can be turned into the ultimate weapon of destruction, thus fulfilling Duke Red's goal of world domination.

Also on Laughton's trail is Rock, an orphan boy raised (but not loved) by Duke Red. He's a member of the Malduks, a fascistic band of vigilantes who terminate robots breaking Metropolis's strict rules of segregation. When Rock finds out about Tima he determines to destroy her, motivated by a mixture of jealousy and fierce loyalty to his adoptive father, whom he believes should be the one controlling the Ziggurat rather than the robot.

Rock remains a few steps ahead of Ban and Kenichi as they venture into the lower zones of Metropolis in search of Laughton. They're accompanied by a police robot which they nickname Pero, a character that

Tezuka's star system

If you think that detective Shunsaku Ban in *Metropolis* looks suspiciously similar to Astro Boy's teacher then you're spot on. Ban is a member of Osamu Tezuka's "star system" – a gallery of characters who have played different roles in his many manga and anime. In the 1950s Tezuka even went as far as to compile a directory that included descriptions of his leading manga characters with clippings of their images from different manga and even the "salary" they were paid to appear in each new story.

Among the star system characters appearing in *Metropolis* are Kenichi, Duke Red, Acetylene Lamp, Notarin and Rock Holmes. This last character, who was not present in the original *Metropolis* manga, is among Tezuka's most interesting and complex. His debut was as an idealistic, heroic boy in the manga *Detective Boy Rock Holmes* in 1949. But over the subsequent decades Rock grows up into a morally warped sociopath. As Ada Palmer notes in her insightful essay about Rock, on the Tezuka in English website (www.tezukainenglish.com), his development from hero to villain mirrors the darkening of Tezuka's philosophical themes in his work.

illuminates the fragile nature of Metropolis's social make-up and how robots are treated like slaves. Ban and Kenichi arrive at Laughton's laboratory just after Rock has killed the doctor and set fire to the facility. Kenichi and the newly "born" Tima escape the conflagration but are separated from Ban. Together they attempt to reach the upper levels of Metropolis, avoiding the murderous Rock as they go. Kenichi thinks that Tima is a normal girl who has lost her memory – he teaches her to be human and, in the process, Tima comes to love Kenichi.

This only partial summary of the plot indicates there's a lot going on in *Metropolis* – and certainly not just in the detail-saturated background art. The episodic script by **Katsuhiro Ōtomo** (of *Akira* fame) is packed with incident, moral quandaries and philosophical debate about the nature of man and machine. It also draws inspiration from the themes of the silent Fritz Lang movie that Tezuka hadn't actually seen when he wrote his manga.

Set to a rambunctious Dixieland jazz soundtrack, the incredible design of a retro-styled, futuristic city, stratified into several levels, is particularly reminiscent of that created for the Lang movie. It's an intricate CGI marvel that's equal parts Prohibition-era Chicago and futuristic *Bladerunner* LA.

Millennium Actress

Sennen Joyû; 千年女優

dir Satoshi Kon, 2001, 87m

scr Satoshi Kon, Sadayuki Murai *m* Susumu Hirasawa *cast* Fumiko Orikasa/Regina Reagan: Chiyoko Fujiwara teens; Mami Koyama/Regina Reagan: Chiyoko Fujiwara (20s–40s); Miyoko Shoji/Regina Reagan: Chiyoko Fujiwara (70s) ; Kōichi Yamadera/David Kitchen: Man with the Key; Shozo Iizuka/John Vernon: Genya Tachibana; Masaya Onosaka/Stuart Milligan: Kyōji Ida cameraman

Official site www.millenniumactress-themovie.com

The scene is a space station on the moon, overlooking earth. A determined female astronaut prepares to blast off in a rocket despite the protests of her male colleague. It looks like the familiar territory of anime sci-fi, but the scene then shifts slightly, to reveal that what is actually happening is a film within a film. It is typical of the ingenious structure of *Millennium Actress*, a multilayered story told in a succession of beautifully composed, movie-inspired moments, which traces the fortunes of Japan during the twentieth century through the prism of the experiences of screen star Chiyoko Fujiwara.

It's the turn of the millennium and for the last thirty years Chiyoko has been living in Garbo-esque seclusion, her final film before sudden retirement being that space saga. The buildings of Ginei, the studio for which Chiyoko worked, are being demolished and the film producer Genya Tachibana is making a documentary about his favourite actress's career. Together with his cameraman, a laconic youth, he has come to interview Chiyoko in her forest-set retreat. As a prelude to the interview, Genya returns a key that once belonged to Chiyoko – it proves to be the catalyst that unlocks the actress's memories, right back to her first involvement in the movies during the politically turbulent years preceding World War II.

On the same day that the head of Ginei comes to ask Chiyoko's disapproving mother for permission to allow her teenage daughter to star in a movie in Japanese-occupied Manchuria, Chiyoko also has a fateful meeting with a political dissident and artist on the run from the authorities. Chiyoko never learns the man's name, nor sees him that clearly, but she fast develops a crush on the dissident, who gives her a key to guard. Determined to find the

Pictures within pictures: the mult-faceted tale of *Millennium Actress* has many levels

man, who has escaped to Manchuria, she overrules her mother and takes the part in the movie.

Chiyoko's relentless pursuit of her romantic phantom continues for the rest of her life and it's tempting to see it as a metaphor for a star's chasing of fame. As the story unfolds, Genya and the cameraman – in a device blurring fantasy and reality that is *very* Satoshi Kon – become physically transported into key scenes from Chiyoko's life and movies. One moment Chiyoko is depicted aboard a Manchurian train besieged by Chinese rebels in a flashback to an event in her past, the next moment she's playing a warrior princess in twelfth-century Japan – then a geisha in nineteenth-century Kyoto. As the documentary-making duo struggle to keep pace, it's revealed that Genya has had his own crucial part to play in Chiyoko's life.

Kon is far too interesting a director to settle for a conventionally happy conclusion to Chiyoko's quest. He litters her path with earth-shattering events (sometimes even literally – Chiyoko is born during the Great Kantō Earthquake of 1923, and there are several other major tremors during the course of the movie) perpetually reducing her world to rubble. Through it all Chiyoko perseveres, acknowledging in her final moments that what has motivated her perhaps more than love of a man is love of the chase itself.

Mind Game

マインドゲーム

dir Masaaki Yuasa, 2004, 104m

scr Masaaki Yuasa *m* Shinichirō Watanabe *cast* Koji Imada: Nishi; Sayaka Maeda: Myon; Seiko Takuma: Yan; Takahashi Fujii: Ji-san; Tomomitsu Yamaguchi: Ryō; Toshio Sakata: Myon & Yan's Father

Official Japanese site www.mindgame.jp

So you think you know about anime – what it looks like, what it's about? Think again. *Mind Game* is an adrenaline-fuelled head-trip into a surreal world unlike anything you may have previously encountered. It's tremendous fun: a tsunami of amazing multicoloured visuals rendered in a patchwork of traditional and CGI animation with bits of live action thrown in; all so inventive that what comes next is a constant surprise.

A pre-credit montage of seemingly unconnected scenes, set to ominous music, provides an overture for the movie. Nothing seems to make sense but, by the closing credits, if you've been paying attention, the pieces fall into place. For all its visual pyrotechnics, *Mind Game* actually has a logical plot, based on a manga by Robin Nishi, who is the literal model for the film's slacker hero Nishi, an aspiring manga artist. He has finally got up the courage to ask his childhood sweetheart Myon to marry him, only to discover that she already has a fiancé, the handsome Ryō.

At the family *yakitori* bar where Yan, Myon's spunky elder sister, works, Nishi meets Ryo and resigns himself to the situation. However, the sisters' feckless father is being hunted by a gang of yakuza, who are sore at being cheated over tickets for the 2002 soccer World Cup. When the gangsters drop by the yakitori bar Nishi ends up being blasted away, and in the most delicate place possible.

In heaven Nishi meets God, but isn't quite ready to die. He claws his way back to life to rescue Myon and Yan as God urges him to "live for all [he's] worth". Following his new-found credo, Nishi and the girls escape. A furious car chase ensues, climaxing in a headlong dive off a bridge straight into the conveniently open mouth of a passing whale. Inside the whale's belly they meet a resourceful old geezer who's

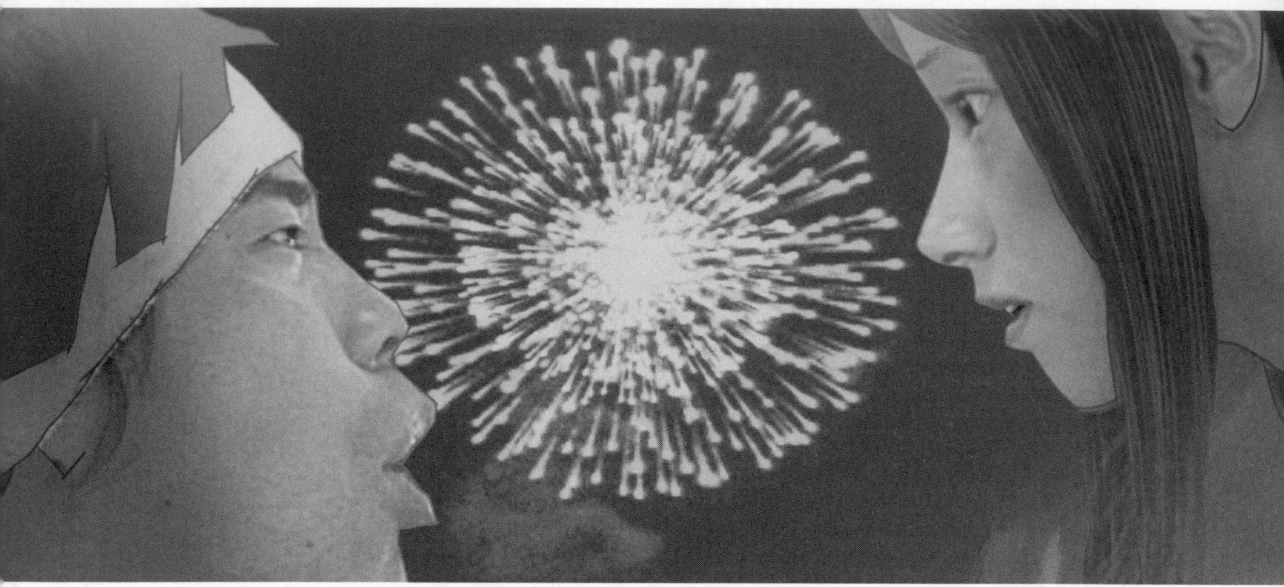

As Nishi and Myon close in for a kiss errupting fireworks are the least of their problems in Masaaki Yuasa'smind-blowing *Mind Game*

been stranded there for thirty years and created his own world out of swallowed garbage. Passing time as they work out how to escape, the four of them entertain each other, mull over their lives and discover surprising connections.

Director **Masaaki Yuasa** got in practice for this very adult anime, peppered with sex and violence, with his previous movie *Cat Soup*, an equally weird and somewhat disturbing short. *Mind Game* is a far more accomplished and complex movie that works not only on a visual level but also in terms of character and story development. The wild anarchic images are not just airy bubbles devoid of meaning but often crucial clues from each character's memory, fizzing up as in a free-flowing dream.

As the movie builds to its energetic finale, with Nishi and co making a grab for freedom, the underlying message about seizing chances and living life to the full resurfaces. *Mind Game* is an arthouse anime, for sure, but it's also a masterclass in the rewards of breaking away from stereotypes and cliché in a spirit of creative ambition.

Mobile Suit Gundam

Kido Senshi Gundam; 機動戦士ガンダム

dir Yoshiyuki Tomino, 1979–80, 43 x 25m

scr Hiroyuki Hoshiyama, Kenichi Matsuzaki, Yoshihisa Araki, Yoshiyuki Tomino, Yu Yamamoto *m* Takeo Watanabe, Yuji Matsuyama *cast* Tōru Furuya/Brad Swaile: Amuro Ray; Shuichi Ikeda/Michael Kopsa: Char Aznable; Hirotaka Suzuoki/Chris Kalhoon: Bright Noah; Fuyumi Shiraishi/Cathy Weseluck: Mirai Yashima; Yō Inoue/Alaina Burnett: Sayla Mass; Rumiko Ukai/Kristie Marsden: Fraw Bow

Official Japanese DVD site www.gundam.jp

Gundam official site www.gundamofficial.com

Credited with introducing the "real robot" genre, *Mobile Suit Gundam* is a much-beloved sci-fi series that spawned one of the medium's most lucrative and long-running franchises. Despite showing its age visually and dragging in pace compared to peppier follow-ups (of which there have been plenty), the original *Gundam*'s status as a classic is unassailable. Its battling protagonists – the idealistic seeker of justice Amuro Ray and the enigmatic and equally determined Char Aznable – are one of the iconic duos of anime, neither one being fully hero or villain, and their mobile suits of multifunctional electronic armour have become the de facto blueprint for all subsequent giant robots.

In the Universal Century 0079, the colony of Zeon is seeking independence and coming into conflict with other colonies loyal to the Earth Federation. Thanks to their superior Zaku mobile suits – gigantic mass-produced human-shaped armour with laser-charged firepower – under the leadership of the masked Char (a.k.a. The Red Comet), Zeon has the upper hand in the One Year War. On the planet Side 7, fifteen-year-old Amuro Ray has to work out how to pilot one of the Federation's newly enhanced Gundam mobile suits to defend the colony against an attack by rogue Zeon forces.

Having proved his innate piloting talents, Ray is taken aboard the Federation's White Base battleship where the commanding officer is Bright Noah. Here he's thrust into battle as the Federation's top warrior, a role the immature Amuro initially has trouble accepting or excelling at. Over the course of the series Amuro's skills improve as he discovers that he is a Newtype – someone born on a higher plane of human evolution, with superior

The Char and Amuro Factor

The duelling heroes of *Mobile Suit Gundam* have taken on a unique life of their own as two of the most famous and commercially exploited anime characters in Japanese culture. Over the years there have been Char custom tennis shoes, blue jeans, electric guitar series, motorcycle helmets, Pocky (a phenomenally popular Japanese snack food), cellphones, bathrobes, massaging gel face masks, even full-size forklift trucks. Amuro's image has been no less ubiquitous. In 2007 the government of Yamagata prefecture in northern Japan even hired Osamu Wakai, a famous Amuro cosplayer (lookalike), to appear in costume on posters and TV spots to encourage voter turnout in an upcoming election.

intuitive and psychic skills. His conflict with archnemesis Char reaches fever pitch when Amuro accidentally kills Lalah Sune, a gifted Newtype whom Char had rescued from an Indian brothel.

Much like its hero Amuro, *Mobile Suit Gundam* was initially something of an underdog, struggling to find a sufficiently large audience on its first screening in Japan, thus having its planned 52-episode run slashed to 39. However, the subsequent success of the toys based on the series, and of the three theatrical-release movies edited from the original episodes, established a rock-solid foundation for a franchise that has since run and run. The latest instalment was *Gundam 00* during 2007 and 2008.

It would take the better part of this book to describe the myriad permutations of *Gundam* down the years. The attempt would be largely futile as, for all their individual twists, each successive series incorporates the same mix of character types and dramatic elements from the original's winning formula. Above all *Gundam* is – and always has been – chiefly about those massive mechanized suits of armour, exactly the sort of thing you'd expect a samurai from the future to wear. Japan's **Science and Technology Agency** have estimated that it would cost about ¥79.5 billion ($730 million) to build a real Gundam suit. That they bothered to even make such a calculation is a sign of the esteem in which this series is held.

My Neighbour Totoro

Tonari no Totoro; となりのトトロ

dir Hayao Miyazaki, 1988, 86m

scr Hayao Miyazaki *m* Joe Hisaishi *cast* Noriko Hidaka/Dakota Fanning: Satsuki Kusakabe; Chika Sakamoto/Elle Fanning: Mei Kusakabe; Shigesato Itoi/Timothy Daly: Tatsuo Kusakabe father; Sumi Shimamoto/Lea Salonga: Yasuko Kusakabe mother; Tanie Kitabayashi/Pat Carroll: Granny

(*English cast refers to the Disney dub*)

He's got sharp-looking claws. His mouth is as big as a whale's, packed with teeth, and emits bone-rattling roars. Most people, if they had just tumbled down a hole in the forest and encountered this fantastic furry creature, as big as a hot-air balloon, would be scared rigid, especially if they were a four-year-old like Mei Kusakabe. But Mei shows no fear. She hugs the cuddly beast, laughs out loud and calls him Totoro. In *My Neighbour Totoro* Miyazaki climbs inside a child's head and shows, thirteen years before Disney's *Monsters Inc.*, that a monster can be a friend rather than foe.

Totoro is a children's classic on a par with *The Railway Children* and *Mary*

Totoro's legacy

The enormous and ongoing merchandising success of *My Neighbour Totoro* since the film's release means that cuddly toys of the giant forest spirit and fellow characters are found in many family homes in Japan and overseas. Another spin-off is the full-scale re-creation of Satsuki and Mei's house that was the star attraction of the Nagoya EXPO in 2005; see chapter seven for visiting details.

More significantly, in 1996 Miyazaki helped establish a foundation to save from development a 1500-square-metre patch of land adjacent to the Fuchi no Mori forest on the border of Tokyo and Saitama prefecture. This forest is near where Miyazaki grew up and is the inspiration for the locations of *My Neighbour Totoro*. Locals call it Totoro's Forest and in October 2007, ¥72 million had been raised (including ¥25 million donated by the general public) to ensure its protection. See the websites of the Totoro no Furosato Foundation (www.totoro.or.jp) and Totoro Forest Project (totoroforestproject.org) for details.

Waiting for the Catbus in *My Neighbour Totoro*

Poppins, a story that unfolds gently and subtly from a child's perspective. The central characters are Mei and her nine-year-old sister Satsuki, who at the start of the film are moving to the countryside with their father, an academic, so as to be closer to their mother who is recuperating from an unspecified illness in a nearby sanatorium. The sisters soon discover that their new home and the surrounding fields and forests are inhabited by wonderful creatures – not just the titular giant Totoro (O-Totoro) but also the medium-sized blue Chu Totoro, the tiny white Chibi-Totoro, a flying "Catbus" with twelve legs and a huge grin, and an army of soot sprites, looking like floating black dandelion heads with eyes.

One of the curious aspects of *Totoro* for a Western audience is how readily each of its characters accepts the existence of such spirits even if, unlike the children, they cannot actually see them. Such attitudes are far from uncommon in Japan, since the culture's major religion is **Shinto** (see p.204), a tenet of which is a belief in thousands of different spirits. The giant Totoro lives inside a sacred camphor tree, beneath which is a small wooden Shinto shrine which the Kusakabe family visit to offer prayers.

Miyazaki has said that "*Totoro* is where my consciousness begins." Although it's not spelled out, the illness that Mrs Kusakabe suffers from is most likely tuberculosis – the same deadly disease that Miyazaki's own mother caught when he was a child of Mei's age. That great fear of losing a parent underlies *My Neighbour Totoro*, providing a serious base note to an otherwise whimsical tale of childhood wonder in nature. The sisters may play joyfully and be delighted by their discovery of new forest friends, but one ominous-sounding telegram from the hospital is enough to send them both into tearful panic and kick off the movie's most dramatic episode.

There's much to admire in *Totoro*, not least the beautiful, light-dappled background art of Kazuo Oga, one of Studio Ghibli's most talented artists. His detail-packed vistas conjure up an innocent Japan of the 1950s, devoid of neon, concrete and electronic technology, and are as essential to establishing the pastoral mood of *Totoro* as Joe Hisaishi's delightful musical score.

The film became so popular that Studio Ghibli adopted Totoro as the company mascot. The character has made a brief cameo appearance in Studio Ghibli's 1994 release *Pom Poko* (as well as in an episode of Hideaki Anno's TV series *His and Her Circumstances*) while Mei features in *Mei and the Baby Catbus*, a thirteen-minute short specially created for screening at the Ghibli Museum in Mitaka.

Nausicaä of the Valley of the Wind

Kaze no Tani no Nausicaä; 風の谷のナウシカ

dir Hayao Miyazaki, 1984, 116m

scr Hayao Miyazaki *m* Joe Hisaishi *cast* Sumi Shimamoto/Alison Lohman: Nausicaä; Goro Naya/Patrick Stewart: Lord Yupa; Yoshiko Sakakibara/Uma Thurman: Kushana; Ichiro Nagai/Edward James Olmos: Mito; Yoji Matsuda/Shia LaBeouf: Asbel

Nausicaa.net www.nausicaa.net/miyazaki/nausicaa

When Hayao Miyazaki started work on his manga *Nausicaä of the Valley of the Wind* in 1982, one of the conditions he made with the publisher Tokuma was that it would not become an animation. Yet within a couple of years the popularity of this epic story – which took its eclectic inspirations from an old Japanese folk tale about a princess who loved insects, a mythological Grecian heroine called Nausicaä and the ecological disaster wrought in Japan's Minamata Bay in the 1950s – had reached such a point that Miyazaki was forced to change his mind. The thrilling, thought-provoking result was not only the first insight into his full range of talents as an artist, scriptwriter and director, but also formed the foundation for the establishment of **Studio Ghibli**.

Glider-flying princess Nausicaä is the archetype of Miyazaki's typically gutsy heroines and the film's ecological, anti-war themes and man-versus-nature dilemmas would also echo through several other Ghibli features. A catastrophic conflict a thousand years ago has left Nausicaä's world in a precarious balance with the Sea of Corruption, a polluted jungle of toxic spores, acid lakes and giant insects, such as the tank-like *ohmu* creatures.

Nausicaä's home, the Valley of the Wind, is a verdant haven populated with a peaceable people. Even though the valley is protected from the toxic wastes by the prevalent winds (hence its name), Nausicaä is secretly conducting her own research to better understand and find a solution to the relentlessly spreading Sea.

The Valley of the Wind's calm is shattered when a warship from the kingdom of Tolmekia crashes into it. Inside is an embryo of the massive God Warrior. Not about to lose this superweapon, which when developed promises to grant ultimate power to the owner, the Tolmekians – led by the ruthless Kushana – invade the valley, killing Nausicaä's father and taking Nausicaä captive. Returning to Tolmekia, Kushana's fleet is attacked by Asbel, the Prince of Pejite, a rival kingdom. Nausicaä escapes and together with Asbel discovers the key to solving the ecological crisis. But will she be able to share this knowledge before war and the rampaging *ohmu* trample everything she holds dear?

This synopsis only hints at *Nausicaä*'s rich complexity, which includes multifaceted, fallible characters. The animation, while not quite up to Miyazaki's later movies, is streets ahead of almost anything else. Particularly well done are the graceful twirls of Nausicaä's glider, the lumbering *ohmu* and the resurrected God Warrior (an early job for *Evangelion*'s creator **Hideaki Anno**, see p.150). The background art of the weird flora in the Sea of Corruption is also beautiful, as is Joe Hisaishi's symphonic score.

There's one unnecessary step in the direction of cuteness, in the form of Teto. A rather annoying creature that's a cross between a fox and squirrel, Teto is tamed by Nausicaä in the movie's initial scenes, then carries it around on her shoulder. But other than that there's little to complain about. Whether you choose to ponder *Nausicaä*'s various messages or be swept away by its adventure and sense of the fantastic, it is a science-fiction classic.

Nausicaä nagivates the Sea of Corruption, with a giant insectoid *ohmu*

Neon Genesis Evangelion

Shin Seiki Evangelion; 新世紀エヴァンゲリオン
dir Hideaki Anno, 1995–96, 26 x 25m

scr Hideaki Anno, Akio Satsugawa *m* Shiro Sagisu *cast* Megumi Ogata/Spike Spenser & Greg Stanley: Shinji Ikari; Kotono Mitsuishi/Allison Keith: Misato Katsuragi; Megumi Hayashibara/Amanda Winn: Rei Ayanami; Yuko Miyamura/Tiffany Grant: Asuka Langley Sohryu; Akira Ishida/Kyle Sturdivant: Kaworu Nagisa; Fumihiko Tachiki/Tristan MacAvery: Gendō Ikari

Official Gainax site www.evangelion.co.jp

ADV Platinum release site www25.advfilms.com/titles/evangelion

Commonly called *Evangelion* (which, in turn, is shortened to *Eva*), *Neon Genesis Evangelion* is a brilliant conundrum. Some find it difficult to get beyond the whiny lead character Shinji Akari, the most annoying teen in anime. Sci-fi purists are infuriated by the apparent paradox of a technologically advanced future that has conventional cars, trains, payphones and Walkman cassette-tape players coexisting alongside subterranean cities and the giant biomechanical Eva units. The plot is practically impenetrable and comes with a fancy wrapping of Christian symbolism (drawing in particular on the Book of Revelation) and Freudian psychobabble bordering on the pretentious.

For others, these factors are what make *Evangelion* so special. The basic premise – the world's fate is in the hands of a few specially chosen teenagers who are pitted against alien invaders known as Angels – is a clear homage to previous anime landmarks such as *Mobile Suit Gundam* and Anno's own *Gunbuster*. But the execution is anything but standard, with angst, trauma, abuse and despair galloping through the proceedings like the Four Horsemen of the Apocalypse. Addictively perplexing, the series is a bravura remixing of anime stereotypes.

Shinji is a gangly, neurotic fourteen year-old who's the antithesis of the fearlessly brave hero. He is called to Tokyo-3 by his estranged father Dr Gendō Ikari, head of the NERV organization, which built the Eva units. He's the Third Child, one of a handful of dysfunctional teenagers capable of piloting these ultimate killing machines. The others are the fragile, blue-haired, red-eyed and demure First Child, Rei Ayanami, and her personality opposite, the

Eva Unit 1, piloted by anime's whiniest teen, Shinji Ikari, prepares to kick butt in *Neon Genesis Evangelion*

fiery redhead Second Child Asuka Langley Soryu, of mixed German-Japanese blood. Against his will Shinji goes into battle against the terrifying Angels, which have the ability to take on a variety of forms.

Some much-needed comic relief is provided by the busty Misato Katsuragi, NERV's hard-living chief operations officer, who becomes an unconventional mother figure to Shinji when she takes him in as her room-mate. For all her braggadocio, Katsuragi is just as screwed up as her charge; like most of *Evangelion*'s cast, she's engaged in a titanic struggle with her inner demons, while at the same time trying to make sense of a complex, stressful situation. Practically no part of this convoluted story is served on a plate. Just when the fog starts to clear, and the audience is prepared for a conventional apocalypse, Anno abruptly changes gear with a pair of final episodes that are a self-consciously arty and abstract examination of the main characters' inner thoughts and demons.

Legend has it that the highly unusual, predominantly static montage of images that bombards the viewer in these controversial episodes was the result of Gainax running out of money and time on the series. Anno protested that the outcome was just as he had planned, and, love it or hate it, there's nothing quite like it. Until, that is, you watch the various alternatives that Gainax went on to provide, apparently demanded by fans desperate for a more conventional conclusion – although most likely produced to keep milking what had, by this point, become a phenomenal success.

Out of all these pick-and-mix conclusions, the one not to miss is *End of Evangelion* (1997), which provides not only the all-guns-blazing showdown absent from the original but also a fully realized vision of a surreal post-apocalyptic world in which Asuka and Shinji appear to be the sole survivors. In true *Evangelion* style, Asuka's final words are enigmatic, but it's obvious she's none too happy to have Shinji for company – understandably after what he'd pulled off over her comatose body at the start of the film. It's confrontational stuff and further proof, as if any more were needed, of *Evangelion*'s ability to provoke debate like no other anime.

Rebuilding Evangelion

For all its creative experimentation, the quality of animation in *Evangelion* reflects its roots as a low-budget TV series. The follow-up movies offer technical improvements, but the best version yet is currently underway with the "Rebuild" series of four state-of-the-art theatrical releases produced by Anno's new Studio Khara in partnership with Gainax. The first film of the four is *Evangelion: 1.0 You Are (Not) Alone* (*dir* Hideaki Anno, Kazuya Tsurumaki, 2007, 98m), a condensed shot-for-shot remake of the first six episodes of the original given a CGI gloss and more graphically violent battles.

Apart from the chance to utilize new technology in its production, one of the stated objectives for revisiting *Evangelion* is to make the famously complicated plot more accessible for a new audience. Anno has also cited his desires "to fight the continuing trend of stagnation in anime" and push Japan's "exhausted" anime industry into the future as reason for returning to his magnum opus. To this list should certainly also be added "making money", especially when all the merchandising spin-offs are considered, not to mention the somewhat spurious new *Petit Eva: Evangelion @ School* series, which presents all the major characters in super-deformed mode.

Night on the Galactic Railroad

Ginga Tetsudô no Yoru; 銀河鉄道の夜

dir Gisaburō Sugi, 1985, 105m

scr Minoru Betsuyaku *m* Haruomi Hosono *cast* Mayumi Tanaka/Veronica Taylor: Giovanni; Chika Sakamoto/Crispin Freeman: Campanella

The World of Kenji Miyazawa www.kenji-world.net/english

Night on the Galactic Railroad is based on a Japanese literary classic written by **Kenji Miyazawa** (1896–1933), an ambitious and unusual writer and poet for his era, who only saw two of his books published before his untimely death. This story was not among them and first appeared in an anthology of Miyazawa's works in 1933. Sometimes translated as *Night on the Milky Way Train*, four different drafts of it existed. Although its main protagonists – Giovanni and Campanella – are children and its plot is a fantastic one about their dreamlike journey on a mysterious train across the starry heavens, the story is so packed with symbolism, allegory and subtle meaning that it appeals to all ages.

It's rewarding to find out about this anime's literary origins, but it's not a prerequisite for enjoying **Gisaburō Sugi**'s slow-paced but mesmerizing film. For his adaptation, Sugi called on the talents of avant-garde playwright **Minoru Betsuyaku** and artist **Hiroshi Masamura**, who had already turned the story into manga form, making all the main characters into cats. Sugi uses this feline device in the film, thus disguising a high-concept arthouse animation as a children's film. Don't be fooled. For all his wide-eyed cuteness and blue-coloured fur, Giovanni is no **Doraemon** and neither is his pink, nattily dressed friend Campanella.

The story looks and unfolds like a child's picture book. Giovanni, whose father is away on an extended fishing expedition and so has to work tedious jobs before and after school to support his sick mother, is teased by all but one of his classmates – Campanella. On the night of the Festival of the Stars Giovanni hopes to meet up with his friend in the town square. Instead, after running around trying to get some milk for his mum, Giovanni lays down to rest in a field. Looking up at the stars, he suddenly sees a steam train approaching him out of the sky. Curious, he climbs aboard. Much to his delight he's soon joined by Campanella. But something is not quite right. Campanella is inexplicably brushing water off his clothes and later he says, from nowhere: "I hope my mother forgives me for this. I tried my best."

As the train chugs across the galaxy it pauses at surreal locations and picks up a bizarre set of passengers, including a bird-catcher (who breaks the legs off the herons in one of his sacks and feeds them to the two boy-cats as candy) and three young victims from the sinking of the *Titanic* – the only characters to appear in the movie in human form.

Gradually it becomes clear that for many of those aboard, including Campanella, this is a one-way journey. Just as his friend jumps off the train into a black hole, Giovanni wakes up. Returning to the town he discovers the awful truth of what had really happened to Campanella earlier in the evening.

Night on the Galactic Railroad is a tragic tale, to be sure, but one that also has a powerful message about the importance of finding happiness in this life, not in the hereafter. If watching it makes you curious about Kenji Miyazawa's other works, a fine anime to follow up with is the artful *Spring and Chaos* (*Kenji no Haru*, 1996, 53m) in which director Shoji Kawamori also uses cat characters for his biography of the author's short life. Miyazawa also wrote the story on which Isao Takahata's *Gauche the Cellist*, see p.173, is based.

Ninja Scroll

Jûbei Ninpûchô; 獣兵衛忍風帖

dir Yoshiaki Kawajiri, 1993, 92m

scr Yoshiaki Kawajiri *m* Kaoru Wada *cast* Kōichi Yamadera/Dean Elliot: Jubei Kibagami; Emi Shinohara/Wendee Lee: Kagerō; Daisuke Gōri/Richard Epcar: Genma Himuro; Takeshi Aono/Rudy Luzion: Dakuan; Toshihiko Seki/Andrew Philpot: Yurimaru

Ninja Scroll the series www.ninja-scroll.com

Samurai dramas, animated or otherwise, tend to follow a tried-and-trusted recipe. First take your hero, a freelance warrior or ronin, whose rapier wit is an equal match for his fighting skills. Throw in an assorted cast of villains (preferably including a blind swordsman), a wily Buddhist monk who's not all he seems, and a decent pinch of political intrigue. Don't stint on the blood and gore – the more the better. Finally, season with some gratuitous sex scenes.

Ninja Scroll gets the recipe just about right and improves on it by wrapping up the package with imaginative and often striking visuals, decent characterization, high production values and a crazy plot that's just about coherent. For these reasons it has become one of the most popular of this genre of anime, spawning a thirteen-part TV serial in 2003. There's been talk, but no confirmation, of a movie sequel too.

Sometime during the **Tokugawa Era** (1600–1868), a mysterious plague takes a lethal toll, leaving the streets of Shimoda littered with rotting corpses. A lone survivor staggers to the next village and, in a hypnotic trance, tells of the tragedy before collapsing dead herself. The local lord Koga sends in his crack team of ninjas to investigate, but on approaching Shimoda, the warriors are massacred by the stone-clad giant Tessai who, in one of the anime's most memorable and grisly scenes, rips apart the ninja leader and laps up the blood pouring from his severed arms.

The sole survivor is the plucky ninja girl Kagerō who, in her role as Lord Koga's food taster, has ingested so much poison that she's become poisonous herself. She's rescued from Tessai's lascivious grip by *Ninja Scroll*'s hero, Jubei Kibagami, a masterless samurai, first encountered, in a precursor to the main action, dispatching a couple of assailants while munching on a rice ball. The two team up with the scheming monk Dakuan to solve the mystery of Shimoda, in

Yagyū Jūbei Mitsuyoshi: master swordsman

The character of Jubei is a homage to a real person: a samurai from the seventeenth century called Yagyū Jūbei Mitsuyoshi. It's unclear whether this real Jubei was a ninja, but his reputed prowess as a swordsman means he certainly could have been. The ninjas were Japan's most feared warriors, employed by lords as assassins and spies. They practised ninjutsu, "the art of stealth", which emphasized non-confrontational methods of combat. Black-clad and moving like fleeting shadows, they used a variety of weapons, such as the projectile metal stars known as *shuriken* employed to deadly effect in several scenes of *Ninja Scroll*.

the process of which they must defeat the eight devils of Kimon.

This octet of fantastic creatures, all of whom do the bidding of the chief villain Genma, are particularly creative inventions. They include the seemingly invincible Tessai, the snake-tattooed Benisato, the hunchback Mushizo (whose hump conceals a hive of wasps), and the blind swordsman Mujuro. Jubei's lightning-fast sword fight with Mujuro in a serene bamboo forest is one of the anime's highlights. The movie's most interesting character, however, is Kagerō; her toxicity is an essential plot point and motivation for her character. It's refreshing to see a woman in a strong central role (even if she is, disappointingly, turned into just a sex object at two different points in the story).

Only Yesterday

Omohide Poroporo; おもひでぽろぽろ

dir Isao Takahata,1991, 118m

scr Isao Takahata *m* Masaru Hoshi *cast* Miki Imai: Taeko Okajima (adult); Yōko Honna: Taeko Okajima (5th grade student); Toshiro Yanagiba: Toshio; Michie Terada: Mrs Okajima; Masahiro Itō: Mr Okajima; Yorie Yamashita: Nanako Okajima; Yuki Minowa: Yaeko Okajima; Chie Kitagawa: Grandma Okajima

Only *Yesterday*, a rare example of an animated film made principally for an adult audience, is among the best work of director Takahata. The Japanese title means "memories falling like raindrops" and that's exactly what you get in this beautifully drawn, expertly paced and delicately nuanced film. The story follows 27-year-old office worker Taeko Okajima as she takes a break from city life for a working holiday in the countryside of Yamagata prefecture in northern Japan. During her journey, memories of her family and school life as a fifth-grade student in 1966 come flooding back to her.

Some of these memories are funny and some are apparently insignificant, yet they have an anecdotal charm. There is the time her family, which includes two older sisters and her grandmother, sample a fresh pineapple – an exotic delicacy for that era in Japan. The fruit is hard and dry, but Taeko, who had been so excited at the prospect of eating it, munches on gamely. But there are painful memories too, as when Taeko's father forbids her to take part in a play, even though she's proved herself to be a talented little actress, or when Taeko's truculent behaviour provokes her father to slap her.

In the countryside, the grown-up Taeko finds herself confiding these childhood episodes to the young farmer Toshio, an ebullient chap who has given up city life to work with a friend on an organic farm. He is clearly keen on her, and his careful listening and perspective on her memories gradually make Taeko reassess the past and sparks a romantic interest that drives the latter part of the film.

The original manga (by **Yuko Tone** and **Kei Okamoto**) on which the film is based only concerned itself with Taeko's childhood. Takahata's masterstroke is to set these stories in the context of what turns out to be a

Taeko's childhood memories are brought to hazy but vivid life in *Only Yesterday*
© 1991 Hotaru Okamoto – Yuko Tone – GNH

life-changing journey for Taeko. The subtle way that Takahata handles the switches between the two timeframes is indicative of his directorial brilliance. The 1966 scenes often have hazy edges and bleached-out colours. They are also the only parts of the movie in which fantasy sequences come into play, such as when Taeko floats dreamily up into the sky after a boy she's got a crush on speaks kindly to her.

In stark contrast, the present day scenes are highly detailed and vividly coloured, achieving a precise photo-realism. In an unusual process for Japanese animation, Takahata pre-recorded the voices of grown-up Taeko and Toshio and videoed the voice actors so as to capture their facial movements; usually voices are recorded after animation has finished. The animators then worked from these recordings to create uncannily realistic performances for the lead characters.

The director also took the production team on location, as it were, to a safflower farm in Yamagata prefecture like the one in which Taeko goes to work. The meticulous images that resulted are stunning, entirely justifying the use of animation for a story that could easily have been made as a live-action movie. There's a scene in the film when Toshio explains how the "natural" scenery of fields and forests that Taeko so admires is, infact, entirely man-made. Similarly when Takahata and his team animate sunrise over the safflower farm, you realize the hand-drawn images appear more beautiful than any real dawn could be.

Panda and the Magic Serpent

Hakujaden; 白蛇伝

dir Taiji Yabushita, Kazuhiko Okabe, 1958, 78m

scr Taiji Yabushita, Shin Uehara *m* Masayoshi Ikeda, Chuji Kinoshita *cast* Hisaya Morishige: Xu-Xian; Mariko Miyagi: Bai-Niang
(*English dub* Marvin Miller: Narrator)

Tōei Animation www.toei-anim.co.jp/lineup/movie/hakujaden

Anyone interested in the history and development of anime should watch *Panda and the Magic Serpent*, the first feature-length Japanese animation in colour. The film sets everything else that follows in context and gives a fascinating insight into the ambitious motivations of the industry. Consider, for example, why Tōei Animation chose, for such a prestigious movie, to animate a Chinese folk tale rather than a Japanese one. The answer lies in Tōei president Hiroshi Okawa's desire for the movie to be a kind of peace offering to one of the neighbouring countries that Japan had occupied during World War II.

The fascinating story is a kind of Asian *Little Mermaid* meets *Romeo and Juliet*. The star-crossed lovers are Bai-Niang, a white snake that has been transformed into a beautiful girl, and Xu-Xian, the original *bishōnen* (beautiful) male anime lead – all delicate features and gestures. Xu-Xian had played with the white snake as a child, but his concerned parents had disapproved and the two were separated. The white snake is turned into a human following a violent storm, leaving the way clear for the two music lovers (she strums a Chinese lute, he plays a flute) to be reunited, helped by Bai-Niang's maid Xiao Chin (a fish who also got zapped into human form in the same storm as her mistress) and Xu-Xian's pets Panda and Mimi (a red raccoon-like creature).

The latter pair of characters, who sing and dance and get into scrapes with the White Pig Gang, show the influence of Walt Disney on the project. But overall the art design and the plot – which grows darker as Xu-Xian is banished to a far land and forced into hard labour by a meddling priest-cum-wizard named Fa Hai – stick faithfully to their Oriental source material. The *Little Mermaid* correspondence kicks in towards the movie's climax as Bai-Niang sacrifices her spirit status to save Xu-Xian's life.

The animation used in *Panda* puts many much more recent works to shame. The movie's images were hand-drawn, and required 13,590 staff over a two-year period. It was typical of Tōei's craft-like modus operandi, in which the best and brightest animators were hired and a system put in place to create a high-quality product. (The vast cost of it all might explain why only two actors were used to provide the voices for all the different parts.) While the animation is not quite perfection itself, the fluid movement in some scenes (such as the dragon statue taking flight, or the beautifully realized festival scene) and the composition of others (take note of the detail as Xu-Xian enters Bai-Niang's mansion near the start) is quite beautiful.

Also known as the *Legend of the White Serpent* or *Tale of the White Serpent*, the film gained the title it is best known by for its US release – most likely to play up the role of the cute panda. Legend has it that Hayao Miyazaki became interested in animation after seeing this film. *Panda* has plenty of things going for it but, if for nothing else, everyone should be grateful to this movie for having inspired one of the masters of the medium today.

Paprika

パプリカ

dir Satoshi Kon, 2006, 86m

scr Satoshi Kon, Seishi Minakami *m* Susumu Hirasawa *cast* Megumi Hayashibara/Cindy Robinson: Dr Atsuko Chiba/Paprika; Akio Ōtsuka/George C. Cole: Detective Toshimi Konakawa; Tōru Furuya/Yuri Lowenthal: Dr Kosaku Tokita; Katsunosuke Hori/David Lodge: Dr Toratorō Shima; Toru Emori/Michael Forest: Dr Seijiro Inui; Kōichi Yamadera/Doug Erholtz: Dr Morio Osanai

Sony official site www.sonyclassics.com/paprika

What dreams reveal about the subconscious mind is the main theme of *Paprika*, Satoshi Kon's most visually splendid and mentally challenging movie to date. Told in disjointed images that are often hard to fathom, the film is like a vivid reverie. Its fascinating mix of sci-fi, fantasy and thriller elements resolves into a poignant love story. To fully understand what's going on repeated viewings are highly recommended.

Atsuko Chiba is the team leader of a psychotherapy unit developing the DC Mini, a revolutionary device that allows doctors to enter into the dreams of patients and record them, with the aim of discovering the roots of their neuroses. In the pre-credit sequence we see the dark-haired, no-nonsense Atsuko in entirely different guise – here she is Paprika, the frisky redhead of the title, who is unofficially trialling the DC Mini on an anxiety-stricken police detective, Konakawa. Paprika/Atsuko dives into Konakawa's dreams and finds them to be an intriguing montage of classic movie moments referencing the circus, Tarzan, James Bond and knockabout romantic comedy.

The DC Mini's inventor, a naïve genius who looks like a flabby Michelin Man, is Dr Kosaku Tokita and we first meet him squashed in an elevator, on his way to tell Chiba that several of the DC Mini prototypes have been stolen. Chiba and her immediate superior, the kindly Dr Shima, are desperate to get the devices back as they fear they could be used for terrorism. The sinister wheelchair-bound chairman of the institute, Dr Inui, agrees and thinks the device should never have been invented in the first place.

Suddenly Shima starts spouting nonsense and nearly kills himself by jumping out of a window. Someone is using the DC Mini to make Shima dream about a nightmarish carnival, the depiction of which is one of the most mind-boggling things you will ever see captured on film. In an interview Kon has referred to it as the "parade of everything under the sun" – which is exactly what it is with trumpeting frogs, samba-dancing postboxes and vending machines, marching temple gates and a Technicolor army of dolls, statues and robots. Like many of the movie's scenes, it blends 2D and 3D CGI animation to dazzling and lifelike effect.

But it is not so flashy as to detract from the story, or from the personalities of the characters, who remain believable amid the increasingly anarchic dream world they come to inhabit. Seiyu superstar Megumi Hayashibara puts in one of her best voiceover performances as both the serious scientist Chiba and the capricious Paprika, while Tōru Furuya (the voice of *Gundam* hero Amuro Ray), contributes a vulnerable quality to the giant genius Tokita. Together they make credible one of the most unlikely romantic couples in anime history.

A nice touch is Kon's casting of himself as a tall thin bartender alongside a short fat colleague voiced by Yasutaka Tsutsui, whose novel is the basis for the movie. Their Laurel and Hardy turn is one of many familiar images in *Paprika* deliberately and skilfully plundered from the biggest dream factory of all – Hollywood.

Paranoia Agent

Môsô Dairinin; 妄想代理人

dir Satoshi Kon, 2004, 13 x 30m

scr Seishi Minakami *m* Susumu Hirasawa *cast* Mamiko Noto/Michelle Ruff: Tsukiko Sagi; Haruko Momoi/Carrie Savage: Maromi; Daisuke Sakaguchi/Sam Regal: Shōnen Bat/Lil' Slugger; Shōzō Iizuka/Michael McConnohie: Detective Keiichi Ikari; Toshihiko Seki/William Markham & Liam O'Brien: Mitsuhiro Maniwa

Adult Swim site www.adultswim.com/shows/paranoia

Geneon site www.paranoiaagent.com

In December 2000, a seventeen-year-old boy who had quarrelled with his father ran amok in the central Tokyo district of Shibuya severely injuring eight people with a baseball bat. A spate of similarly shocking crimes involving teenagers – Japan is a comparatively law-abiding country – provided the inspiration for *Paranoia Agent*, a movie helmed by master anime filmmaker Satoshi Kon. The social commentary that is never far from the surface in Kon's movies comes right to the fore in this creepy, engrossing TV series that plumbs the murky depths of urban Japan's stresses, fears and traumas.

Intricately constructed, each episode focuses on a different character (or characters) and situations but also progresses the overall story forward, like a kind of narrative relay race. *Paranoia Agent* kicks off with an attack on Tsukiko Sagi, a meek designer of mascot characters, who claims her assailant was a young boy in baseball cap and golden inline skates wielding a crooked baseball bat.

Sagi is the creator of Maromi, a pink dog with floppy ears, huge black eyes and no mouth (just like Japan's favourite cute icon Hello Kitty) and she has been under intense pressure from her company to come up with an equally successful follow-up.

With little evidence to go on, the detectives assigned to Sagi's case – world-weary senior Keiichi Ikari and the idealistic youngster Mitsuhiro Maniwa – suspect she may be making it up. Then the mysterious assailant – nicknamed Shōnen Bat (Lil' Slugger in the English dub) by the media – strikes again. And again and again. Victims include a reporter following up Sagi's case, an overachieving schoolboy bullying target, a corrupt policeman under pressure from loan sharks, and a professor's assistant who moonlights as a prostitute. When Ikari and Maniwa arrest a suspect who fits the bill of Shōnen Bat it seems like the case is closed. But the attacks continue.

Much of *Paranoia Agent*'s appeal is that it can be enjoyed either as a straightforward mystery or as a series of critiques of a pressure-cooker society that drives people to find some kind of release. On the one hand, some people find succour in the fetishization of reassuring, cute childhood mascots like Maromi; on the other, a youth becomes a murderous thug getting his kicks beating people's brains out. In the most unsettling episode in the series, three strangers – a ten-year-old girl, a sad homosexual and an elderly man – engage in an online suicide pact. Another story, about the members of an animation production team struggling to make a series based on the Maromi character, provides an interesting insight into who does what on such shows, as well as making a not-so-sly dig at the unrealistic deadlines and budgets of such enterprises.

There is one particularly telling episode, in which concerned housewives spread wild, hysterical rumours about the past attacks of Shōnen Bat. It illustrates how easily such public menaces become urban myths; these agents of paranoia can then provide convenient excuses for those unable or unwilling to take responsibility for their lives. By the apocalyptic

Sometimes what you *don't* show is far more scary than what you do: just who is the baseball-bat-wielding *Paranoia Agent*?

conclusion of the series, which loops back to focus on Tsukiko Sagi, the true origins of Shōnen Bat and the increasingly malevolent Maromi become clear. It's an unsettling, often surreal journey which poses plenty of questions along the way. One of them being: why can't more anime TV series be as ambitious and good-looking as this one?

Patlabor

Kidô Keisatsu Patlabor; 機動警察パトレイバー

dir Mamoru Oshii, Naoyukui Yoshinaga, 1988–89, 7 x 25m

scr Kazunori Ito, Mamoru Oshii *m* Kenji Kawai *cast* Ryunosuke Ōbayashi/Michael Schwartz: Kiichi Gotō; Yoshiko Sakakibara/Adriana: Shinobu Nagumo; Miina Tominaga/Elisa Wain: Noa Izumi; Toshio Furukawa/Dan Green: Asuma Shinohara; Daisuke Gōri/Chunky Mon: Hiromi Yamazaki; Issei Futamata/Jonny Asch: Mikiyasu Shinshi; Michihiro Ikemizu/James Wolfe: Isao Ōta; Yō Inoue/Debora Rabbai: Kanuka Clancy

Patlabor movie sites www.bandaivisual.us/patlabor

Patlabor The Movie 3: WXIII www.bandaivisual.co.jp/patlabor

Minipato www.productionig.com/contents/works_sp/12_/index.html

Schaft Enterprises A Patlabor members.iimetro.com.au/~mwhitley/index.htm

Inserting giant robots into the format of the classic urban cop show *Hill Street Blues* was a stroke of genius by **Mamoru Oshii** and his co-conspirators in Headgear, the creative group convened to produce *Patlabor*. In a parallel-universe Tokyo, giant robots called "labors" are used for major construction projects. (One of them showing an impressive eco-awareness for the late 1980s: the reclaiming of land from seas that have risen because of the melting of the polar icecaps.) Terrorist and criminal abuse of labors has necessitated the creation of Special Vehicles Unit Section 2 (SV2) of the metropolitan police, equipped with its own patrol labors, shortened to pat-labors.

Intricately drawn as these pilotable robots are, the show's real focus is on the daily lives of the poorly paid, overworked and underappreciated staff who operate them. The female captain of SV2's Division I is the super competent and cool-headed Shinobu Nagumo. Division II's leader is the seemingly laid-back (but actually super-switched-on) bloke Kiichi Gotō, who silently carries a torch for Nagumo. Under their command are a ragtag crew comprising, among others, enthusiastic rookie Noa Izumi, who nicknames her labor Alphonse, the quick-firing, hot-headed Ōta, gentle giant Hiromi Yamazaki, and rebel rich kid Asuma Shinohara, whose family business manufactures the labors.

It's the interaction between this ensemble cast – none of them typical hero material – and the skill with which each of the characters is developed that makes *Patlabor* really shine. The balance of comedy, drama and action is finely balanced within an ongoing plot about industrial espionage and corruption. Oshii also directed the highly regarded follow-up features *Patlabor The Movie* (1989, 98m) and *Patlabor The Movie II* (1993, 107m), both of which take the series in a more serious direction. The second movie has a distinctly darker tone, portraying a Tokyo under martial law and giving the characters and visuals a photorealistic makeover. The film's brooding atmosphere and theme of technology abused for political ends foreshadows Oshii's *Ghost in the Shell*.

Patlabor's spin-offs

The success of both the original video series and movies led to a 47-episode TV series, and a 16-episode video series, neither of which was directed by Oshii. There's also a generally inferior third Patlabor movie, *WXIII* (*dir* Fumuhiko Takayama, 2001, 107m), in which the beloved members of SV2 only make cameo appearances as a couple of new detectives investigate a series of attacks on labors by a mutant monster.

Released alongside *WXIII*, the hilarious *Minipato* is a trio of shorts, all written by Oshii, which affectionately lampoon the Patlabor universe. Made in the style of old paper puppet theatre but given a snazzy digital spin, the shorts feature Captain Gotō providing a lecture on firearms, maintenance supremo Shigeo Shiba's musings on the history of anime robots, and Captain Nagumo breaking silence on SV2's eating habits – all in all it's a worthy coda to one of anime's most accomplished franchises.

Perfect Blue

Yume nare sarete; パーフェクトブルー
dir Satoshi Kon, 1997, 80m

scr Sadayuki Murai *m* Masahiro Ikumi *cast* Junko Iwao/Ruby Marlowe: Mima Kirigoe; Rica Matsumoto/Wendee Lee: Rumi; Shinpachi Tsuji/Gil Starberry: Tadokoro; Tsubasa Shioya/Jimmy Theodore: Shibuya

Manga Entertainment site www.perfectblue.com

Geneon Entertainment site www.geneon-ent.co.jp/rondorobe/perfect-blue

With three short words – "Who are you?" – Mima Kirigoe begins her big break into TV acting, following her successful career as a pop starlet. But inside the psychologically fragmented world of *Perfect Blue*, the gripping debut feature of Satoshi Kon, they have several other meanings. Later, when called upon to act out a vicious rape scene, Mima's desire to be a serious actress threatens to smash her virginal image as a sugar-sweet singer, and both she and her audience must re-evaluate exactly who she is. The fans, socially awkward males who obsess over their idol's every move, don't want Mimarin – their pet name for Mima – to change. One particularly creepy fan seems to be taking his obsession too far. Mima receives heavy breathing phone calls and an anonymous note accusing her of being a traitor.

Another note that she receives has a curious reference to "Mima's Room". Rumi, a former idol singer and one of Mima's managers from the talent agency, informs Mima that it's a website. Initially, Mima is delighted by the online diary on the site, written as if by herself; but then she starts to notice how eerily accurate the blog is. Not only is she being stalked, but the author also seems to be able to read her mind. Her question recurs: "Who are you?" she demands of her mysterious tormentor.

When a small letter bomb explodes, meant for Mima but opened by Tadokoro, the boss of the talent agency, the situation rapidly gets more serious. Shibuya, the screenwriter of the psycho-thriller series *Double Bind*, in which Mima is starring, is gruesomely murdered; a sleazy photographer who takes some provocative photos of Mima is the next victim; and clothes covered in blood turn up in Mima's closet. The line between what's happening in the real world and the fictional one of the TV series begins to blur as the increasingly distressed and mentally disturbed Mima wonders whether she, in fact, might be the author of Mima's Room after all, and – like her onscreen character – a schizophrenic killer.

It's easy to see why *Perfect Blue* has been compared to the films of **Alfred Hitchcock**. Kon's psychologically unbalanced heroine in peril is reminiscent of *Marnie* or *Rebecca*. We see Mima reflected in mirrors, windows, shiny surfaces and TV screens: stark visual metaphors for her split personality. The reflections eventually take on a life of their own, as Mima confronts an imaginary doppleganger in a pink pop-idol costume who taunts the real Mima and skips away over the tops of the streetlights like a malevolent fairy. This flight of fancy is particularly striking given that the rest of the film is meticulously accurate and true to life, in what has become a trademark style for Kon. The urban landscape of Tokyo with its trains, giant advertising boards and jumbled landscape of housing and office blocks is ultra-precisely rendered. So too is Mima's typically cluttered and cramped apartment.

"I don't know anything about myself anymore," says Mima's character towards the end of *Double Bind*. Kon's skill in transferring the novel by Yoshikazu Takeuchi into animation keeps the audience guessing, right up until the bloody conclusion, exactly who Mima is, too.

Fitting together the pieces of an enigma: perfect who?

Porco Rosso

Kurenai no Buta; 紅の豚

dir Hayao Miyazaki, 1992, 94m

scr Hayao Miyazaki *m* Joe Hisaishi *cast* Suichiro Moriyama/Michael Keaton: Porco Rosso; Akemi Okamura/Kimberly Williams-Paisley: Fio; Akio Ōtsuka/Cary Elwes: Curtis; Tokiko Kato/Susan Egan: Madame Gina; Tsunehiko Kamijo/Bill Fagerbakke: Mamma Aiuto Boss; Sanshi Katsura/David Ogden Stiers: Grandpa Piccolo

Many of Miyazaki's anime revel in the wonders of flight – think of Nausicaä on her glider, Kiki astride her broom, Totoro spinning up into the trees, or the flying scenes in both *Castle in the Sky* and *Howl's Moving Castle*. *Porco Rosso*, in which daredevil seaplane pilots dogfight over the Adriatic between the world wars, is an adventure from Miyazaki that spends even less time on the ground and is, by his own admission, one of his most personal films.

The movie was inspired by his manga *Hikōtei Jidai* (*The Age of the Flying Boat*), which was created for a hobby model magazine, *Model Graphix*, and ran in February, March and April 1990. The movie's intended audience was, according to the director, "tired, middle-aged men". Perhaps that's why Marco Pagott's snout-faced alter ego Porco, with his well-padded midriff, belted mackintosh and ever-present cigarette, recalls both a rumpled salaryman and Humphrey Bogart. In the movie it's never spelled out how or why Marco, an Italian World War I flying ace, has morphed into Porco, a bounty hunter and pig who lives rough on a secluded island. Studio Ghibli's book *The Art of Porco Rosso* explains that the transformation was brought on by Marco's loss of innocence and comrades during wartime.

What is made clear is that Porco prefers being a pig to being a fascist. His rejection of the era's dangerous politics provides a serious undercurrent to an otherwise frivolous plot revolving around his duel with brash American aviator Donald Curtis and jousts with the hopeless Mamma Aiuto gang of aerial pirates led by Boss, a dead ringer for Bluto in *Popeye*. Just how pathetic this unwashed band of cartoon brigands is becomes clear in the movie's initial hilarious scenes when they are easily outflanked by a class of perky toddlers they have kidnapped who, far from being afraid, find the whole thing a hoot.

Romance raises its head in the form of Gina, a glamourous chanteuse who runs a hotel where Porco and other aviators hang out and has long held a torch for Porco. In one of the movie's most memorable scenes, she croons the haunting nineteenth century ballad "Les Temps des Cerises". Also angling for Porco's affections, although in a more fatherly way, is Fio, the spunky seventeen-year-old granddaughter of Piccolo, the owner of an aviation company. She helps redesign and rebuild Porco's plane and might just be the girl to unfreeze the aviator's heart. Miyazaki's subtlety on this point, by not explicitly showing whether her final kiss turns Porco back into Marco, is brilliant. Similarly in Fio's voiceover at the movie's end she keeps mum on whether Gina and Porco finally get it together. Eagle-eyed viewers, however, will spot Porco's distinctive red plane moored by Gina's island hotel.

Ultimately it's *Porco Rosso*'s magnificent flying machines that are the star turns here. Their sleek designs, based on 1920s Italian models, and their thrilling animation are where Miyazaki's imagination really takes flight.

Pigs really can fly: could romance be in the air for the hero of *Porco Rosso*?

Princess Mononoke

Mononoke Hime; もののけ姫
dir Hayao Miyazaki, 1997, 133m

scr Hayao Miyazaki *m* Joe Hisaishi *cast* Yoji Matsuda/Billy Crudup: Ashitaka; Yuriko Ishida/Claire Danes: San; Yuko Tanaka/Minnie Driver: Lady Eboshi; Kaoru Kobayashi/Billy Bob Thornton: Jigo; Akihiro Miwa/Gillian Anderson: Moro; Sumi Shimamoto/Jada Pinkett-Smith: Toki

Miramax site www.princess-mononoke.com

The concerns that previous Miyazaki movies had shown about man's uneasy relationship with nature come to the fore in his magnificent epic *Princess Mononoke*. Medieval Japan is a battleground between the ancient giant gods of the forest, such as the mother wolf Moro and the blind boar Okkotonushi, and humans intent on progress at practically any cost. It's a complex, legendary tale, but one that is easy to follow, thrillingly exciting, and never less than beautiful to look at – like a detailed painting brought to life.

Ashitaka is a young prince of the Enoshi tribe, who are clearly modelled on Japan's aboriginal Ainu people. Saving his village from Naga, an enraged boar god, Ashitaka becomes scarred by the cancerous evil that had turned the animal into a demon. The village soothsayer tells him he will eventually die from the wound. With his trusty red elk steed Yakul, Ashitaka rides off to the west, clutching the one thing that might lead him to a cure – the clue of an iron bullet found within the carcass of the dead boar.

It transpires the bullet was forged in Irontown, a settlement established on the edge of the sacred forest by Lady Eboshi. She's a woman determined to master nature – which puts her and her community in direct conflict with the forest gods, as well as Moro's adopted human daughter, San – the Princess Mononoke of the title.

Ashitaka's first sight of this feral yet regal girl provides one of the movie's most striking images – a brave young woman sucking blood from the wound of the giant wolf Moro. In Irontown Ashitaka discovers that Lady Eboshi is a far more complex character than at first would seem the case. She rescues prostitutes and lepers from the uncaring wider society, treating them with respect and giving them useful work. In turn the people of Irontown are fiercely loyal to her. Ashitaka tries to be a bridge between this world and that of the forest, ruled over by the life-giving Shishigami deer god. However, Jigo, a duplicitous monk working for the emperor, is after the Shishigami's head and his attempts to get it, aided by Lady Eboshi, spark the ultimate battle between man and nature.

Unlike other Miyazaki movies this one is not for small children – there's too much violence, bloodshed and death for that. The demon-possessed boar is as scary as anything in a horror movie and the battle scenes are brutally realistic. But there is peace and beauty in the film as well: the wonderfully evoked forest, so lush and colourful that you feel you could touch it; the *kodama*, charming tree sprites who help Ashitaka find his way to safety; and the growing love between Ashitaka and San.

A parable about the perils of disrespecting nature, the destructiveness of anger and the healing power of forgiveness, *Princess Mononoke* is an artistic and philosophical high point of Miyazaki's illustrious career. Though it was his subsequent effort, *Spirited Away*, that won the Oscar, *Mononoke* is probably more worthy of it.

San takes the side of the wolves in *Princess Mononoke*

Puss 'n Boots

Nagagutsu o Haita Neko; 長靴をはいた猫
dir Kimio Yabuki, 1969, 80m

scr Hisashi Inoue, Morihisa Yamamoto *m* Seichiro Uno *cast* Susumu Ishikawa: Pero; Toshiko Fujita: Pierre; Rumi Sakakibara: Princess Rosa; Asao Koike: Lucifer

Tōei site www.toei-anim.co.jp/lineup/movie/nagagutsu

Decades before a similarly dressed cat in a plumed hat and oversized footwear stole scenes in the *Shrek* movies, there was Pero – the original Puss 'n Boots. **Tōei**'s highly entertaining comic romp takes the musketeering feline created by eighteenth-century French author **Charles Perrault** and throws him into a story that's partly faithful to the original but which also plunders ideas from *Beauty and the Beast* and *Cyrano de Bergerac*.

It's straight into the action as our outlaw hero goes on the run for refusing to kill mice, with the bumbling cat police in hot pursuit. Happening on a cottage in the forest, Pero finds refuge with the kind-hearted peasant boy Pierre, who's been tricked out of his inheritance by two conniving elder brothers. The resourceful Pero decides this male Cinderella is just the lad to win the hand of the beautiful Princess Rosa, even though the wimpish Pierre is initially a far from willing suitor. With the aid of some mice grateful for Pero's pacifist inclinations, the cat kits out Pierre in princely garments and talks him up to the king as the Marquis de Carabas, a prospective son-in-law for his daughter. However, Prince Lucifer, a giant buffoonish ogre with a skull-shaped necklace that grants him magical powers, also has the hots for Rosa and warns the king of dire consequences if he doesn't get his way.

Just as Pierre finds the courage to woo Rosa, and she falls for him, the young lovers are separated as Lucifer kidnaps the princess to his castle. Pierre, Pero and their mouse comrades mount a rescue mission leading to an action-packed finale in which everyone is chasing everyone else around the wacky castle.

Barely pausing for a handful of musical numbers as it gallops from one action scene to another, *Puss 'n Boots'* simple cartoonish visual style is reminiscent of both **Hanna & Barbera** and the more sophisticated look of **Disney**'s *101 Dalmations*.

Many Tōei staff worked on this movie after the long and difficult gestation of the studio's previous production *Little Norse Prince*. Their accumulated artistic skill – not to mention the relief they must have felt to be contributing to something so effervescent and fun – shines through.

Animated by veteran **Yasuo Otsuka**, the movie also featured the work of a young **Hayao Miyazaki**, who drew the storyboards and also later penned a manga based on the film for a weekly magazine. The film's acknowledged highlight is the climactic chase sequence; Miyazaki students will see several similarities between this scene and the final fight between Lupin and Count Cagliostro in *Lupin III: Castle of Cagliostro*.

Puss 'n Boots is about as deep as a saucer of milk, but no less enjoyable for that. Kids will adore the comic escapades and slapstick while adults can admire the colourful, inventive animation. The movie was such a hit with Japanese audiences in 1969 that Pero was adopted as Tōei Animation's mascot and went on to star in a couple of sequels: *Three Musketeers in Boots* (1972) and *Puss 'n Boots Travels Around the World* (1976).

Revolutionary Girl Utena

Shôjo Kakumei Utena; 少女革命ウテナ

dir Kunihiko Ikuhara, 1997, 39 x 25m

scr Noboru Higa, Ryoe Tsukimura, Jugo Kazayama, Kazuhiro Uemura, Yoji Enokldo
m Shinkichi Mitsumune, J.A. Seazer *cast* Tomoko Kawakami/Rachael Lillis: Utena Tenjō; Yuriko Fuchizaki/Sharon Becker: Anthy Himemiya; Aya Hisakawa/Jimmy Zoppi: Miki Kaoru; Jūrōta Kosugi/Josh Mosby: Akio Ōtori; Kotono Mitsuishi/Mandy Bonhomme: Juri Arisugawa

Enoki Films site www.enokifilmsusa.com/library/ursula.htm

Based partly on the manga by Chiho Saitō, *Revolutionary Girl Utena* (usually shortened to *Utena*) has its roots in such genre-defining manga/anime as *Princess Knight* and *Rose of Versailles* (see p.217). It's an iconoclastic, post-modern fairy tale, about how myths can trap people in gender roles from which the only escape is revolution. Overloaded with symbolism, what keeps *Utena* from drowning in a sea of pretentions – particularly in the movie version, which is even more expressionist and dramatically intensified – is its distinctive visuals, strikingly beautiful characters, dramatic subtexts and flashes of bizarre humour.

In childhood, the recently orphaned Utena Tenjō is consoled by a gallant prince who gives her a ring with a rose crest. Instead of falling in love with the prince, the tomboyish Utena decides she'd like to be one herself. Thus when she enrols at the Ōtori Academy she dresses and behaves in a regal and masculine way, causing consternation among her tutors and a sensation with her fellow students.

No ordinary school, the Ōtori Academy turns out to be a volatile petri dish of seething, pubescent hormones where schoolwork takes a poor second place to fencing matches and poisonous gossip. Members of the academy's elite Student Council fight duels over "ownership" of the Rose Bride – the nickname given to a dusky-skinned, frighteningly passive schoolgirl named Anthy Himemiya.

Utena is pulled into one such duel, winning Anthy's hand and triggering a cascade of events that lead in as many unexpected directions as the academy's labyrinth of corridors, staircases and duelling grounds.

Not nearly as heavy going as it may sound, *Utena*'s tone is lightened by two shadow puppets who pop up before each episode's commercial break to comment on the action and foreshadow future events. There's also the comic relief of student Nanami Kiryū, the "class clown" who in one especially surreal episode morphs into a cow.

Art Nouveau-style roses are a recurring motif in *Utena*, symbolic of beauty, danger and rampant sexuality. Only those wearing rose crest rings can take part in the duels. The Rose Bride pins roses to the duellists' chests before each match – the winner is the first to strike the flower off with their blade. In key scenes, roses swirl around the characters, mimicking the florid style of shōjo manga.

Utena can be viewed as a coming of age story, one that watches teenagers maturing into adults, shedding their innocence along the way. Sexual desire and gender roles are treated as being fluid and complex – as much as Utena wants to become the valiant prince, the pink-haired heroine clings to her feminine traits just as tenaciously. Darker themes, including incest, sexual abuse and rape, that are only hinted at in the TV series, are made more explicit in the movie version, which loosely retells a condensed version of the series before veering off to a radically different conclusion. In a bid to escape the confined world of the academy, Utena morphs into a turbo-charged pink getaway car in which Anthy is the driver.

Samurai Champloo

サムライチャンプル

dir Shinichirō Watanabe, 2004–05, 26 x 25m

scr Dai Sato, Seiko Takagi, Shinji Obara *m* Fat Jon, Force of Nature, Nujabies, Tsutchie *cast* Kazuya Nakai/Daniel Andrews: Mugen; Ginpei Sato/Kirk Thornton: Jin; Ayako Kawasumi/ Kari Wahlgren: Fuu

Official site www.samuraichamploo.com

In the deep south of the Japanese archipelago are the **Okinawan islands**, once the separate Ryūkyū kingdom. The islands' culture, distinctly different from that of the mainland, reflects influences as diverse as ancient China and the US, whose forces have been stationed on the islands since the end of World War II. A typical Okinawan dish is the veggie stir-fry *champuru*, a local word meaning "to mix up": referencing all this is *Samurai Champloo* – an eclectic sampling of the samurai genre for the hip-hop generation, that has an Okinawan native (Mugen) as one of its lead characters.

Samurai Champloo adopts the guise of a typical *chambara* (samurai sword fight) series, and is set somewhere around the late seventeenth century. However, from the way the characters talk and move, not to mention some of the things they encounter – such as baseball and rap music – you'd be forgiven for thinking that this was a twenty-first century theme park of Tokugawa-era Japan. Series creator Shinichirō Watanabe makes no apologies for such anachronisms. This was his intention: to present a story that is set in a historical era, but told in a way that has maximum appeal for its contemporary target audience.

Mugen is a street-cool ruffian who energizes his sword-fighting skills with break-dancing moves and accessorizes his baggy shorts with tattoos on his wrists and ankles, earrings and a frizzy Afro hairdo. In stark contrast is the Zen-calm loner Jin, another lethal swordsman, who wears a men's kimono with panache and peers at the world through designer spectacles. Rounding out the principal trio is the most traditional anime character of all – spunky, ditzy Fuu, who's sassy enough to get the two boys to stop brawling so they can help her search out the mysterious "samurai who smells of sunflowers" (one of the series' jokes being that sunflowers have no smell).

As with his previous hit *Cowboy Bebop*, Watanabe uses a striking visual style, great character design and music (in this case mainly hip-hop), to tap into contemporary trends and give the show a distinctive edge. The sampling style of the music is appropriate for a series that borrows elements of Tarantino as well as *Enter the Dragon*, Akira Kurosawa's classic *Yojimbo* and Beat Takeshi's similarly anachronistic *Zatoichi* for plot references.

For all its self-conscious cool and post-modern tricks (at one point Mugen breaks out of the action to challenge the narrator), *Samurai Champloo* is above all a well-told, old-fashioned story not too far removed from the reverential samurai dramas of yore. In its telling, it speaks to foreign fans who know nothing of, and probably don't care much about, the Shimabara Rebellion, the sexual mores of Tokugawa Japan and the impact that ukiyo-e woodblock prints might or might not have had on Van Gogh – just to mention three other issues that *Samurai Champloo* casts into the mix.

Samurai X: trust and betrayal

Rurouni Kenshin: Tsuiokuhen; るろうに剣心：追憶編

dir Kazuhiro Furuhashi, 1999, series 4 x 30m, movie 120m

scr Masashi Sogo *m* Noriyuki Asakura *cast* Mayo Suzukaze/J. Shannon Weaver: Kenshin Himura; Junko Iwao/Rebecca Davis: Tomoe Yukishiro; Shūichi Ikeda/Richard Epcar: Seijiro Hiko; Tomokazu Seki/Corey M. Gagne: Kogoro Katsura; Nozumi Sasaki/Brian Gaston: Enishi Yukishiro

Samurai dramas that rise above the banal clichés of successive sword fights are a rare breed. Even rarer are follow-up videos that actually improve on their source material. *Samurai X: Trust and Betrayal* is one such rarity – a richly textured piece with beautiful imagery, a complex plot and realistic character development, that, despite being a prequel to the main action of the series *Rurouni Kenshin* (see p.218), requires no prior knowledge of the characters or story to come. Such is the stylistic chasm in tone and approach between the two that it's almost like you're watching a different series entirely: it's the anime equivalent of an Akira Kurosawa movie.

Released straight to video, thus unbound by both the budgetary and censorship requirements of television, *Samurai X* pitches the viewer straight into a cinematically realistic depiction of the violent trauma that starts nine-year-old Shinta on his evolution into the cold-blooded assassin widely known as Hitokiri Battōsai ("man slayer"). The sole survivor of a bloody massacre, Shinta is adopted, and renamed Kenshin Himura by his saviour, the enigmatic lone master swordsman Seijuro Hiko.

Kenshin proves himself as talented a swordsman as his teacher, who warns that this skill will eventually destroy him. These are turbulent times in Japan and the headstrong teenager leaves Hiko to join one of the rebel groups fighting against the ruling shogunate (see box overleaf).

As the group's unblinking assassin, Kenshin kills many people, including the fiancé of Tomoe, the daughter of a samurai. Seeking revenge, Tomoe agrees to take part in a plot by the shogun's forces to kill Kenshin, by infiltrating the rebel group. However, sent by Kogoro Katsura, the rebel leader, to live undercover in the countryside as husband and wife, Tomoe and Kenshin fall in love. Under Tomoe's discreet influence, Kenshin sees the error of his violent ways. The tragic conclusion explains not only how Kenshin receives the distinctive cross-shaped scar on his cheek (hence the series' English title *Samurai X*) but also why by the start of *Rurouni Kenshin* he has foresworn bloodshed.

The emotional power of *Samurai X* comes from its rich variety of themes, including the loss of innocence, betrayal, the numbing effects of violence and the redemption offered by love and forgiveness. It's all played out against a gorgeous background of images drenched in traditional symbolism, including the changing of the seasons and the fleeting beauty of flowers. Most memorably, in one scene crimson camellia blossoms fall across the bodies of Kenshin's victims and in another Kenshin and Tomoe are glimpsed from a bird's-eye view walking beside a river reflecting the blood-orange skies. Characters are drawn realistically, actually appearing Japanese, save for Kenshin's distinctive red hair.

Samurai X: Trust and Betrayal is best viewed in its original format as two separate DVDs, each with two episodes. The *Director's Cut* movie version combines all the episodes but only adds in a few extra minutes of new footage (mainly at the end) and crops the picture to make it appear as if the series was made for the cinema – although, in terms of animation quality, it certainly could have been.

While *Samurai X: Trust and Betrayal* easily stands on its own, there are a

The dawn of the Meiji era

The fiction of *Samurai X* and *Rurouni Kenshin* is grounded in actual historical events leading up to and after the Meiji Restoration in 1868. From 1600 for over 250 years Japan was ruled by the shoguns (military generals) of the Tokugawa clan from the administrative capital of Edo, the former name of Tokyo. The emperor, stripped of any real power, was confined to the palaces of the ancient capital of Kyoto.

Although the Tokugawa shogunate provided Japan with over two centuries of peace in which to prosper, the regime was essentially despotic, particularly in the way it stratified society and shut the country off from the outside world. By the mid-nineteenth century, the shogunate had grown weak and, as foreign powers sought to establish their presence and influence in Japan, rebel forces seized their chance to restore power to the emperor.

The character of Kenshin is loosely based on the assassin Kawakami Gensai, who fought for the revolutionaries in this period of civil war that led to the fall of the shogun and the imperial restoration of fifteen-year-old Mutsuhito. The new era was called Meiji, meaning "enlightened rule". So rapid were the changes to society that some rebel groups continued to fight, most famously the warrior general Saigō Takamori – whose story forms the basis for the Tom Cruise movie *The Last Samurai*.

couple more DVDs in the *Samurai X* series that are better experienced after some familiarity with *Rurouni Kenshin*. *Samurai X: The Movie* (1997) follows directly on from the events of the earlier series of which it is a stylistic companion. The action shifts to Yokohama, where Kenshin helps foil a plot to destabilize the new Meiji government. Adopting the same realistic, high-quality style of *Trust and Betrayal*, *Samurai X: Reflection* documents the latter years of Kenshin's life, covering events during his later marriage to Kaoru (a key character from the TV series), including the birth of their son Kenji, a showdown with Tomoe's revengeful brother Emishi and a tear-stained conclusion with Kenshin and Kaoru on their deathbeds.

Serial Experiments Lain

シリアルエクスペリメンツレイン

dir Ryutaro Nakamura, 1998, 13 x 25m

scr Chiaki Konaka *m* Reiichi Nakaido *cast* Kaori Shimizu/Ruby Marlowe: Lain Iwakura; Ayako Kawasumi/Patricia Ja Lee: Mika Iwakura; Rei Igarashi/Celeste Burch: Miho Iwakura; Ryunosuke Ōbayashi/Gil Starberry: Yasuo Iwakura; Yoko Asada/Emily Brown: Alice Mizuki; Sho Hayami/Sparky Thornton: Masami Eiri

Official Japanese site www.geneon-ent.co.jp/rondorobe/anime/lain

Thought Experiments Lain www.cjas.org/~leng/lain.htm

It starts with a teenage suicide, involves several more self-inflicted deaths and ends with the heroine abandoning her corporeal self for life in cyberspace. Or does it? This beguiling sci-fi series paints a disturbingly sinister vision of modern Japan and of that perennial anime peril: technology's encroachment on human existence. At the same time the series questions exactly what reality is. Might it all have been a dream after all?

This much seems clear. Introverted Lain Iwakura, she of the kooky haircut, hides away at home in the comfort blanket of her bear-suit pyjamas. Practically ignored by her family – her creepy workaholic dad, disinterested mum and her sneering older sister – she turns to her computer, or "Navi". It's here, on the "Wired", as it's known in *Serial Experiments Lain*, that she receives a beyond-the-grave communication from Chisa, the suicide teen who was in her class at school. Not particularly fazed by this weird turn of events, shy Lain agrees to join some of her schoolfriends, including the kindly Alice, at a popular nightclub called Cyberia, where the kids get their kicks by popping dangerous technologybased drugs. Strangely, some of them recognize Lain even though she's never been there before; one is so disturbed by her he blows his brains out in front of her. Again, Lain seems barely moved by this trauma, but from thereon increasingly retreats into the virtual reality of the Wired where she eventually encounters Masami Eiri, the mysterious and seemingly all-powerful entity who created it.

With its dense plotting, involving conspiracies and philosophical questions, *Lain* is beloved by anime intellectuals for being imbued with an eclectic range of references

Suicide society

Star-crossed lovers sealing their fate in a death pact. Samurai committing *sepaku* (ritual self-disembowelment) rather than living in shameful dishonour. World War II's kamikaze pilots dive-bombing their planes into Allied ships. Suicide has a long and glorified history in Japan – which partly explains why the country continues to have one of the highest suicide rates in the world (thirty thousand a year). It's a miserable fact reflected in the plots of more anime than just *Serial Experiments Lain*.

In *Paranoia Agent*, for example, there's one episode devoted to the very real phenomenon of internet suicide-pact clubs. *Evangelion*'s Asuka Langley is also traumatized by witnessing her mother's suicide as a child. Suicide, it appears, can even be played for laughs, as demonstrated by the wickedly black comedy series *Sayonara Zetsubō Sensei* (*dir* Akiyuki Shinbo, 2007, 12 x 25m). Its suicidal central character, a morose teacher who adopts the guise of a tragic young poet, is contrasted with one of his eternally optimistic teenage students – it's similar to *South Park*, but funnier and more inventive.

to figures and events as diverse as **Vannevar Bush** (a prophetic computer expert of the 1940s), the Roswell UFO incident and Marcel Proust. It is also visually distinctive with off-kilter character designs by **Yoshitoshi Abe** and scenes that flip between the blinding fluorescent white of day and the kaleidoscopic computer-generated world of the web. The idea that all of Tokyo is trapped in an enormous web is strengthened by frequent cutaway shots of the power cables strung above the streets, humming with a malevolent energy.

Space Battleship Yamato

Uchû Senkan Yamato; 宇宙戦艦ヤマト

dir Leiji Matsumoto, 1974–75, 26 x 25m

scr Keisuke Fujikawa, Eiichi Yamamoto *m* Hiroshi Miyagawa *cast* Gorō Naya/Gordon Ramsey: Captain Jūzō Okita/Abraham Avatar; Kei Tomiyama/Kenneth Meseroll: Susumu Kodai/Derek Wildstar; Yōko Asagami/Amy Howard: Yuki Mori/Nova Forrester; Shūsei Nakamura/Tom Tweedy: Daisuke Shima/Mark Venture

Star Blazers official site www.starblazers.com

The giant battleship *Yamato* was a seemingly impregnable behemoth and symbol of Japan's pride. When it sank following a suicidal operation at the end of World War II the psychological trauma was similar to that experienced in the West after the loss of the *Titanic*.

But you can't keep one of the largest and most powerful ships ever built down forever and, thirty years later, the Yamato was resurrected in anime form as a technologically advanced spaceship dispatched on another do-or-die mission to the furthest reaches of the galaxy.

Best known to non-Japanese fans in its late 1970s dubbed version as *Star Blazers*, this is the series that redefined sci-fi anime, establishing conventions that still resonate today. Envelope-pushing at the time for its serious, multilayered storyline, its allusions to World War II and appeal to a more mature audience, plus its detailed production design, *Space Battleship Yamato* can, however, seem corny as hell today. Scientific credibility is an early casualty with tiny details like the lack of air and gravity in space not getting in the way of the visual pyrotechnics of battle. One of the lead characters, Captain Okita (Avatar), looks like he just strolled in from a Bird's Eye Fish Fingers ad, and the baddies – the blue-faced Gamilas (Gamilons) – could be from *Star Trek* central casting.

Even so, the series' influence on future generations of animators was profound and is reflected in the shape of other totemic sci-fi anime including *Macross*, *Mobile Suit Gundam* and *Neon Genesis Evangelion*. Despite the inclusion of comic relief from the robot Analyzer (IQ-9) and the sake-guzzling Dr Sado (Dr Sane), it proved that anime wasn't just for little kids, and could provide audiences with a show that was not only visually exciting but also had a morally complex plot including flawed heroes and villains who were not all bad.

In the year 2199, the world's population has been driven underground, the surface of Earth having been made uninhabitable by the radioactive planet bombs of the attacking Gamilas. Humanity's last hope lies with the crew of the retooled *Yamato* (Argo in the English dub), including young hotshot Susumu Kodai (Derek Wildstar), his buddy Daisuke Shima (Mark Venture) and curvaceous nurse Yuki Mori (Nova Forrester) who falls for Kodai.

They all have just a year to make a return journey to the distant planet of Iskandar, where its sole survivor Stasha (Starsha) holds the key to Earth's salvation. Along the way they not only have to outsmart the Gamilas led by Desler (Desslock) but also deal with on-board tensions: Kodai blames Captain Okita for allowing his brother Mamoru (Alex) to die on a previous mission.

With its precision-drawn spaceship, based not only on the original *Yamato* and World War II aircraft carriers, but also fighter jets used during the Vietnam War, *Space Battleship Yamato* was instrumental in the rise of the otaku subculture (see p.271). Scheduled against Isao Takahata's hit *Heidi*, the series suffered in the ratings when originally screened in Japan and had its run truncated to 26 episodes. However a couple of cinema-screen versions, including *Farewell to Space Battleship Yamato – In the Name of Love* (1978), released around the time of *Star Wars* and drawing on the craze that film ignited for all things sci-fi, gathered legions of new fans and extended the life of the franchise.

In true anime revisionist style, the fact that most of the characters and the *Yamato* seemed to have perished at the end of *Farewell to Space Battleship Yamato* was conveniently ignored and the series continued for two more seasons through to 1981 and several more movies capping off with *Final Yamato* in 1983. Projects related to the original series after this were dogged by a decade-long copyright battle between the producer Yoshinobu Nishizaki and Leiji Matsumoto.

In 2008, however, with all rights settled, Nishizaki announced a revival of the franchise with a new series set 21 years after the events of the original *Yamato* and starring Susumu Kodai who's now captain of the unsinkable spaceship. It's scheduled to hit screens in 2009.

Steamboy

スチームボーイ

dir Katsuhiro Ōtomo, 2004, 106m

scr Katsuhiro Ōtomo *m* Steve Jablonsky *cast* Anne Suzuki/Anna Paquin: Ray Steam; Katsuo Nakamura/Patrick Stewart: Lloyd Steam; Masane Tsukayama/Alfred Molina: Eddie Steam; Manami Konishi/Kari Wahlgren: Scarlett O'Hara; Kiyoshi Kodama/Oliver Cotton: Robert Stephenson

Official Japanese site www.steamboy.net

Sony Pictures site www.sonypictures.com/movies/steamboy

Anime is a frequent visitor to the fantasy sub-genre of steampunk – stories typically set in the Victorian steam-driven era but with plenty of science-fiction and alternative history elements. **Hayao Miyazaki**'s *Castle in the Sky* is a good example and **Rintarō**'s *Metropolis*, mixing 1920s retro style with advanced robotics, also falls into the category. The ultimate steampunk anime has to be *Steamboy*, **Katsuhiro Ōtomo**'s long awaited follow-up to *Akira*.

It's a good but flawed film that's overlong and which could have done with a bit more attention being paid to improve the often clichéd script. In its favour, however, are its impressive visuals – from fascinating steam-powered inventions to the immensely detailed backdrops (this is what you get when you spend $20 million and a decade working on a movie). There's also the tense dynamic between the principal characters, three generations of the Steam family.

Teenager Ray Steam's natural talents as an inventor of steam-driven contraptions comes from his grandfather Lloyd and his father Eddie, also inventors, who are first seen in the movie labouring in a cave in Iceland and later working on a disastrous experiment in steam power in Alaska. From these far-flung locales, the scene switches to Manchester in 1866, where Ray is living in a cosy cottage with his mother and siblings that seems way too comfy for someone who also labours in one of the era's satanic stream-driven cotton mills. Eagle-eyed viewers will notice that a pub in the background of a street scene is called The Rover's Return – a reference to *Coronation Street*, a long-running British soap opera set "up north", and proof of how thoroughly the artists working on this film did their research.

A package arrives for Ray from his grandfather with a mysterious

Teen hero Ray Steam uses his steam-powered inventions to save Victorian London from disaster

note insisting that Ray guards its contents – a powerful steam ball – especially from representatives of the O'Hara Foundation, who have been funding Lloyd and Eddie's research. Sinister O'Hara Foundation agents swiftly follow, causing Ray to scarper on a steam-driven monocycle. In a kinetic action scene involving a dirigible and a speed train, Ray gets to meet up briefly with Robert Stephenson (real-life inventor of the steam engine) before being kidnapped by the agents and removed to London.

Installed in the giant steam castle, next to the site of the Great Exhibition at Crystal Palace, Ray is reunited with his physically scarred father. He also meets the heiress of the O'Hara Foundation, a spoilt American brat by the name of Scarlett, who takes a shine to Ray. The foundation wants to use the Steam inventions for military purposes, something that has brought the idealistic Lloyd and his more realistic son to blows. As full-scale battle breaks out between the foundation's "steam troopers" and British bobbies (policemen), Ray is torn between loyalty to both father and grandfather. He also has to find a way of stopping the flying steam castle from exploding over the centre of London.

Essentially, the movie's an origin story of how young Ray Steam evolves into a Victorian crusader who flies through the air wearing a steam-powered jet pack – the Steamboy of the title. By the movie's conclusion, with all the main characters intact, but half of London in ruins, the stage has been set for a follow-up, elements of which are hinted at in the closing titles. So far, there has been no sequel, though.

Spirited Away

Sen to Chihiro no Kamikakushi; 千と千尋の神隠し
dir Hayao Miyazaki, 2001, 125m

scr Hayao Miyazaki *m* Joe Hisaishi *cast* Rumi Hiiragi/Daveigh Chase: Chihiro; Miyu Irino/James Marsden: Haku; Mari Natsuki/Suzanne Pleshette: Yubaba/Zeniba; Yumi Tamai/Susan Egan: Rin/Lin; Bunta Sugawara/David Ogden Stiers: Kamaji

Official Australian site www.spiritedaway.com.au

Set mainly in a fantastic bathhouse, catering to Japan's weird and wonderful pantheon of Shinto gods and ruled over by a bejewelled, hook-nosed sorceress, this Oscar-winning film is a richly imagined fairy tale, seasoned with Miyazaki's usual concerns for the environment. It is these **Shinto** spirits who are the visual centrepiece of *Spirited Away*. At the same time Miyazaki also constructs a masterclass in character-building and good manners for overly whiney young children.

To be fair, Chihiro, the rosy-cheeked star of this *Alice in Wonderland*-style story, does have some reason to be sulky as the movie commences. Leaving behind her schoolfriends, she is being driven by her parents to a new home. On the way, Dad takes a wrong turn and ends up at the entrance to what appears to be an abandoned theme park, dominated by a giant bathhouse. Chihiro finds the deserted place creepy and when her ravenous parents discover a delicious-looking banquet refuses to join in the feast.

This is a wise move as the food is meant only for the spirits who, come nightfall, arrive to refresh and relax in the bathhouse. As a punishment, her greedy parents are transformed into pigs.

Desperate to find a way out of this nightmare, Chihiro is inducted into the bathhouse with the assistance of Haku, a kindly yet mysterious young boy who for some reason knows her name. He tells her the only way she'll survive in this alternative world and find a way to lift the spell on her parents is to get a job. Chihiro digs deep to find the courage to approach the fearsome witch Yubaba, empress of the bathhouse, who is compelled to employ all who ask her for work – even annoying little human girls.

Yubaba renames her new employee Sen and sets her horrible tasks such as assisting the toxic Stink Spirit in taking a bath. A rusty old bicycle is

Transfigured parents, stinky river gods and ghostly spirits populate the comic but haunting *Spirited Away*

Apart from the multitude of spirits, other denizens of the bathhouse include the no-nonsense worker Lin, the boiler-man Kamaji who has six arms, a gigantic baby, a trio of bouncing bald heads and an army of soot sprites. Haku sometimes turns into a flying dragon to do Yubaba's bidding. When he returns from one assignment battered, bloody and seemingly close to death,

Chihiro is determined to save him, even if it means she has to put a hold on rescuing her parents. This entails her taking a journey on a one-way train to return a stolen seal to Yubaba's twin sister Zeniba. In a colourful, energetic film it's this calm, serene scene, with an antique locomotive skimming over a shallow lake reflecting the dusky skies, that is one of the most beautiful and memorable.

yanked out of the spirit, followed by a mountain of other rubbish, revealing it as a river god; it's a sequence inspired by a real-life clean-up of a river that Miyazaki took part in.

Tarō the Dragon Boy

Tatsunoko Tarô; 龍の子太郎

dir Kirio Urayama, 1979, 75m

scr Kirio Urayama, Takashi Mitsui m Riichiro Manabe cast Junya Kato: Tarō; Sayuri Yoshinaga: Tatsuya; Miina Tominaga: Aya; Kazuo Kumakura: Red Oni

Tōei Animation corp.toei-anim.co.jp/english/film/taro_the_dragon_boy.php

Based on an ancient Japanese myth, *Tarō the Dragon Boy* is a throwback to the glory days of Tōei Animation in the 1960s, with splendid animation, elegantly conceived artwork and distinctively local roots. Its little boy hero, the rosy-cheeked, indefatigable Tarō, and its supporting cast of friendly forest animals, are designed to appeal to children but, as with the best anime of this kind, the film also contains much to appeal to adult tastes.

At the start of the film Tarō is shown to be a lazy, somewhat selfish little boy, reprimanded by his fellow villagers for not helping with the farm work, and is teased by others for being the son of a dragon. Tarō's not all bad, though; he shares his food with the forest animals and plays with them, teaching them sumo wrestling moves. A *tengu* – long-nosed goblin – appears and, impressed with Tarō's bravery, grants him a sip of sake that bestows upon the little boy the strength of a hundred men.

A little later Tarō learns from his grandmother that his mother, who had mysteriously been turned into a dragon just before his birth, might still be alive, living in a lake to the north. Tarō vows to find her, and the rest of the film follows his quest, introducing us to several colourful characters he meets en route, including the pretty flute-playing Aya, the Red Oni thunder god and a cunning old woman who tricks him into farming her lands for a year. In the process Tarō learns many lessons, not least of which is the value of sharing, and unselfish actions.

Kirio Urayama, better known for his live-action films, was tasked by Tōei with directing the project in place of the unavailable Isao Takahata who had suggested animating the fable years earlier. He makes a great job of it, producing a gently paced film that stays faithful to Japan's ancient history and culture without straying into romanticizing or sentimentalizing it.

The harsh life of the poor farmers in the mountainous region where Tarō lives is not given a whitewash. There's also a refreshingly unprudish approach to nudity: Tarō's party trick, established in the credits, is to do a handstand, his tunic falling to reveal a lack of underwear – hardly unusual for a poor boy in rural Japan of centuries past. Later in the film an old witch approaches Tarō, her sagging breasts falling out of her gown, while in the final scene Tarō's mother is revealed in all her natural glory.

The film's beauty really comes across in the production design, which favours delicate compositions in muted greys and blues for the backgrounds, in the style of traditional *sumi-e* ink paintings. Such a setting enables the clean-lined, colourful characters to stand out. There is some lovely animation work here, particularly when the ghostly snow-women pursue Tarō, and in the final scenes with Tarō riding the dragon – an image recycled in Miyazaki's *Spirited Away*. Some of this animation is the work of **Reiko Okuyama**, an alumnus of Tōei from the 1950s and one of the very few women to make her mark in the male-dominated world of anime (see p.151).

Tekkon Kinkreet

Tekkon Kinkuriito; 鉄コン筋クリート

dir Michael Arias, 2006, 111m

scr Anthony Weintraub *m* Plaid *cast* Kazunari Ninomiya/Scott Menville: Kuro/Black; Yū Aoi/Kamali Minter: Shiro/White; Min Tanaka/David Lodge: Suzuki, a.k.a. Rat; Yusuke Iseya/Rick Gomez: Kimura

Official Sony site www.sonypictures.com/homevideo/tekkonkinkreet

A prime example of the creeping internationalization of anime, *Tekkon Kinkreet*, shows how non-Japanese talents can bring a different energy, point of view and burst of creativity to the medium. In his directorial debut, Michael Arias uses his skills as a visual effects and computer graphics specialist to immerse the viewer in the richly imagined 3D streets of Treasure Town, the battleground between spunky young street kids, gangsters and aliens.

The film's heroes are a gang of two orphans who go by the name

You lookin' at me? Black (right) and White (left) the heroes of *Tekkon Kinkreet*

of The Cats. Black is the experienced Artful Dodger to White's idiot savant Oliver. Picking pockets to get by, the boys make their home in an abandoned car beneath the expressways on the edge of Treasure Town, an island territory they fiercely protect against intrusions from outside gangs. Bounding off buildings, across rooftops and between speeding cars, heedless of their nine lives, it's clear how the duo came by their feline gang name. But when yakuza thugs start to muscle in on Treasure Town, acting for Snake, the sinister developer of the planned Kiddie Kastle theme park, the battles turn deadly. Black's violent response provokes Snake to unleash a trio of giant alien assassins to deal once and for all with the irritating kids.

Given to wearing odd shoes and funny hats, the perpetually snotty-nosed White thinks all will be fine if he can get the seed from his apple to grow. Black knows better, but also clings on to White's naïvely optimistic hopes of a better future for them both. Mirroring this duo are two other couples: the cops Fujimura and Sawada, who care for White after his near-fatal stabbing; and the battle-weary yakuza Suzuki (The Rat) and his overly ambitious sidekick Kimura.

More fully realized than any of these characters is the fantastic environment which they inhabit. Not unlike the Asakusa area of Tokyo, spiced up with architectural elements from across Asia, Treasure Town is a mishmash of ancient and modern. A giant Ganesh statue pops out of the clock tower, the bulbous domes and rocket-like minarets of a mosque burst through a tangle of electricity and telephone wires, and the polyglot scripts of Sanskrit, Japanese and English jostle for attention on shop signs and posters. Superlative computer graphics enable the audience to see it all from every angle, including the point of view of Black and White as they are pursued through streets.

Treading a fine line between whimsy and the avant-garde, particularly in its closing straight, *Tekkon Kinkreet* adopts the sharp, graphic style of the manga by Taiyō Matsumoto on which it is based, resulting in one of the most distinctive animated films of modern times. Arias has said he was aiming for the feel of a "documentary shot inside a hand-drawn, hand-painted world". Some eighty percent of *Tekkon Kinkreet* (the title is a pun on the Japanese for reinforced concrete) was created using computer graphics, but you'd hardly know it such is the care and attention to detail lavished on each scene which mimic the rougher, more organic look of traditional cel-based animation.

Tokyo Godfathers

東京ゴッドファーザーズ

dir Satoshi Kon, 2003, 92m

scr Satoshi Kon, Keiko Nobumoto *m* Keichi Suzuki *cast* Aya Okamoto: Miyuki; Toru Emori: Gin; Yoshiaki Umegaki: Hana

Sony Pictures site www.sonypictures.com/cthe/tokyogodfathers

Transvestites, drunks and feisty teenagers are not uncommon characters in anime, but taking one of each and making them homeless and living together in a cardboard box beneath the glittering towers of the Tokyo Metropolitan Government Building is something unique. Such is the setup for *Tokyo Godfathers*, Satoshi Kon's joyous twist on the old "three vagrants and an abandoned baby" theme. Kon's sympathetic depiction of the circumstances that shape such people's unfortunate lives provides the comedy's emotional core. It's a funny, charming and beautifully composed movie about families, however unconventional they may be, and reunions set in the week between Christmas and New Year's Day.

Following a nativity play and soup-kitchen meal, Hana, a washed-up transvestite with delusions of being a mother, and Gin, a gruff middle-aged alcoholic bum, return with food for Miyuki the tough-talking teenage runaway they've been looking after for the past six months. Hana also has some books to give Miyuki as a Christmas present but, while looking for them in the trash dumpster, the trio instead happen upon a baby. It seems like a miracle to Hana, and though Gin and Miyuki want to take the newly born infant to the police, he convinces the other two that it is they who must find the parents of the child, whom he names Kiyoko.

A locker key left with the baby turns up some clues to its identity, including photos of a couple and business cards for a massage parlour. Slogging through the snowbound streets, the trio set off to find out if the mother may work there. On their way they rescue a mobster who is trapped beneath the wheels of his car. He turns out to not only know the massage parlour's owner but also is about to become his father-in-law as his daughter is marrying him later that day.

In narrative terms, while this is Kon's most conventional film to date, the director liberally uses such chance encounters, outra-

© Madhouse Productions

geous coincidences and plot twists to drive *Tokyo Godfathers* towards its happy conclusion. Along the way the baby's plight shines a light on the past lives of Hana, who never knew his real mother as a child; Gin, who is consumed with guilt about his estrangement from his daughter; and Miyuki, who following a violent row with her policeman father is afraid to return home.

The film is packed with memorable scenes, from a slow-motion assassination attempt at the wedding, to the action hero finale which sees Gin furiously pedalling a bike to catch up with a speeding lorry in which the stolen baby is being carried. Best of all are the believable central characters – even the drama queen Hana whose super-elastic facial movements strike the most cartoonish moments in a film that otherwise strives for photo-realism, particularly in its background animation of the snowy cityscape. Kon captures the beguiling neon glow of Tokyo in the film's many night scenes, turning the city into a magical setting for a tale of Christmas miracles.

A Christmas miracle: a baby is found left in the garbage in *Tokyo Godfathers*

Urusei Yatsura

うる星やつら

dir Mamoru Oshii and others, 1981–86, 218 x 25m

scr Mamoru Oshii and others *m* Fumitaka Anzai, Micky Yoshino, Shinsuke Kazado *cast* Fumi Hirano: Lum; Toshio Furukawa: Ataru Moroboshi; Akira Kamiya: Shūtaro Mendō; Ichirō Nagai: Sakuramboo Cherry; Saeko Shimzu: Shinobu Miyake; Machiko Washio: Sakura

Studio Pierrot site pierrot.jp/english/title/urusei.html

The title of this fantasy/sci-fi sitcom can be translated as *Those Obnoxious Aliens*, but there are few extraterrestrials as appealing as Lum, the cutie in tiger-print bikini and kinky boots who's the show's star and an iconic pin-up of anime. The first, and best, of Rumiko Takahashi's riotous manga adventures to make the leap from page to screen, the series is a knockabout farce with a vast cast of human and alien characters who constantly find themselves in the most bizarre of adventures cherry-picked from the manga's nine-year run.

Lecherous layabout teenager Ataru Moroboshi from Tomobiko is selected by computer to be the human representative in a crucial game of tag between Earth and the far from fearsome *oni* (devil) aliens, represented by the lovely princess Lum. Thanks to a stolen bikini top and a misinterpreted proposal of marriage, Ataru wins the race and finds himself shackled to Lum, who moves into his home, much to the bemusement of Ataru's despairing parents, and attends his high school where she meets his friends including super-rich kid Mendō and Ataru's previous girlfriend Shinobu.

For all Lum's obvious charms, Ataru is not about to suddenly change his philandering ways. The jealous Lum constantly strikes back with electric shocks to her "Darling" (her pet name for Ataru) and serves up disastrous attempts at Japanese cooking. To make things even more complicated, Lum's alien relatives and friends frequently drop by, as does the meddling monk Cherry, whose niece, Sakura, is the school nurse and also happens to be a powerful Shinto priest.

With its rich variety of appealing characters and farcical, slapstick setups it's very easy to enjoy *Urusei Yatsura* as a straightforward romantic comedy. The series is also packed with direct and satirical references to Japanese culture, history and behaviour that makes it a fun way to learn about life in the country. The excellent subtitles and copious liner notes on the DVDs produced by US distributor AnimEigo help decode the subtext of what's going on for the uninitiated.

Not counting the straight-to-video releases, there have been six *Urusei Yatsura* movies. The most interesting is *Urusei Yatsura 2: Beautiful Dreamer* (1984, 90m) directed by **Mamoru Oshii**, who was also the chief director of the series for its first three years. Even by the series' wacky standards, *Beautiful Dreamer* is particularly offbeat, throwing Tomobiko's residents into a surreal time-loop that sees Ataru, Lum and co constantly repeating the day and night before the school festival. The second half of the movie makes clear how the predicament is related to the folklore tale of Urashima Taro (see p.206). Oshii uses the setup to allow the characters to riff on concepts of time, space and dreams – a trial run for the philosophizing that goes on in his later films.

Whisper of the Heart

Mimi o Sumaseba; 耳をすませば

dir Yoshifumi Kondō, 1995, 111m

scr Hayao Miyazaki *m* Yuji Nomi *cast* Yōko Honna/Britney Snow: Shizuku Tsukishima; Issei Takahashi/David Gallagher: Seiji Amasawa; Takahashi Tachibana/James B. Sikking: Yasuya Tsukishima Dad; Shigeru Muroi/Jean Smart?: Asako Tsukishima Mum; Yorie Yamashita/Courtney Thorne-Smith: Shiho Tsukishima (elder sister); Maiko Yoshiyama/Ashley Tisdale: Yūko Harada; Keiju Kobayashi/Harold Gould: Shirō Nishi; Shigeru Tsuyuguchi/Carey Elwes: The Baron

As Shizuku Tsukishima discovers early on in *Whisper of the Heart*, it's tough putting an original spin on an old standard. She's attempting to write new lyrics for the Olivia Newton-John hit "Country Roads" for her and her friends to sing at their junior high school graduation.

Similarly, when Yoshifumi Kondō and Hayao Miyazaki came to adapt the *shōjo manga* (girls' comic) by Aoi Hiiragi they had to find a way to make something fresh and different out of what could easily have been just another stereotypical tale of the trials of young love. They strike their magic formula by carefully building up realistic characters and situations to match the meticulously detailed background art and atmosphere, a homage to the approach adopted by Isao Takahata in *Only Yesterday*. With the contrast between bright light and shadow and the chirping of cicadas you really feel immersed in a Japanese summer.

In a vivid opening sequence that sets the quality bar high, we follow Shizuku, a bright, confident bookworm, as she returns from school through her suburban Tokyo neighbourhood to a cramped flat that she shares with her librarian father, mature student mother and crabby elder sister. Shizuku should be studying for exams, but she's distracted by the fairy-tale books she loves to read. Noticing that the books always seem to have been previously borrowed from the library by Seiji Amasawa, she starts to fantasize romantically about who this boy could be.

In a setup worthy of Jane Austen, she's fairly certain it's not the annoying fellow student who discovers the lyrics she absent-mindedly leaves on a park bench and gently teases her about them. However, fate finds her following an intriguing stray cat off a train and across the city to end up at the antique shop of the kindly old man Nishi. It turns out that Nishi is the grandfather of Seiji who is also the boy who teased her earlier.

Once she gets over her anger,

Shizuku and her artistocratic feline friend The Baron, later to return in his own movie

Shizuku begins to find much to admire about Seiji who's an aspiring violin maker. In one of the movie's best scenes she jams with Seiji and his grandpa's band on an impromptu version of "Country Roads". Seiji reveals his love for Shizuku, but he has also set his heart on learning to craft violins in Cremona, Italy. When he travels there for a two-month trial apprenticeship, Shizuku dedicates herself to testing her own talent as a fiction writer. Her schoolwork suffers but her parents, though concerned, encourage her to pursue her goal.

Shizuku bases her story around the model of a dapperly dressed cat, known as the Baron, that she's enchanted by in Nishi's shop. The Baron reappears in Studio Ghibli's *The Cat Returns* (see p.147), a prequel to this movie and it's tempting to imagine how Kōndo might have handled that story. Sadly, this would be the highly talented animator's only directorial effort before his untimely death at the age of 47, three years after *Whisper*'s release.

Wings of Honneamise

Ôritsu Uchûgun Oneamisu no Tsubasa; 王立宇宙群オネアミスの翼

dir Hiroyuki Yamaga, 1987, 125m

scr Hiroyuki Yamaga, *m* Ryuichi Sakamoto *cast* Leo Morimoto/Robert Matthews: Shitotsugh Lhadatt; Mitsuki Yayoi/Melody Lee: Riquinni Nonderaiko

Gainax official site www.gainax.co.jp/anime/honeamis

Imagine they held a space race, but only one side turned up and nobody particularly cared, including the vast majority of the participants. That's the satirical premise behind *The Wings of Honneamise,* the debut feature of Gainax. For a first shot, *Wings* is an amazing achievement, not least because of the risk the Gainax boys were taking by going with wholly original material. No fall-back on previous manga success for them. A flop on initial release, *Wings'* reputation has grown over time to the point where it is justly heralded as a classic of the medium.

The workaday hero of the piece is Shitotsugh Lhadatt who is first glimpsed running through the snow and looking up at the jet planes soaring into the skies from the deck

The Right Stuff: Shitotsugh Lhadatt (middle) is the astronaut hero of *Wings of Honneamise*

of an aircraft carrier out at sea. As a child Lhadatt wanted to be one such pilot, but his average grades and abilities landed him instead in the Royal Space Force (RSF), a backwater of the military that everyone, including most of its members, treat as a joke. Suffering from lingering depression following the death of one of his colleagues, Lhadatt is drawn towards Riquinni, a plain but passionately religious girl who preaches to the deaf ears of passers-by in Honneamise's fleshpots. Riquinni's friendship and enthusiasm for his work gives Lhadatt renewed confidence to volunteer as the pilot of the first manned flight into space. It's a highly risky move given the past catastrophic fumblings of the RSF, not to mention covert machinations to turn the rocket launch into a pretext for war with a neighbouring hostile nation.

All the characters – some of whose looks are said to have been modelled on Hollywood stars such as Harrison Ford, Lee Van Cleef and Treat Williams – are distinct. Plain-looking Riquinni is practically unique in the anime world – she's dowdy, yet her devout and forgiving nature give *Wings* a moral centre. Boyishly bedraggled for most of the movie, Lhadatt cuts himself while shaving, throws up after his first bumpy outing piloting a plane and, in spite of his easy-going nature, attempts to rape Riquinni. That hard-hitting scene adds to rather than diverts from the anime's central theme – that humankind may have base and violent instincts but is capable of nobler things – making it one of *Wings'* great achievements.

The other is the film's phenomenal production design. Honneamise

Wings of Honneamise: a production that prided itself on its meticulously realistic depiction of spacecraft and landscape

may look a lot like somewhere on Earth, but practically everything, from the architecture, numbers and written language to the fashions and money has been invented anew for this fantasy kingdom. The animators visited Cape Kennedy and the National Air and Space Museum in the US and made many sketches adding veracity to the retro rocket technology. The modern Greek meets Ruritania uniforms of the RSF are also an inspired touch. Rounding off the inventive package very nicely is Ryuichi Sakamoto's catchy electronic score, for which it's said he was paid ¥100 million – apparently over 10% of the total cost of the whole film.

Given the initial lukewarm reception for the film, financial backers Bandai might have initially rued letting loose a bunch of novices with so much cash. However, the subsequent successful video release of *Wings* proved the potential for that format, leading to profits for all involved.

The good, the bad and the ugly

For every genuine anime classic there's innumerable dross. Sifting through the mountains of dirt for rare diamonds is a full-time job for Jonathan Clements and Helen McCarthy, authors of *The Anime Encyclopedia*.

"There are many hours of my life spent watching awful hentai that I am never going to get back. I keep telling myself, I'm watching this now so that nobody else ever has to," says Clements who also writes several monthly columns on anime and manga. "Many TV series, including the most popular ones, are just lazy rehashes of old hits, predicated on the fact that most children grow out of anime within a few years," adds McCarthy.

Who better, then, than Clements and McCarthy to bestow the Golden Turkey awards for anime shockers? Clements' top five picks are: *The Gigalo* ("So bad that its distributor couldn't even spell its name"); the "infantile" cop show *Mad Bull 34* ("one of the most puerile anime ever made"); the gang leader redeemed by baseball series *Butchigiri* ("so bad that its own makers set the storyboards on fire when it was completed"); the "disappointingly trite adaptation of Yasuaki Kadota's SF novel" *Psychic Wars*; and the unintentionally funny *Sins of the Sisters* – "prime candidate for the most mind-boggling plot in anime".

McCarthy also nominates *The Gigalo* and *Mad Bull 34* ("so bad it's hard to imagine how anyone watches it"). Other picks include *Landlock* ("a horrific mess of an anime" with a very tenuous connection to Masamune Shirow) and *Balthus: Tia's Radiance* – a porn version of Miyazaki's *Castle in the Sky*.

The duo also have some forthright views on the subject of "best" anime, particularly those chosen for **award ceremonies** such as the Mainichi Film Awards and in **fan polls.** "There's often more commercial or political significance in awards than anything remotely related to artistic merit," says McCarthy. "Awards are only as good as their voters, " Clements adds, "and the average anime viewer still only knows an incredibly detailed amount about a tiny fragment of the larger anime world. Usually just the anime made in a 24-month bubble around their self-identification as a 'fan'."

When asked to nominate their own personal favourites, the top picks are *Gunbuster* for Clements, and *My Neighbour Totoro* for McCarthy who considers it "the most magical film ever made." Both of them put the TV series *Escaflowne* and *Patlabor* in their top fives, with Clements rounding out his nominations with *Kiki's Delivery Service* and *Neon Genesis Evangelion*, while for McCarthy its *Porco Rosso* – "anime for the middle-aged – a recognition that dreams never die" and *Tokyo Godfathers* – "a love letter to a Tokyo most anime fans wouldn't even recognize".

3

Creating anime

a look behind the scenes

Like all filmmaking, the creation of an anime is a collaborative process, combining the talents of hundreds of people including animators, background artists, voice actors, musicians, writers and film technicians. Studios have the task of assembling the production team and appointing a director, who provides leadership and shapes the project's vision. This chapter shines a light into the production process, picking out some of the star players in the anime firmament.

These days computers are integral to making an anime. However, the essential theory and workflow of production remains the same as in the days of hand-drawing and total **cel animation**. Cel stands for celluloid – the transparent sheets of film onto which animators transfer the thousands of slightly different images needed to give the impression of movement when filmed in sequence and projected at speed.

All anime starts with an idea that leads to a project proposal and eventually a script. The project

proposal will cover things such as the target audience of the anime, the names and designs of key characters, machinery and robotics (or **mecha**) if they're part of the story, and possible merchandising spin-offs. If the proposal piques the interest of various sponsors, including TV stations and video distributors, it gets the green light. A production team is pulled together and a script is written. From this a series of **story-boards** (called e-conte, where "e" is the Japanese for picture and "conte" an abbreviation of continuity) are drawn up. Often it's the director who creates the storyboards.

From the storyboards a team of key animators and **inbetweeners** work to create the anime. The key animators use the storyboards to lay out the anime, drawing the major or key frames for each scene. As their name implies, the inbetweeners fill in the gaps, laboriously sketching the minor changes between each of the key frames. Finally the drawings are transferred to the cels and painted in.

Computer-generated imagery (CGI) has taken much of the grunt work out of this process. Once fed with key frames, a computer can automatically draw the additional images needed to make the movement fluid in a process called **tweening**. Computers can also be used to ensure that colourization of each frame is consistent and to create specific film effects – in fact, cels are hardly ever painted by hand now as so much of an anime is created digitally. The same goes for the actual "filming" (or **compositing**) of the images when all are complete. The camera is part of the old process; most compositing is now done within computers.

While all this is going on the **soundtrack**, including vocals, music and sound effects, is being created. If time is tight (as it often is in anime production), the soundtrack may be created to a rough, un-colourized cut of the finished work, which might even be as simple as the story-boards shown sequentially in the show's time frame.

Eventually everything is edited together – if the anime is for TV broadcast there's a set format to be followed including second-specific running times and a break for ads. At each and every stage the director will check that the anime, as initially imagined, is being created. The producer is also there to ensure that the crew are doing their jobs on time and to budget.

The studios

The first wave

Small Japanese animation studios have existed since the 1920s, but it was with the formation of Tōei Dōga in 1956, later renamed **Tōei Animation** (www.toei-anim.co.jp), that the industry began to get serious. Among Tōei's back catalogue of over 8500 titles are Japan's earliest full-length animated feature films, many highly impressive works for their time, including classics such as *Little Norse Prince* and *Puss 'n Boots* (see Canon for both), the lead character of which became the company mascot.

In the early 1970s Tōei began to concentrate on producing anime for TV and many of its animators, including **Hayao Miyazaki** and **Isao Takahata** left to join second-generation studios such as A-Production and Nippon Animation. Tôei's TV hits, all of which have had spin-off movies, include *Sailor Moon*, *Dragon Ball*, *Digimon* and, mostly recently, the pirate romp *One Piece*.

Specializing in TV series, particularly those with a science-fiction or action theme, is **Tatsunoko Productions**, or Tatsunoko Pro (www.tatsunoko.co.jp). Founded in 1964 by the Yoshida brothers, its biggest international hits have been *Speed Racer*, *Gatchaman* (a.k.a. *Battle of the Planets*) and *Macross* (a.k.a. *Robotech*), but in Japan it's also known for scores of other series including *Time Bokan*, in which a team of heroes use a time machine (the Time Bokan) to search for its lost inventor Dr Kieda, encountering villains on their way. The final image of each episode – a mushroom cloud explosion in the shape of a giant skull – served as an inspiration for the multimedia artist **Takeshi Murakami** (see p.246). In Japanese, one of the word *tatsunoko*'s several meanings is seahorse, which is the company's logo. As with Tōei, Tatsunoko provided a training ground for staff members who would go on to launch successive generations of studios, such as **Studio Pierrot** (www.pierrot.jp) in 1979, producers of the hit shows *Naruto* and *Bleach*, and **Production I.G**.

In the wake of the financial meltdown of Mushi Production Inc. in 1973 Osamu Tezuka's other company, **Tezuka Productions** (en-f.tezuka.co.jp), created to manage his manga works, fought to retain the rights to develop his massive library of cartoon creations into anime. This has been the company's aim ever since and has resulted in series based on characters such as Unico the unicorn, the renegade surgeon Black Jack and an adaptation of Tezuka's magnum opus of life, death and rebirth down the centuries *Phoenix* (see p.181).

© Tōei Studios; courtesy of FUNimation Entertainment

Yo ho ho: *One Piece* is among the latest hits from long-running studio Tōei Animation

Recent works of his include the 2003 update of *Astro Boy* and the *Astro Boy* CGI movie with Hong Kong-based studio IMAGI (see p.244).

In 1977 Tezuka's original anime studio was resurrected as **Mushi Production Co Ltd** (www.mushi-pro.co.jp) with the Tezuka-appointed Satoshi Ito in charge. The reborn Mushi Pro retains rights to some of Tezuka's older animated properties, including the original *Astro Boy* and *Kimba the White Lion* series and the non-Tezuka-scripted production *Tomorrow's Joe* (see p.231). Its output in recent years has been very limited, but includes the feature *Nagasaki The Angelus Bell 1945* (2005), about a doctor coping with the aftermath of the nuclear explosion, similar to *Barefoot Gen* (see Canon). The anime was funded by the city of Nagasaki as a memorial to the historical event.

Animal Treasure Island

Dōbutsu Takarajima

dir Hiroshi Ikeda, 1971, 78m

Hayao Miyazaki played a crucial role in the character design and concepts of this energetic romp, loosely based on the Robert Louis Stevenson classic. Plucky young Jim is joined by pet mouse Gran and his baby brother Baboo on a quest for the buried treasure marked on Captain Flint's map. Captain Long John Silver (a pig) and his duplicitous crew are also after the loot and Jim has to deal not only with them but also Flint's gutsy granddaughter Kathy, a prototype of strong-willed Miyazaki heroines to come. Made to celebrate Tōei's twentieth anniversary, this is one of their funniest films, ideal entertainment for kids and adults alike.

Karas

dir Keiichi Satō, 2003, 6 x 30m

Revisiting the demons-versus-humans battleground of *Wicked City*, *Karas* – a special fortieth anniversary project for Tatsunoko Pro – was based on a comic book created by Americans Phil Amara, Nuria Peris and Sergio Sandaval. Into the mix are thrown *X-Files* references, with a team of police officers following a trail of murders committed by the army of mechanized demons created by the renegade *karas* (spirit warrior) Eko. It's a hyper-stylish production, mixing 2D and 3D animation, with an "Asian Gothic" look applied by director Satō to modern-day Tokyo.

The second and third waves

In the 1970s a second generation of studios was born, several founded by former staff of industry stalwarts Tōei and Tatsunoko Pro, others rising from the ashes of Mushi Pro. Two such studios, still in business, are **Sunrise** (www.sunrise-inc.co.jp) and **Madhouse** (www.madhouse.co.jp) both established in 1972. Part of the Namco Bandai toy and game group since 1994, Sunrise has many hit shows to its credit, its output ranging from the *Mobile Suit Gundam* series to *Cowboy Bebop* and *Inuyasha*. Madhouse is particularly associated with the work of directors Rintarō (*Metropolis*) and Yoshiaki Kawajiri (*Wicked City* and *Ninja Scroll*) and has produced all of Satoshi Kon's films as well as his TV series *Paranoia Agent* (see Canon).

The 1980s witnessed the rise of a third wave of studios, the most famous of which is **Studio Ghibli** (www.ghibli.jp), pronounced "zhibli", and named after the Italian scouting planes of World War II, which were themselves named after a wind that blows across the Sahara. Ghibli was set up to provide an invigorating breath of fresh air to the local animation industry, dedicating itself to making high-quality theatrical release features.

The studio's founding fathers are **Hayao Miyazaki** and **Isao Takahata**, but a major driving force behind its success has been **Toshio Suzuki**, the former editor of *Animage* magazine, who originally commissioned Miyazaki's manga *Nausicaä of the Valley of the Wind* and persuaded him to turn it into an animated film. *Animage*'s publisher **Tokuma Shoten** was the company that bankrolled Studio Ghibli.

Suzuki, who has acted as producer on many of Ghibli's films (as well as Mamoru Oshii's *Ghost in the Shell 2: Innocence*), formally joined the company in 1991 as the executive

Life can be hectic when you're a motorbike-riding alien in *FLCL*

managing director. He's credited as the financial brains behind the studio's lucrative merchandising spin-offs, enabling Ghibli to make a mint off character goods from *My Neighbour Totoro;* he was also the broker of a distribution deal with Disney that protected the integrity of the studio's works after some disastrous earlier deals with foreign partners. In January 2008 Suzuki stepped down as Ghibli's president to concentrate on being a producer for the studio.

The other major production house to emerge from the 1980s is **Gainax** (www.gainax.co.jp), founded by a group of anime fans and junior-level industry workers, including **Hideaki Anno** (see p.150). The studio will forever be associated with the blockbuster series *Neon Genesis Evangelion*, although anime aficionados hold in high regard the short films made by Gainax's founders for the Ōsaka-based science-fiction convention Daicon in 1981 and 1983. (For more information on these never commercially released videos see www.cjas.org/~leng/daicon.htm and www.gainaxpages.com/anime/daicon.php.) One of Gainax's best productions is its very first, the movie *Wings of Honneamise* (see Canon).

The Cat Returns

Neko no Ongaeshi

dir Hiroyuki Morita, 2002, 75m

A charming fairy tale in which Morita, who worked as an animator on *Akira*, proves he has the skill to follow in the giant footsteps of his Studio Ghibli mentors. Haru is a bumbling schoolgirl who has the ability to communicate with cats. After saving a princely feline from being run over, Haru is transported to the Cat Kingdom – where the Cat King fancies her as his daughter-in-law. To the rescue comes the Baron, a debonair cat who appeared in the earlier Ghibli movie *Whisper of the Heart* (see Canon). The shift between the real and fantasy worlds is deftly handled, particularly in the wonderful scene in which Haru trails the fat cat Muta through the city's back alleys to the Baron's Cat Bureau.

FLCL

dir Kazuya Turamaki, 2000, 6 x 30m

Pronounced "furi kuri", this wacky video series, thumping along on a persistent guitar beat, is a riot of surreal visuals and in-jokes which, even by the experimental standards of Gainax, are seriously out there. Naota has problems that no twelve-year-old should have to deal with. There's an ominous factory in the shape of an enormous steam iron in his town, and his home has been invaded by an aggressive rock chick who rides a motorbike and claims to be an alien on the hunt for an intergalactic outlaw. His elder brother's girlfriend flirts shamelessly with him. And what's he going to do about the robot that has popped out of his forehead?

The fourth wave

The industry has matured to the point where the second- and third-generation studios are now spawning offspring. Former employees of Gainax, for example, formed **Gonzo Digimation Holding**, or **GDH** (www.gdh.co.jp) in 1992, a studio that specializes in high-quality digital animation calculated to appeal to an international market. GDH have made it something of a habit to dress classic works of a literature and film in new anime clothes: good examples being *The Legend of Moby Dick* (*Hakugei Densetsu*), which sends its Captain Ahab in obsessive pursuit of the sentient spacecraft Moby Dick; *Gankutsuō* (see Canon), a chic, stylized reworking of *The Count of Monte Cristo*; and *Samurai 7*, a steampunk adaptation of Akira Kurosawa's classic movie, featuring robots, flying castles and other futuristic anachronisms. Their hip-hop influenced *Afro Samurai* was co-produced with the Hollywood actor and anime fan Samuel L. Jackson (see p.236), who also voices the lead character.

Kurosawa gets cyberpunked up: *Samurai 7*

Production I.G (www.production-ig.com), established in 1987, is a spin-off from first-generation studio Tatsunoko. The I.G comes from the initials of the surnames of its founders Mitsuhisa Ishikawa and Takayuki Goto.

From its inception the studio has nurtured its collaborative relationship with the director Mamoru Oshii, working first on his *Patlabor* movies, and later on *Ghost in the Shell*. The global success of this franchise, and Production I.G's dedication to similar top-quality anime, many using state-of-the-art digital techniques, has secured it brand recognition abroad practically on a par with Studio Ghibli. A major coup for I.G came about in 1997 when Quentin Tarantino chose the studio to animate a key section of *Kill Bill: Volume 1*.

Founded in 1986 by producer Eiko Tanaka, **Studio 4°C** (www.studio4c.co.jp) really began to shape up as an exciting new studio in the late 1990s with its theatrical release *Memories* and its work in 2003 on *The Animatrix*, a joint production with Warner Bros (see p.238) that was an animated spin-off of *The Matrix* movie franchise.

Constantly innovative in its output, the studio's projects range from music clips, advertisements and computer games to acclaimed feature-length productions such as *Mind Game* (see Canon) and *Tekkon Kinkreet* (see Canon) and award-winning shorts. The name references the temperature at which water chills to its maximum density, the studio's mission being to create works that are "dense with substance and extreme quality".

Samurai 7
Samurai Sebun

dir Toshifumi Takizawa, 2004, 26 x 25m

Filmed in "high definition", with an often dazzling but not always successful combination of 2D and 3D animation, this is Gonzo's twenty-first-century spin on Akira Kurosawa's 1954 movie, the basis for Hollywood's *The Magnificent Seven*. In a feudal yet futuristic world recovering from war, seven impecunious warriors for hire are recruited to protect a rice-farming village against a gang of mecha-enhanced villains. Character design is great, with light relief provided by a samurai who is literally a tin man – complete with an exhaust pipe on his head to let off steam.

Ghost Hound
Shinreigari

dir Ryūtarō Nakamura, 2007, 22 x 25m

Production I.G pulled in some big guns for its twentieth anniversary show, including top manga artist Masamune Shirow, who provided the plot, and director Nakamura who made his mark with *Serial Experiments Lain* (see Canon). Set in the forested mountains of Kyūshū, the eerily atmospheric series offers a mystery that's somewhere in between *Twin Peaks* and *Stand By Me*, as repressed memories of traumatic events set up a kind of portal to a supernatural spirit world for a trio of teenagers.

Spooky: teenagers are plagued by the supernatural in *Ghost Hound*

Directors and animators

Like a general marshalling the troops, a director guides the production crew, harnessing their talents to realize the final product. The director is usually a seasoned professional who has risen through the ranks, essaying most creative stages of the anime production process. It's a role that shouldn't be confused with that of the animation director, also known as the production supervisor, who oversees all the technical aspects of the animation and ensures the consistency of such things as character design and background art.

Hideaki Anno

The subversive director Hideaki Anno, born in 1960, is a hero for a generation of otaku. His maverick reputation was sealed by *Neon Genesis Evangelion* (see Canon), a show whose startling images and themes derived from the four years in which Anno suffered from depression.

Anno's anime debut was *Macross* (see Canon) in 1982. Two years later he was hired by **Studio Ghibli** to work on *Nausicaä of the Valley of the Wind* (see Canon). The same year he was one of the founders of Gainax and took on the animation direc-

Women working in anime

There are women working in anime, but the long hours, low pay and hierarchical studio systems of the past have made the upper echelons of anime production – and directing in particular – a peculiarly male-dominated area.

Reiko Okuyama and **Kazuko Nakamura** were a couple of pioneering female animators from the late 1950s and 1960s. Okuyama debuted as an inbetweener on *Hakujaden*, and rose quickly through Tōei's ranks, working on practically all the studio's major cinema features of the 1960s and early 1970s, as well as moonlighting on Mushi Pro's *Tragedy of Belladona*. She became Tōei's head animator in the 1970s, before going freelance and teaching. Her last major work was a contribution to the award-winning *Winter Days* in 2003, which also featured work by her old Tōei compatriot Isao Takahata. She died in 2007.

Nakamura also hailed from Tōei, and she worked on the first three of their cinema features before being poached by Osamu Tezuka to work at Mushi Pro. There she filled the role of director on many of the company's TV series as well as being the chief animator on *Arabian Nights* and *Cleopatra*.

Several women have made major contributions to the animation of Studio Ghibli's films. They include **Makiko Futaki**, who has worked on practically every Ghibli film, as well as *Night on the Galactic Railroad*, and **Atsuko Tanaka**, who animated *Mon-Mon the Water Spider*, a delightful fifteen-minute short screened at the Ghibli Museum, Mitaka (see p.278). **Eiko Tanaka** started out as a producer (on *My Neighbour Totoro* and *Kiki's Delivery Service*), founded Studio 4°C, and ran her company for many years as a one-woman operation. In May 2007 the entertainment trade paper *Variety* listed Tanaka as one of the sixty people who will shape the future of the Cannes Film Festival.

tor's role in the studio's *The Wings of Honneamise* (see Canon). This led to full directorial duties on *Gunbuster* (see Canon) and *Nadia: Secret of Blue Water* (see below), and the experience of working on it is said to have sparked his breakdown.

Shrugging off death threats by crazed fans enraged by the surreal closing episodes of *Evangelion*, Anno next directed the wacky high school comedy *His and Her Circumstances*. He has also tried his hand at experimental live-action films – first *Love & Pop* in 1998 and *Shiki Jitsu* (*Ritual Day*) in 2000, a movie about a burnt-out director played by Shunji Iwai, another leading light of Japanese contemporary cinema, and produced by Studio Kajino, an offshoot of Studio Ghibli. Anno has also directed a live-action version of *Cutie Honey* by Go Nagai and acted in *Funky Forest*, an omnibus of shorts directed by Katsuhito Ishii, Hajime Ishimine and Shinichiro Miki.

In 2006 Anno set up Studio Khara specifically to make a "rebuild" of *Evangelion* as a completely new four-part movie, with a different ending – the fourth so far for his eternally morphing magnum opus.

Nadia: Secret of Blue Water

Fushigi no Umi no Nadia

dir Hideaki Anno, Shinji Higuchi, 1990, 39 x 25m

Sprung from a story originally conceived by Hayao Miyazaki, which was itself very loosely based on Jules Verne's *20,000 Leagues Under the Sea*, this was Gainax's first anime series,

The bumbling villains of *Nadia: Secret of Blue Water*

produced for the NHK, Japan's public broadcaster. As such, the level of creative control granted to Anno was limited – besides which Miyazaki had already cherry-picked many of the details for his own *Castle in the Sky* (see Canon). Still, Anno and co-director Higuchi manage to have some fun and stamp wacky Gainax trademarks on this jaunty tale of teenage inventor Jean and circus acrobat Nadia, who team up with Captain Nemo to search for the lost continent of Atlantis.

Osamu Dezaki

Anime directed by Osamu Dezaki, born in 1943, tend to have a distinct visual style, the leitmotifs of which include split screens and freeze-frames which often dissolve from simple animation into a more detailed painting, like a photo coming into sharp focus. Dezaki's career started in 1963 when he joined Tezuka's Mushi Pro studio as an animator on *Astro Boy*. Directorial duties on hit shows such as the boxing saga *Tomorrow's Joe* and the tennis drama *Aim for the Ace* in the early 1970s established his reputation.

Not content to sit in the sports anime box, Dezaki went on to tackle a range of other genres including the historical romance *Rose of Versailles*, the pulpy thriller *Golgo 13* (see p.194) – the first anime to include a digital sequence – and its follow-up *Queen Bee*. More recent projects have included the movie and series based on Tezuka's *Black Jack* manga and the movies *Air* and *Clannad*, both of which started life as computer games.

Black Jack: The Movie
Burakku jakku

dir Osamu Dezaki, 1996, 93m

Brooding, enigmatic Black Jack – with his scarred face, badger-like streak of white hair and Dracula-style cape – is one of Osamu Tezuka's most popular manga characters. Having successfully directed a series of straight-to-video episodes faithfully based on the manga, Dezaki brought his hard-boiled style to bear on this feature-length film. Jack is a brilliant unlicensed surgeon who here teams up with the equally talented, morally compromised scientist Jo Carol Brane to try to help the genetically altered and fatally flawed "super humans" she has created.

Yoshiaki Kawajiri

Born in 1950, Yoshiaki Kawajiri is yet another alumnus of Mushi Pro where he worked on *Cleopatra*. Other earlier work as an animator includes a couple of features with Rintarō (*Dagger of Kamui* and *Harmagedon*), as well as with Hayao Miyazaki on *Future Boy Conan*.

Kawajiri is best known for the stylish ninja horror flick *Ninja Scroll* (see Canon), although it was his 1987 feature *Wicked City* (see below) that brought him to prominence. Kawajiri was an early recruit to the anime studio **Madhouse** in the early 1970s, where he cut his directorial chops on the sci-fi adventure *Lensman* (1984), which has similarities to *Star Wars* but is actually based on the novel *Galactic Patrol* by E.E. Smith, first published in 1937.

Kawajiri's style avoids the wide-eyed cuteness of much anime, instead favouring edgier material, bold graphics and brooding, cold-blooded protagonists. Also on his résumé are *Demon City Shinjuku* (1988), based on a horror novel by Hideyuki Kikuchi (the author of *Wicked City*; *Vampire Hunter D: Bloodlust*, the 2000 entry in the *Vampire Hunter D* series) and one of the segments in the *Matrix*-themed anime *The Animatrix* (see p.238). His latest project is *Highlander: The Search for Vengeance* , based on the live-action fantasy sword-fight saga *Highlander*.

Wicked City

Yōjū Toshi

dir Yoshiaki Kawajiri, 1987, 82m

Sexually voracious demons and the human agent Renzaburo Taki battle it out on the streets of Tokyo in this noirish horror thriller. Taki's partner is the slinky fashion model Makie, a turncoat demon who appears in human form. The multiple sexual abuses and rapes she suffers during the course of the action are the nadir of an otherwise imaginative and darkly atmospheric anime. It's most memorable for a groin-tingling scene in which Taki's one-night stand almost turns out to be his last.

Satoshi Kon

From his dazzling debut *Perfect Blue* to his mind-blowing *Paprika*, Satoshi Kon has proved himself to be one of Japan's most creative and talented directors. He makes films on subjects not typically tackled by anime, such as the homeless in his comedy-drama *Tokyo Godfathers* and frequently ventures into the hazy territory between dreams and reality. An artist by training, Kon makes films that look splendid and have a polished, cinematic quality.

Born in 1963, Kon's entry into anime was through drawing manga with mentor **Katsuhiro Ōtomo**, with whom he would later work as a set designer on both *Roujin Z* and *Patlabor 2: The Movie* (see Canon). Having penned the script for one segment of *Memories* (see below), he was offered the chance by Madhouse, the studio for which he has always worked, to helm *Perfect Blue*.

Two more classics – *Millennium Actress* (see Canon) and *Tokyo Godfathers* – followed, after which Kon successfully turned his hand to TV anime with the adult-oriented series *Paranoia Agent* (see Canon). *Paprika* toured the world's cinema festival circuit in 2007, gathering praise and awards in its wake. Although he is probably the most serious contender to inherit the mantle from Hayao

Satoshi Kon's *Paprika*: a mind-blowing visual riot

© Madhouse Ltd.

Miyazaki as the emperor of anime, Kon has yet to create a movie specifically for children. It's a gap in his CV that he intends to correct with his latest venture, *Dreaming Machine* (*Yume-miru Kikai*), which, from initial promotional posters, appears to have the retro visual style of 1960s Tezuka anime.

Memories

Memorīzu

dir Kōji Morimoto, Tensai Okamura, Katsuhiro Ōtomo, 1995, 113m

Of this glossy anime's three segments – all based on Katsuhiro Ōtomo's stories – it's the first, *Magnetic Rose*, that is the best. Morimoto, who also directed a segment of *The Animatrix*, and scriptwriter Satoshi Kon fashion a space-bound ghost story that tips its hat to *Alien* by way of *Sunset Blvd.* and then, with its murderous holographic diva heroine, heads off in an entirely different direction. *Stink Bomb* – a jaunty satire about a company employee (blissfully unaware that an experimental drug he's accidentally taken has turned him into a walking disaster zone) determined to make it to Tokyo on company business – is an entertaining filling in a sandwich topped off with the Ōtomo-directed *Cannon Fodder*, a bleak tale following a day in the life of a family living in a totalitarian regime fighting an eternal, pointless war.

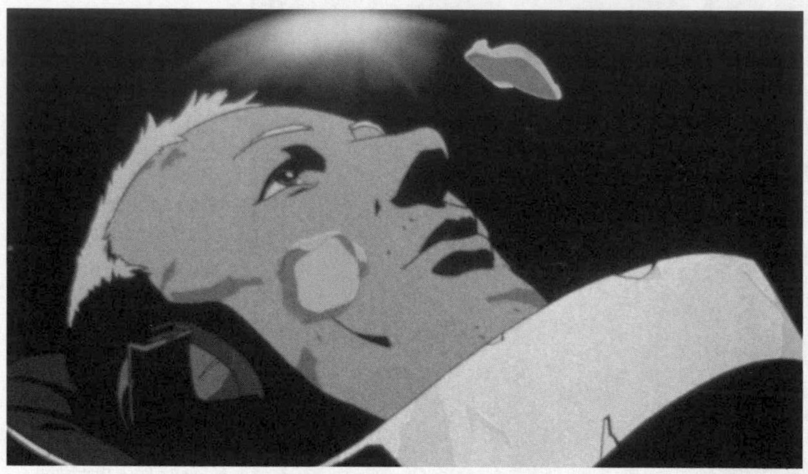

A still from the striking "Magnetic Rose" section of the portmanteau movie *Memories*

Leiji Matsumoto

Characters created by Leiji Matsumoto, such as the space pirate **Captain Harlock** and the blonde beauty Maetel, are as beloved in Japan as Mickey Mouse and Donald Duck are elsewhere. Born Akira Matsumoto in 1938, Leiji prefers the phonetic version of his pen name rather than the romaji-correct Reiji. Like his near contemporary, Osamu Tezuka, Leiji was an established manga artist before he started turning his stories into anime in the 1970s. Matsumoto's directorial credits are few but he's often been closely involved in the adaptation of his manga into anime.

His first big anime hit, *Space Battleship Yamato* (see Canon), set the mould for a generation of space sagas to come. Follow-ups included various incarnations of the *Captain Harlock* and *Galaxy Express 999* series. Among his recent projects has been making a series of music videos for the French electronica group **Daft Punk**, based on their album *Discovery*. These were combined in 2003 to create the anime movie *Interstella 5555*, in which Matsumoto trots out his trademark character designs of supermodel hero and heroine and squashed-down sidekick.

The anime promoters

The global market for anime didn't spring out of nowhere. It was nurtured over several decades by a hard-core group of fans and several visionary TV producers and writers who realized the crossover potential of the medium.

Midwife for the debut airings of several iconic series in the US, and subsequently elsewhere, was **Fred Ladd** (born Fred Laderman in 1926). Ladd was the US producer of Tezuka's *Astro Boy* and *Kimba the White Lion*, as well as Yokoyama's *Gigantor* in the 1960s, and in the 1990s he was a consultant on the *Sailor Moon* series. Credited with giving both of Tezuka's leading characters their Western names, Ladd's skill at "localizing" anime provided a sturdy foundation for its eventual worldwide popularity.

In 1977 the promotional baton was passed from Ladd to TV producer **Sandy Frank** who snapped up the epic space-based series *Kagaku Ninja-tai Gatchaman* and reworked it into the more *Star Wars*-friendly style *Battle of the Planets*. The success of this series in the US led to *Robotech* in 1985, a show produced for Harmony Gold by **Carl Macek**, who cobbled it together from three separate anime: *Macross*, *Southern Cross* and *Mospeada*.

Macek was pilloried by some hard-core anime fans at the time for his practice of redubbing anime rather than using subtitles, a debate that in these multi-language DVD days is archaic. If anything, Macek's work at Harmony Gold and later through his Streamline Pictures (one of the first companies to import, translate and distribute anime on video in the US), was another crucial step in the medium's progression to the mainstream of global pop culture.

Arcadia of My Youth

Waga Seishun no Arcadia

dir Tomoharu Katsumata, 1982, 130m

Leiji Matsumoto's scar-faced space pirate Captain Harlock took a quarter of a century to make the leap from manga to anime, first appearing in the 1978 series directed by Rintarō. This Robin Hood of the thirtieth century has starred in a string of follow-up series, usually alongside other stalwarts of Matsumoto's repertoire including the master engineer Tochiro, designer of Harlock's spaceship the *Arcadia*, and buccaneering queen Emeraldas. His finest hour came in the feature *Arcadia of My Youth* in which the romantic figure becomes a freedom fighter against the alien Illumidans occupying Earth. It's a slow-moving, melodramatic but often startlingly arty production, the tragic story underscored by the mournful music of Toshiyuki Kimori.

The Cockpit

dir Yoshiaki Kawajiri, Takashi Imanishi & Ryosuke Takahashi, 1993, 90m

There's an anti-war theme running through these adaptations by three different directors of a trio of Leiji Matsumoto's manga set during World War II. The styles differ between each segment but all are beautifully animated, with particular attention given to the combat scenes involving planes and motorcycles. Two stories focus on the heroic but doomed efforts of Japanese soldiers in the war. The third, opening the video and directed by Kawajiri zones in on a disgraced Luftwaffe pilot who sacrifices the woman he loves to save the UK from an attack by a Nazi-developed atom bomb.

Hayao Miyazaki

Even without the international credibility bestowed by his Oscar win for *Spirited Away*, Miyazaki's reputation as one of Japan's living national treasures rests on a remarkable, unparalleled series of movies, which have proved as popular – if not more so – with the paying public as with critics.

Born in 1941, Miyazaki learned his craft from the ground up, joining Tōei Animation as an inbetweener in 1963, the same year he graduated with a degree in economics and political science from Tokyo's prestigious Gakushuin University. At Tōei he met **Isao Takahata**, with whom he would first work on *The Little Norse Prince* (see Canon). During the early 1970s the pair would collaborate on several entries in the *World Masterpiece Theater* series. His directorial work on the TV series *Future Boy Conan* led to his debut as a feature film director on *Lupin III: Castle of Cagliostro*.

Although many of the films Miyazaki has made for **Studio Ghibli** (the company he founded with Takahata in 1985) are for children, the director's work has plenty of adult appeal. Concern for the environment, an abhorrence of war and violence, and strong female characters are recurrent themes and motifs. Miyazaki has been attracted to European and American literary works throughout his career, but some of his best films, including *My Neighbour Totoro, Princess Mononoke* and *Spirited Away*, are set in Japan and deeply rooted in Japanese culture; his latest film *Gake no ue no Ponyo* is set in a Japanese fishing village.

Future Boy Conan

Mirai Shōnen Konan

dir Hayao Miyazaki, 1978, 26 x 30m

Set just twenty years in the future from its original screening date, *Future Boy Conan* envisages a post-apocalyptic world in which the seas have overwhelmed the land. A handful of humans, including the eleven-year-old boy hero of the title, struggle to survive on an island, following an abortive attempt to flee into outer space. The simple yet expressive design of the main characters, Conan and his ESP-gifted playmate Lana, and the anti-war and pro-environmental themes would resurface in subsequent Miyazaki movies such as *Castle in the Sky* (see Canon).

Go Nagai

In the late 1960s, Go Nagai – who had served as an apprentice to **Shōtarō Ishinomori** – smashed the polite, child-focused mould of manga with his ultra-violent comic strips. In the early 1970s he took his hard-edged vision into anime with envelope-pushing shows such as *Devilman*, controversial because of its demonic possession theme (in line with the same era's live-action movie *The Exorcist*). *Devilman* was revived in 1987 for a straight-to-video production, before being recast in female form in 1998 in the confusingly titled *Devilman Lady*, and revisited again in 2000's ultra-violent *Amon: The Apocalypse of Devilman*.

Nagai's piloted robot show *Mazinger Z* (see p.19) became the inspiration for everything from *Mobile Suit Gundam* to *Neon Genesis Evangelion* and Hideaki Anno, *Neon Evangelion*'s director, made his own Nagai tribute in 2004, with a live-action version of *Cutey Honey*, a titillating twist on the magical girl genre: when Honey transforms into her superhero alter ego she briefly goes nude during a midair spin.

Devilman

dir Tomoharu Katsumata, Masayuki Akehi, 1972–73, 39 x 25m

Played out between Tokyo and the Himalayas, this gothic fantasy has a superhero twist: mild-mannered teenager Akira Fudo (looking oh-so-70s with his jaunty cravat) turns into bat-winged Devilman after becoming possessed by a demon controlled by evil Lord Zenon. His affection for classmate Miki is Akira's saving grace, allowing the human side of his nature to triumph over the demonic. The character design and drawing is rough-edged but the hokum is swept along on a wave of dark humour, grizzly demons and feverish energy.

Mamoru Ōshii

Born in 1951, Mamoru Oshii is the Harold Pinter of anime. His atmospheric, otherworldly films ponder life's eternal philosophical questions and, like Pinter's characters, often indulge in extended, near-silent pauses followed by an explosion of action. Best known as the director of *Ghost in the Shell* (see Canon), Oshii has also directed live-action films and written manga, novels and radio plays.

He began his anime career back in the late 1970s working for Tatsunoko Productions. Oshii's big break as a director was on the fantasy/sci-fi sitcom *Urusei Yatsura* (see Canon), based on the manga by Rumiko Takahashi. He directed two movies based on the series, including the surreal *Urusei Yatsura 2: Beautiful Dreamer*, in which the characters find themselves, à la *Groundhog Day*, trapped in a recurring time loop. This freewheeling approach to his source material had Takahashi up in arms, but has since become something of a signature style for Oshii. For example he chose to downplay the comedy that exists in the manga versions of *Ghost in the Shell* and *Patlabor* (see Canon) in favour of exploring deeper, more serious themes and adding entirely new material. *Ghost in the Shell 2: Innocence* was the first anime (and only the sixth animated film) to be shown in the competition at the Cannes Film Festival but it is his obscure, surreal *Angel's Egg* (*Tenshi no Tamago*) video from 1985 that's considered his masterpiece.

A trademark of Oshii's anime has been the cameo appearances made by his pet dogs: basset hound Gabriel and mongrel Daniel, who you can spot in the *Ghost in the Shell* movies, his experimental animated film *Tachigui: The Amazing Lives of the Fast Food Grifters* and his 2008 opus *The Sky Crawlers*, an alternative history fantasy based on the five-part novel by Mori Hiroshi.

Angel's Egg

Tenshi no Tamago

dir Mamoru Oshii, 1985, 71m

With little dialogue and an ambiguous, symbol-heavy plot, Mamoru Oshii's cult movie coasts along a series of surreal, dreamlike images reminiscent of Salvador Dali. Even the director has said he doesn't know really what it's about. This much is clear – a young girl living in what appears to be an abandoned, decaying planetarium, carries around a large egg, wondering what's inside it. She meets a mysterious young man, a Christ-like figure bearing a cross on his back and with bandaged hands, to whom she shows the odd objects that she has collected. To learn more about the film and see some images, go to the fan site www.cultivatetwiddle.com/angelsegg.

Tachigui: The Amazing Lives of the Fast Food Grifters

Tachigui-shi Retsuden

dir Mamoru Oshii, 2006, 104m

Paper-puppet-style theatre is given an eye-popping 3D-CG makeover in this experimental anime project set in a fictional post-World War II Japan and based on a novel by Oshii that's part of his *Kerberos Saga* (see Canon). A satire on Japanese dining habits and trends over the last fifty years, the quirky mockumentary details the outlandish culinary escapades of the grifters, including the wonderfully named Moongaze Ginji, Foxy Croquette O-Gin, Cold Badger Masa and Beefbowl Ushigoro, as they attempt to scam various fast-food vendors.

Katsuhiro Ōtomo

The global success of both the manga and anime of *Akira* (see Canon) secured Katsuhiro Ōtomo's place in Japan's pop culture hall of fame. This talented artist, born in 1954, began to make his name in the 1970s and early 1980s with ultra-realistic manga such as *Domu* and *Nippon Sayonara*. Like Oshii, Ōtomo's films typically take a wry, intelligent look at the impact of technology on society, focusing in particular on the development of weapons. His striking, meticulous style of visual presentation has also singled him out as one of anime's innovators as well as big spenders: the budgets for his major features, *Akira* and *Steamboy*, both broke records.

Ōtomo contributed character designs to Rintarō's 1983 effort *Harmagedon*. Although Ōtomo's frustrations with the quality of animation on this film is said to have inspired him to do things very differently on his own *Akira*, it was not so sour an experience that it prevented him from working with Rintarō again on the Tezuka homage *Metropolis*, for which he contributed the script. Prior to *Akira*, he honed his directorial chops on the compilation movies *Neo-Tokyo* and *Robot Carnival*. His scripts for *Roujin Z* and *Memories* were also filmed in the 1990s.

Apart from anime, Ōtomo has directed several live-action movies, most recently 2006's *Mushi-shi*, based on the popular manga and anime TV series of the same name (see p.186). He's also contributed character and mecha designs for the *Freedom Project* – a series of videos directed by rising anime star **Shuhei Morita**.

Roujin Z

dir Hiroyuki Kitakubo, 1991, 80m

Played mainly for laughs, this sci-fi movie is based on a Katsuhiro Ōtomo script about – of all things – a technologically advanced hospital bed. Code-numbered Z-001, it is programmed to be the ultimate nursemaid but is secretly a military weapon. When the bed's elderly resident Kijuro Takazawa expresses a wish to visit the seaside, the bed sets off in that direction allowing nothing to stand in its way. The crazy scenario is a vehicle for dealing with a range of sophisticated issues, from the mechanized and inhuman treatment of the elderly and infirm to dark dealings within the military-industrial establishment.

Rintarō

Shigeyuki Hayashi, a.k.a. Rintarō, has worked on some of the landmark anime of the last five decades. Born in 1941, Hayashi was recruited to Tōei Animation in 1958 as an inbetweener on *Hakujaden* (*Panda and the Magic Serpent*). He was one of the initial staff at Mushi Pro, where he was singled out by Tezuka to direct episodes of the original *Astro Boy* and *Kimba the White Lion* series.

While working on the *Moomins* series, based on the creations of Finnish author Tove Jansson in the late 1960s, he adopted his nickname

Rintarō – an alternative reading of the Japanese characters making up his name – as his professional moniker. By the time Rintarō made his first feature-length anime, *Galaxy Express 999*, in 1979, he'd been a freelance animator for around a decade.

Rintarō has long been associated with the studio **Madhouse**. Among his best films have been the samurai adventure *Dagger of Kamui*, the apocalyptic thriller *X: The Movie* and the Tezuka tribute *Metropolis* (see Canon). His latest directorial gig, the Japanese-French co-production *Yona Yona Penguin*, aims to bring a distinct anime sensibility to the kind of 3D animation popularized by Pixar.

Dagger of Kamui

Kamui no Ken

dir Rintarō, 1985, 132m

Overly long and with gaping holes in its episodic plot, this is nonetheless an ambitious attempt to give epic breadth to the ninja genre, with the action bounding around Japan, the US and the snowy wastes of Kamchatka. In the tumultuous period at the close of the Tokugawa era (around 1860) half-Ainu, half-Japanese Jiro seeks the pirate Captain Kidd's treasure and attempts to avenge the deaths of both his real and adoptive families at the hands of the villainous priest Tenkai. Rintarō applies arty flourishes such as split screens, wild psychedelic colours and an electro-synthesized musical soundtrack.

Makoto Shinkai

It speaks volumes about the dearth of young Japanese animators with a unique creative vision that so much praise has been heaped on Makoto Shinkai. Most of the former computer-game designer's films have been shorts, but he is such a master stylist that he is already being hailed as a future Miyazaki. Talented as Shinkai undoubtedly is, such comparisons are way too premature for a director born in 1973 who has yet to reach his full potential.

What really made people sit up and watch is that Shinkai crafted his award-winning debut feature *She and Her Cat* (just five minutes long) and the breakout follow-up *Voices of a Distant Star* at home using a personal computer and a variety of software packages. As the buzz about Shinkai grew, proto-studio CoMix Wave stepped in to assist with distribution and help him re-record an improved soundtrack; on the original, Shinkai and his girlfriend provided the voices.

Shinkai's total control over his material – which he has managed to maintain even now that he works in a more collaborative studio environment – has resulted in some of modern anime's most beautiful images, such as those seen in *The Place Promised in Our Early Days* and *5 Centimeters per Second* (see Canon). Before taking time out in 2008 to study English in London, he made *Neko no Shūkai* for NHK's *Ani-Kuri 15* series of anime shorts. In a welcome break from the lonely, lovelorn protagonists of his earlier works, this is a funny piece about a cat who, sick of having his tail trod on by the careless family who own him, imagines fellow felines gathering to summon a Godzilla-sized moggie to wreak revenge.

Voices of a Distant Star

Hoshi no Koe

dir Makoto Shinkai, 2002, 25m

The time-dilating effects of space travel, a prominent theme in the classic Gainax video *Gunbuster*, drive forward this poignant vignette which established Shinkai as *the* hot talent to watch. Winsome teenager Mikako goes into interstellar battle to save humanity, leaving behind sweetheart Noboru. As she ventures further into space, he grows older, she hardly ages and the text messages they exchange take longer and longer to reach their destinations. It sounds trite, but Shinkai's singular artistic vision – he made the original version almost entirely by himself – is astounding and the quality of animation just dazzles.

The Place Promised in Our Early Days

Kumo no Mukō, Yakusoku no Basho

dir Makoto Shinkai, 2004, 91m

Shinkai's first feature-length anime bears his distinctive visual stamp. The island of Hokkaidō (called Ezo), belonging to a hostile power, tantalizes a trio of middle-school friends who long to visit its mysterious giant tower that shoots up into the sky. To achieve this end the boys build a plane but a strange turn of events delays its maiden voyage for three years. The sci-fi spin on a Cold War plot, with references to dreams, separation and the importance of keeping promises, is overly complex and a little nonsensical, but the film is never dull and is frequently breathtaking in its beautiful, detailed visuals and moody atmosphere.

Gisaburō Sugii

Helming popular series and movies on baseball, martial arts and soccer has made Gisaburō Sugii one of the pre-eminent directors of sports-themed anime. Sugii, who was born in 1940, is yet another alumnus of Tōei Animation and Mushi Pro, where he worked on episodes of *Astro Boy* and the short-lived series *Dororo*, about a little girl thief in feudal Japan who teams up with a warrior fighting demons to regain his lost body parts.

His 101-episode baseball series *Touch*, aired from 1985, was a phenomenal success; it's a sensitively told tale of young love and ambition that famously left the audience hanging on whether its hero Tatsuya clinched the championship or won his girl Minami. However Sugii has proved a versatile director, switching effortlessly from the high melodrama of *Mask of Glass* (*Gurasu no Kamen*), about an aspiring actress, to imaginative adaptations of the novels *Night on the Galactic Railroad* and *The Tale of Genji*.

His taking charge of the 2001 entry in the *Captain Tsubasa* soccer franchise (*Captain Tsubasa: Road to Dream*) was a no-brainer, but it is on *Street Fighter II*, Sugii's skilful transformation of a computer game into an all-action anime, that his talents have been best displayed.

Street Fighter II

Sutorito Faita Tsu Mubi

dir Gisaburō Sugii, 1994, 102m

Based on the video arcade and computer game of the same name, this globe-trotting martial arts flick works best during its dazzlingly fluid and imaginative fight scenes. Japanese Ryu and American Ken trained at the same dōjō before going their separate ways. A plot by the crime syndicate Shadowlaw to recruit the world's top street fighters brings them together again, pitting a mind-controlled Ken against his friend. Also along for the ride are the game's roster of fighters including brush-headed Guile and feisty Chun Li, who has the silliest hairdo since Princess Leia.

Isao Takahata

The Studio Ghibli limelight usually falls on Hayao Miyazaki, even though every step of the way beside him has been Isao Takahata, Miyazaki's mentor since their time at **Tōei Animation** in the 1960s. Takahata's choice of movie subjects and artistic styles has been far broader than Miyazaki's, zigzagging from the stark documentary realism of *Grave of the Fireflies* to the beleaguered *tanuki* of *Pompoko* and on to the charming, jovial cartoon figures of *My Neighbours the Yamadas*. The film that best represents his accomplished style is the nostalgic adult drama *Only Yesterday*.

Born in 1935, Takahata's joining Tōei Animation was not the most obvious move for a graduate in French literature from Tokyo University, one of Japan's most prestigious educational institutions. His initial project was assistant director on *The Littlest Warrior* with his debut to full directorial duties on *Little Norse Prince* (see Canon) the movie on which he first teamed up with Miyazaki. It has proved to be an enduring partnership, running through several collaborations in the *World Masterpiece Theatre* series to many of Miyazaki's movies at Studio Ghibli, on which Takahata has acted as producer.

Since *My Neighbours the Yamadas*, Takahata's only animated work has been his brief contribution to *Winter Days* in 2003, a project which brought together 35 animators from around the world to visualize the collaborative poem orchestrated by the famous seventeenth century writer **Bashō**. In 2008 Studio Ghibli announced a new project for Takahata, the subject of which was undisclosed at the time of research.

My Neighbours the Yamadas

Hōhokekyo Tonari no Yamada-kun

dir Isao Takahata, 1999, 104m

Far from the stereotypical polite, reserved Japanese, the Yamadas – lazy mum, bumbling dad, study-shy big brother, cute little sister and grumpy granny – are a breath of comedy fresh air and proof that there's nothing more universal than the daily trials and mini-triumphs of getting along with your relatives. The movie is a series of humorous anecdotes about life *chez* Yamada framed by haiku (poems) relating the seasons. The sketchy watercolour look of the film reflect the roots of the material (a comic strip by Hisaichi Ishii) and it was all created by computer rather than cel animation – a first for Studio Ghibli.

Osamu Tezuka

One of anime's founding fathers, Osamu Tezuka (1928–89) had a love of animation honed from boyhood, when his father screened imported 9mm cartoon shorts on a hand-cranked home projector. By the time

Tezuka's pioneering venture into adult animation: *Arabian Nights*

of his first professional involvement with animation at Tōei, where he was contracted to work on three films, he was already a famous and highly prolific manga artist.

It's been said that while manga was Osamu Tezuka's wife, anime was his mistress: an obsession that he was loath to quit, even when faced with the bankruptcy of his first animation studio, Mushi Pro. For all his success in establishing the industry (albeit at a cost, see box opposite), Tezuka was often frustrated with his TV anime, as broadcasters and overseas producers foisted happy endings on him, and diluted or cut out the more complicated themes and political messages present in the manga versions of his stories.

The experimental films of Osamu Tezuka

Tezuka's debut film was *Tales of the Street Corner* in 1962. This charming wordless story, drawn in an impressionist European arthouse style, involves a little girl, her blue teddy bear, an inquisitive mouse, a wheezy old streetlamp, a mischievous moth and the love triangle between a blowsy bar girl, a demure pianist and a strong-jawed violinist – all characters on fly posters. Its underlying anti-war and cycle-of-life themes were common to several of Tezuka's manga.

Throughout the rest of his career, when not penning new manga or overseeing TV series and other projects, Tezuka would keep returning to making animated short films. Among the highlights are the *Fantasia*-inspired *Pictures at an Exhibition* (1966), ten short episodes illustrating the music of Mussorgsky; *Jumping* (1984) which sees the world from the perspective of a skipping little girl, her jumps getting progressively larger until she's flying over countries; *Broken Down Film* (1985), a comedy about a cowboy made in the black-and-white style of early moving pictures, complete with film scratches and projection glitches; and *Legend of the Forest* (1987), in which two of the four movements of Tchaikovsky's *Fourth Symphony* are set to stories that trace the history of animation. Tezuka's son Makoto announced in 2008 that he plans to complete the final two parts of his father's film.

All of the above, plus eight other shorts, are included on the DVD *The Experimental Films of Osamu Tezuka*, released by Australian anime distributor Madman. Extras include an interview with Tezuka (mainly concerning *Jumping*) and commentary by manga and anime scholar Philip Brophy. All these shorts and others are also available via iTunes in the US.

Tezuka's talents as an animator are best remembered by a remarkable series of short experimental films, kicking off with his initial animation *Tales of the Street Corner* in 1962 and culminating with 1988's *Self Portrait*, his final film. Many of these won awards in animation and film festivals around the world. He was also a pioneer of animation for adults, with *Arabian Nights* and *Cleopatra* in the late 1960s.

Yoshiyuki Tomino

Not for nothing has Yoshiyuki Tomino earned the nickname "Kill 'em all Tomino". From his early 1970s series *Triton of the Seas* to *Space Runway Ideon*, Tomino has demonstrated a ruthless propensity to annihilate almost entire casts of characters before wrapping up with a dubious "happy" ending. He's also famous for developing the concept of "real robots" – in that they are vaguely realistic ones, require maintenance and are generally lacking in super powers, most notably in his signature series *Mobile Suit Gundam* (see Canon).

Born in 1941, Tomino's career in anime began back in the 1960s at Mushi Pro, where he wrote and directed episodes of *Astro Boy*. By the mid 1970s, Tomino had moved on to creating his own sci-fi sagas, such as *Brave Raideen* and *Zambot 3* (which introduced the fiendish concept of unwitting suicide bombers), both of which have giant robots as key characters.

Despite the frequent recurrence of robots in his anime, Tomino has had a complex relationship with the mecha genre, expressing in interviews his frustration at being forced to retread the same ground by producers keen to stick with a successful formula ripe for merchandising spin-offs. For

Tezuka's curse

Because of his importance to the development of both manga and anime, Tezuka will always be a highly revered figure. However, his influence on anime was not entirely for the good. So desperate was Tezuka to get his works animated that he struck what some consider a Faustian bargain with TV companies, by accepting unreasonably low budgets for his shows. This resulted in low wages and production values (see box, p.13), creating compromised working conditions that quickly became the norm – and which to a large extent remain so. In an interview following Tezuka's death in 1989, Hayao Miyazaki accused him of creating the "curse of the animation industry, of constantly low production budgets".

example, robots were shoehorned into his sci-fi/fantasy series *Aura Battler Dunbine* in 1983, despite the fact that they're absent from the source novel *The Wings of Rean*, also written by Tomino.

Shinichirō Watanabe

Born in Kyoto in 1965, Shinichirō Watanabe made his mark with the series *Cowboy Bebop* (see Canon)and *Samurai Champloo* (see Canon), both of which breathe fresh life into the exhausted stereotypical themes and characters of their respective sci-fi and samurai genres. Apart from these series, Watanabe has also contributed two segments to *The Animatrix* anthology of shorts and one to the Studio 4°C project *Genius Party*.

If you're sick of saccharine pop songs in anime, Watanabe's intelligent use of music in his work is an inspiration. Jazz and blues themes power along *Cowboy Bebop* while the characters of *Samurai Champloo* move to a hip-hop beat. He also acted as music director on *Mind Game* (see Canon).

Note: Shinichirō Watanabe is often confused with Shinichi Watanabe (also known by the nickname Nabeshin), the afro-haired director of *Excel Saga*, among other things.

The voices

Computers may have become integral to the creation of anime, but one area where they're unlikely to replace people is the field of **voice acting**. Known as **seiyū** in Japanese, voice actors are a crucial component of an anime, bringing greater personality and emotional range to the characters than images alone. Interestingly, however, voice actors lay down their tracks after an anime has been drawn (not before, as usually happens outside of Japan). Thus they have to fit their performance to the images, not the other way around.

There's a ready supply of specialist voice actors in Japan since, in addition to the great number of anime produced, dubbing of imported films and TV series is also a major business. There are said to be well over one hundred voice-acting schools in the country.

Some actors have made their names as the Japanese voices of certain Hollywood stars, a phenomenon that has been exploited by canny producers hoping that audiences will make the association between the animated character and the real actor whom the *seiyū* typically dubs. For example, the Japanese voice of Clint Eastwood was often provided by Yasuo Yamada; he was also the voice actor who played *Lupin III*,

To be or not to be... accurate

Some of the most fraught (and often pointless) battles in anime fandom are fought over issues of translation. For all non-Japanese-speaking fans of anime, the importance of an accurate translation of the script cannot be underestimated. However, a *good* translation – be it for subtitles or for a voice-acted script – is not down to accuracy alone: translating word for word straight from Japanese to English or another language can misconstrue or entirely miss the nuances, puns and even the true meaning of the original.

There's nothing new about such problems. When the *Astro Boy* and *Kimba the White Lion* episodes were first broadcast in the US, translation issues involved not only the series titles but also characters' names and the overall sense of humour – the Japanese jokes rarely translating well in their trans-Pacific journey. The American producer Fred Ladd (see p.157) is credited with much of the success of this translation effort (even though he didn't speak Japanese), coming up with, for example, Dr Packadermus J. Elefun for the enormous-nosed character Professor Ochanomizu – the straight translation of which would have been Professor Tea Water.

A perennial problem for translators and voice actors has been how to make the mouth movements (or "lip flaps") of the characters speaking Japanese not look odd once an alternative language track is used. From a scriptwriting point of view this can mean adding or subtracting dialogue that existed in the original.

In recent times, the Japanese origins of anime have been held by some to be sacrosanct, leading to a more difficult and time-consuming job for the hapless translator struggling to convey the original meaning and flavour of the dialogue yet not lose an audience unfamiliar with, for example, Japanese honorific expressions or specific cultural traits.

It's also a two-way call on ad-libs to the script by the Japanese cast. Should the English actors be given similar leeway, or should they stick to a faithfully translated script? Both approaches can result in "semantic drift", or a shift from the true meaning. The English ad-libs in the *Lupin III* series have gone down particularly well with overseas fans, as did the authentic English slang inserted into London-based vampire series *Hellsing*, but that's not always the case. When you consider the occasional tendency for an overseas distributor to want to spice up the script with expletives and coarse language to appeal to a more mature market – a process called "fifteening" – it becomes clear how complex the question of accuracy is.

a character the laconic Eastwood might well have played himself. Another form of celebrity casting of seiyū is the use of pop idols: *Gundam Seed*, for example, intentionally cast Japanese pop superstars in key roles in order to secure high ratings and soundtrack sales.

Certain seiyū (mainly women) have long attracted the attention of fans and a few of the most prolific are profiled below. A similar veneration of non-Japanese voice actors is also happening overseas through their appearances at fan conventions. Examples include Monica Rial, the American voice of *Hello Kitty*, Chris Patton, who plays both Greed in *Full Metal Alchemist* and one of the lead roles in *The Place Promised in Our Early Days*, as well as troopers such as Peter Fernandez and Corinne Orr who essayed the roles of Speed and Trixie in *Speed Racer*. By and large such actors hail from North America, the bulk of voice-acting recording being done at studios in Los Angeles, Houston and Vancouver.

However, to many viewers voice actors – particularly the Japanese ones – remain anonymous. The exceptions are the marquee name performers who have been signed up for high-profile theatrical release anime, dating back to Frankie Avalon's appearance on the dubbed soundtrack of *Alakazam the Great* (see p.10) in the early 1960s. The likes of Billy Crystal, Patrick Stewart, Claire Danes, Michael Keaton and Kirsten Dunst have boosted the acting credits for Studio Ghibli's products, while the legendary figures of Jean Simmons and Lauren Bacall were persuaded to add their lustre to *Howl's Moving Castle*, as was Orson Welles to *Transformers: The Movie* (1986).

Megumi Hayashibara

Born in 1967, Megumi Hayashibara is the reigning seiyū superstar, the voice of such iconic characters as Rei Ayanami in *Neon Genesis Evangelion*, Faye Valentine in *Cowboy Bebop* and Ranma Saotome in *Ranma 1/2*. Her debut was in 1996 playing a bit part in *Maison Ikkoku*. Since then Hayashibara has not only displayed a talent to play everything from a penguin (Pen Pen in *Neon Genesis Evangelion*) to the scientist Chiba "Paprika" Atsuko in *Paprika*, but also to sing songs on the soundtracks of many of her anime (most notably the *Slayers* series) and to write song lyrics. In live-action films she has dubbed Drew Barrymore's role in *Scream*, as well as Audrey Tautou's in *Amélie*. Her fame in Japan is bolstered by many top-selling albums, her hosting of a couple of radio shows,

courtesy of FUNimation Entertainment

Listen carefully while watching *Slayers* and you'll hear the singing voice of Megumi Hayashibara

the penning of several books and a column in *Newtype* magazine.

Kikuko Inoue

Partnering with Megumi Hayashibara in the singing group DoCo (who appeared on the soundtrack of *Ranma 1/2*) is the almost as prolific Kikuko Inoue. Born in 1964, Inoue is most famous as the voice of Belldandy in *Oh My Goddess!* and Kasumi Tendo, the eldest sister of the Tendo family in *Ranma 1/2*. This latter role earned her the respectful nickname of *Onē-chan* (big sister).

Takehito Koyasu

The deeply dreamy voice of scores of *bishōnen* (beautiful young men) characters is provided by Takehito Koyasu, born in 1967. He's as hard-working a seiyū as Megumi Hayashibara, having appeared in well over two hundred roles in anime and computer games, including *Revolutionary Girl Utena* (as Kiryū Tōga), *Fushigi Yūgi* (as Hotohori) and *Excel Saga* (as Il Palazzo).

He also wrote the manga *Weiss Kreuz*, which was later turned into an anime (known as *Knight Hunters: Weiss Kreuz* in the US) about four bishōnen florists who are really secret agents!

Pop idols in anime

Cute pop songs have long been part and parcel of anime, preferably with equally cute, sweet-voiced pop singers to perform them. Japanese pop singers are known as idols and in some anime they've become stars of the show.

The heroine of *Macross* (1982) is idol singer Lin Minmei, a woman whose beautiful love ballads are so beguiling that they put a stop to an intergalactic war. Two years later, the computer-simulated singer Sharon Apple turns up in *Macross Plus* to perform the otherworldly songs of Yōko Kanno.

In *Bubblegum Crisis* (1987), one member of the four-woman vigilante group Knight Sabers is rock singer Priss Asagiri, whose songs are voiced by Kinuko Omori. The hard-driven rock 'n'roll musical themes of this video series are said to have been inspired by the 1984 Hollywood movie *Streets of Fire*.

In ß*Gravitation* (1999), Shuichi Shindō is a hyperactive teen struggling to balance his career as a pop idol and his homosexual relationship with a depressed romance novelist. This was the anime that first introduced many US fans to shōnen ai (boys love) or yaoi anime (see p.228).

The ugly side of the pop idol industry is partially revealed in *Key the Metal Idol* (1994). Mima Tokiko (a.k.a. Key) is a girl who may or may not be an android. She takes a stab at becoming a pop singer in Tokyo in a desperate attempt to become human, encountering the burnt-out pop idol Miho Utsuse and her scheming understudy Beniko Komori. Junko Iwao, the **seiyū** who voices Mima, also does duty as psychologically trapped Mima Kirigoe in Satoshi Kon's *Perfect Blue* (see Canon) – an anime that's practically the last word on the pitfalls of pop idoldom.

Minami Takayama

Minami Takayama provided the voice not only of Kiki in *Kiki's Delivery Service* but also of her artist friend Ursula, which meant in several scenes she was talking to herself. She also essayed several roles in the *Escaflowne* series and the boy detective Conan Edogawa in *Detective Conan*. Like other popular *seiyū*, Takayama, born in 1964, can also hold a tune and is one half of the duo Two-Mix.

The music

Anime is nothing if not eclectic in its choice of musical accompaniment, dipping into everything from classical works (Albinoni's *Adagio* for *Arcadia of My Youth,* Beethoven and Handel for *Neon Genesis Evangelion*) to hip-hop and rap (*Samurai Champloo* and *Afro Samurai*). Sometimes a theme song is so striking that it can stop an alien invasion in its tracks as in *Macross*. Occasionally established musicians, such as Ryuichi Sakamoto (*Wings of Honneamise*), David Sylvian (*Monster*) or Jean-Jacques Burnel of the Stranglers (*Gankutsuō*) are hired, typically with excellent results. However, more often than not, vapid and generally unmemorable ditties by pretty, young and ultimately disposable popsters grace an anime's opening and closing credits.

Among the top Japanese composers working in anime a handful of names stand out, in particular **Joe Hisaishi** and **Yōko Kanno** (see below). Kenji Kawai provided highly atmospheric music, including chanting and Eastern tones, for *Ghost in the Shell* and *Patlabor*. Shoji Yamashiro did a similarly impressive job on *Akira*, which also has choral work and metallic percussion. Other composers of note include Michio Mamiya who collaborated with Isao Takahata on *Little Norse Prince*, *Grave of the Fireflies* and *Gauche the Cellist*; Yuki Kajiura who has provided the music for the .hack series; and the jazz musician Yuji Ono for the *Lupin III* series.

In Japan, hundreds of anime soundtrack CDs are released each year. It's not only the opening and ending themes and instrumental background music that sell big, but also the "insert songs" (original vocal pieces composed for action or montage sequences) and "image albums", which include music inspired by the anime or tracks not included in the final cut. It's also become something of a craze for fans around the world to substitute their own choice of music over the director's when creating **anime music videos (AMVs)** – see p.248.

Gauche the Cellist

Sero Hiki no Gōshu

dir Isao Takahata, 1982, 63m

Classical music, including Beethoven's *Pastorale*, has a starring role in this charming film based on a Kenji Miyazawa short story. Set in rural Japan in the 1920s, the young cello player Gauche is the weak link in an orchestra. While practising late at night at home for an upcoming concert he's visited in turn by a cat, cuckoo, raccoon and a couple of mice who each teach him how best to perform. Takahata yet again works magic with a cast of simply drawn but memorable characters who really do look as if they are playing their instruments.

Joe Hisaishi

The winner of five Japanese Academy Awards for best music, as well as many other commendations, is Joe Hisaishi. Born Mamoru Fujisawa in 1950, Joe changed his name in tribute to his mentor, the American jazz musician Quincy Jones. An alternative reading of the kanji for Hisaishi is Kuishi, as close as you're going to get in Japanese to Quincy, and Joe is an abbreviation of Jones.

Since his composition of the music for *Nausicaä of the Valley of the Wind*, Joe has been a key collaborator with Hayao Miyazaki. However, it was the decision of Isao Takahata, the producer of that movie, to bring Joe in as the composer and to retain him for the follow-up *Castle in the Sky*. Joe's compositions have graced all of Miyazaki's movies since, including the latest, *Gake no ue no Ponyo*. Other directors Joe has collaborated with more than once include Yoshikazu Yasuhiko on *Arion* and *Venus Wars* and Takeshi Kitano for several of his live-action films. For more information, see Joe's website www.joehisaishi.com.

Yōko Kanno

One of the most prolific and highly versatile composers in anime is the pianist Yōko Kanno, born in 1964. Among her most memorable works have been compositions for the soundtracks of *Macross Plus*, which included jazz, orchestral, pop and experimental pieces, and *Cowboy Bebop*, in which her exuberant jazz and blues riffs provided much of the show's pizzazz.

With her former husband, Hajime Mizugochi, she composed the music for her first anime *Please Save My Earth* (*Boku no Chiyū o Mamotte*) in 1994, as well as the series *Escaflowne* two years later. She played piano on *Jin-Roh* and was the musical mastermind behind the soundtracks for the *Ghost in the Shell* series *Stand Alone Complex* and *Solid State Society*. Kanno's composing skills are not confined to anime: she has worked across practically the entire entertainment field, contributing music to TV dramas, computer games and commercials.

4

the manga connection

from comic to anime

Anime may be big in Japan but manga is even bigger, and always has been. Around sixty percent of anime are adaptations of already successful manga, an art form which encompasses drawn cartoons, comic books and graphic novels – everything, in fact, from *Lone Wolf and Cub* to *Hello Kitty*.

The medium's history and development is outlined in this chapter, which also turns the spotlight on some of the most popular mangaka (manga artists) whose work has been adapted for the screen.

A pictorial language

Scholars may quibble over the relative importance of Japanese traditional culture against the post-World War II influences on the development of modern manga, but there's general agreement that the Japanese have an affinity for the drawn image that they

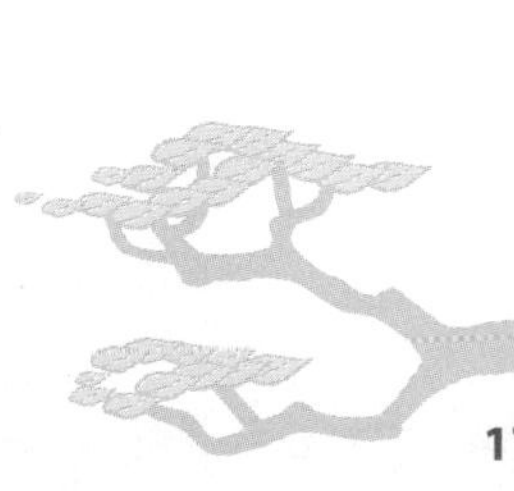

have nurtured over many centuries. Just look at the characters used for the language; the Chinese ideograms *kanji* are essentially simplified and abstract drawings representing different words.

A twelfth-century example of graphic art employed in the service of storytelling is the *Chōjūgiga*, a set of four scrolls, attributed to the priest Toba Sōjō, which depict animals including monkeys, rabbits, frogs and foxes at play. The scrolls are read from right to left, a tradition that continues with manga today. Toba also lent his name to the collections of humorous caricature sketches called *toba-e* that were popular in the earlier half of the eighteenth century. Neither the scrolls nor *toba-e* contain text, relying for their humour on the wittiness of the pictures.

Words were first married with drawings in *kibyōshi*. Literally meaning "yellow covers", these illustrated picture books, produced from woodblock prints, often had satirical or political themes and were a hit among the educated citizens of pre-Meiji era Japan. They share clear similarities with contemporary manga but Adam Kern concluded in *Manga from the Floating World* that the modern art form is far more closely related to Western-style comic books than to *kibyōshi* which, partly due to government censorship, had died out by the mid-nineteenth century.

It's also worth mentioning the highly detailed woodblock prints known as *ukiyo-e*, which were produced as either a single image or in a series of panels. *Ukiyo-e* were massively popular in the eighteenth

Coining the word "manga"

Manga, which has been used to describe comical drawings for at least two centuries in Japan, is written using two *kanji* or Chinese ideograms. The first (man) can be read as meaning "in spite of oneself" or "lax", while the second (ga) means "picture". Idiomatically, you would translate this as "whimsical pictures". The word's invention has typically been ascribed to the great artist Katsushika Hokusai (1760–1849), whose fifteen-volume collection of four thousand humorous sketches entitled *Hokusai Manga* was published in 1814. However, Adam Kern, an associate professor of Japanese literature at Harvard University, links manga's coinage to Santō Kyōden, a *kibyōshi* artist who used the word in print in 1798. So, as Matt Thorn, a Kyoto-based manga scholar, notes, exactly when, and by whom, the word was created remains unclear.

and nineteenth centuries and the vivid, action-packed styles used for some genres such as *shunga* (erotic art) and *yokai* (mythical monsters) are reflected in contemporary manga on similar subjects. One of the most celebrated *ukiyo-e* artists was Katsushika Hokusai.

Early Western-style manga

Kibyōshi and *ukiyo-e* both developed and flourished during the Edo period (1600–1868), when Japan deliberately shut itself off from the world. The doors were flung wide open during the subsequent Meiji period (1868–1912), when the Japanese were encouraged to *oitsuke* and *oikose* – to catch up and overtake. As with other products, such as electrical technology and cars, this axiom was applied to Western-style comic strips, resulting in the debut of *The Japan Punch*, a magazine based on the British weekly *Punch*, launched in 1862.

Caricatures of real people with critical and satirical commentary on current events had been heavily circumscribed during the Edo period, so such comic strips were a novel concept. So too was the multi-panel style of presentation with word balloons for dialogue. Japanese artists were inspired to create their own *ponchi-e* ("Punch-style pictures"), igniting the evolution of the hybrid East-meets-West style of modern manga. Pioneers included Ippei Okamoto, who founded the first Japanese cartoonists' society (*Nippon Mangakai*) and Rakuten Kitazawa, who started the cartoon magazine *Tokyo Puck* in 1905, and whose characters included Donsha, a street urchin, and the thoroughly modern Miss Haneko. Both artists travelled abroad, absorbing comic-strip art, including George McManus' *Bringing up Father*, which proved to be hugely influential when translations were syndicated in Japanese newspapers.

An edition of *The Japan Punch*: a Japanese take on British satirical cartoons

Manga became a mainstay of chunky monthly magazines such as *Shōnen Club* in the 1920s and 1930s. Popular strips, such as *Norakuro* (see p.5) by **Suiho Tagawa** about a puppy who signs up for the army, were compiled into hardback books selling over a million copies. The process is identical today with the most successful strips and serials from manga magazines and newspapers being collected into multi-volume paperback and hardback books known as *tankōbon*.

The impact of Tezuka

It's impossible to read a history of manga and anime without Osamu Tezuka's name quickly popping up. So crucially important was this highly talented and prolific artist to the development of both mediums in Japan that he is frequently referred to as *manga no kamisama* – the "god of manga". The statistics speak for themselves: during his lifetime, he drew nearly one hundred and fifty thousand pages, covering over five hundred different works.

Tezuka grew up in Takarazuka, a town which is famous for its all-female theatrical musical revues (p.249), and his artistic leanings were encouraged by his arts-loving parents. Although he would train as a medical physician, he had been drawing cartoon strips since he was a boy, and he made his professional cartoonist's debut at the age of eighteen in 1946 with a newspaper strip entitled *Mā-chan no nikkichō* (*Ma-chan's Diary*). A year later *Shin Takarajima* (*New Treasure Island*), created in conjunction with the artist **Sakai Shichima**, caused a sensation. Its dynamic approach to comic-book storytelling incorporated cinematic effects such as close-ups, zooms, cutaways and unusual points of view, rather than the full-figure, fixed-distance style of presentation that had been the norm in pre-World War II manga. Published as a cheap *akabon* (a "red book", so called because of their eye-catching red covers), it is said to have sold four hundred thousand copies and influenced a generation of artists including **Shōtarō Ishinomori** (see below) and the duo **Fujiko Fujio**, creators of *Doraemon*.

Tezuka followed up *New Treasure Island*'s success with the even more ambitious three-hundred-page *Metropolis*, inspired by Fritz Lang's classic silent movie. Tezuka hadn't actually watched the movie at the time he sketched out his story, but his imagination was sparked after he saw a picture of the famous image of the robot Maria, and he used this as a basis for his futuristic story of man and machines. *Metropolis*'s gender-switching robot Mitchy (Tima in the anime version, see Canon) is a dry run for Tezuka's most famous character **Astro Boy** (see Canon), who debuted as a character in *Shōnen* magazine in 1951.

Tezuka's dynamic style was a perfect fit for the era's manga publishers, who snapped up his output as quickly as the artist could turn it out. Although several of Tezuka's cinema-style techniques had been used by Japanese artists before **World War II**, in the immediate post-war period, for an audience seeking distraction from poverty, they appeared new and exciting. Other winning factors were Tezuka's emulation of the rounded cartoon character design of popular US comics and animation and his incorporation of adult themes and philosophical musings in his plots and characters. Before the 1950s were over, Tezuka had created several more manga classics, including *Janguru Taitei* (*Jungle Emperor*), the basis for his *Kimba the White Lion* (see Canon), and *Ribon no*

Princess Knight is one of many much-loved manga created by Tezuka that subsequently made it into anime form

Kishi (*Princess Knight*) – one of the first *shōjo*, or manga for girls.

In the same period Tezuka also broke down the creative process of making a manga, establishing a **production system** using assistants so he could increase his productivity. The assistants were given highly specific instructions on how to ink or draw certain elements of the manga after Tezuka provided the character and story outlines. Such production systems are still used in manga today.

Gekiga and the weeklies

Tezuka's style of manga had the biggest impact on the development of the medium in the 1950s and beyond – but it was not the only influence. At the opposite end of the spectrum from Tezuka's largely cutesy images were **gekiga**. The word, meaning "dramatic pictures" and said to have been coined by artist Yoshihiro Tatsumi in 1957, describes the more realistic, hard-edged story strips that were aimed at older readers. As manga scholar Paul Gravett points out, *gekiga* meant that "instead of growing out of comics both readers and creators continued to grow up with them."

Gekiga were a staple of the same *akabon* that Tezuka began his career drawing for. Artists who adopted this style include Takao Saitō (the creator of *Golgo 13*, see below), Go Nagai, whose liberal use of nudity, sex and violence in his 1968 opus *Harenchi Gakuen* signalled a new permissiveness in the medium, and Sanpei Shirato, who drew the bloody saga

Tezuka on Tezuka

In his 1979 autobiography *Boku wa Mangaka (I am a Manga Artist)*, Tezuka explained how his manga style developed:

"I began to introduce cinematic techniques into my composition. The models for this were the German and French movies I saw in my days as a student. I manipulated close-ups and angles, of course, and tried using many panels or even many pages in order to capture faithfully movements and facial expressions that previously would have been taken care of with a single panel ... Also, I thought the potential of manga was more than getting a laugh; using themes of tears and sorrow, anger and hatred, I made stories that didn't always have happy endings."

Ninja Bugeicho in 1959 and *Kamui Den* (*Legend of Kamui*) in 1964 for the monthly magazine *Garo*. *Ninja Bugeicho* was adapted for the screen in *Band of Ninja*, an experimental film directed by Nagisa Ōshima in 1967: he photographed Shirato's static images and added a soundtrack.

Garo, a showcase for avant-garde manga, was never a commercial success: at its peak the circulation hit eighty thousand, which was small fry compared to the millions of copies per week shifted by the likes of *Shōnen Jump*. It closed in 2002, but in the 1960s its reputation and that of the artists it featured were enough to spur the ever-competitive Tezuka in 1967 to publish *COM*, a monthly manga magazine featuring his own *gekiga*. *COM* folded in 1972 but during its run it featured Tezuka's most ambitious work *Hi no Tori* (*Phoenix*). This allegorical epic of twelve separate yet interlinked tales spanning millennia and each examining the cycle of life was described by Tezuka as his "life work". Sadly, it was one he would never finish. The series was the basis for the 1980 feature *Phoenix 2772* scripted by Tezuka and the series *Phoenix* in 2004, as well as a live-action movie and stage musical.

Japan's growing economy in the late 1950s led to the publication of the now familiar format of bumper weekly magazines containing manga. The first of these, *Shōnen Magazine* and *Shōnen Sunday*, both appeared in 1959 and their content was skewed towards the tastes of young boys – namely adventure and science-fiction themed stories. As these young readers grew up, publishers responded by producing *seinen* (young men) manga magazines containing more adult stories and presentations influenced by the *gekiga* style. In 1968 the weekly *Shōnen Jump* first appeared and would rise to become the blockbuster of the publishing sector through relentlessly surveying its readers, offering them what they most liked and constantly taking on and promoting new talents.

phoenix

Hi no Tori

dir Ryōsuke Takahashi, 2004, 13 x 25m

Five chapters from Tezuka's magnum opus are covered in this anime, a co-production between Japan's national broadcaster NHK and the US PBS station WNET. The stories are set in widely different epochs, ranging from the primitive past to the distant future. All take birth, death and renewal as their themes, their characters each seeking the legendary phoenix, whose blood will provide eternal life to those who drink it. The clash of fancy CG and standard cel animation jars, but the stories, faithfully rendered from the original manga, are what's of interest here.

The classic manga recipe

To otaku and other manga initiates, much of what follows will be well known. But if you're new to this particular medium of expression, here's a primer to manga basics.

Manga's major difference with non-Japanese comic books is the layout, which reads right to left, back to front – this means the last page of a book or comic in the West would be the first page of a manga. In their original Japanese form, manga magazines are mainly printed in black ink on white or colour-tinted pages on flimsy recycled paper. They will typically have four hundred or more pages and contain a score of serialized and one-off stories.

Manga magazines are a disposable product, cast away as quickly as they are read. The most popular of the strips get compiled into *tankōbon* – volumes the size of a regular paperback about two or three hundred pages long and printed on better quality paper. A series can run over several volumes amounting to thousands of pages.

Although there's a predisposition to give characters enormous, expressive eyes and wacky hairstyles, a glance through a selection of manga will reveal an enormous range of drawing styles from figures made up of a handful of squiggles to highly detailed, realistic images.

The cinematic style of presentation, popularized by Osamu Tezuka, is common along with graphic "sound effects" and speed lines to emphasize action. One notable difference between *shōnen* (boys) and *shōjo* (girls) manga is the use of jagged straight lines in the former and flowing, more flowery presentation in the latter.

The pacing of the story is usually much slower than that in Western-style comics, with artists often lingering over particular incidents or details to create a mood, stress a plot point or highlight a particular action or emotion. Manga are also defined by their tendency towards long-running plots, multi-layered storytelling and complex, emotionally realistic characters.

The dōjinshi era

By the mid-1990s, the 400-page plus *Shōnen Jump* was selling in excess of six million copies a week, powered along by hit series such as Akira Toriyama's epic *Dragon Ball*, and the basketball saga *Slam Dunk* by Takehiko Inoue. Bestselling *tankōbon* of the popular strips also sold in the millions. Manga cafes – dedicated libraries of books and magazines where readers could sip and browse for hours – were all the rage. Manga were also used to teach subjects in schools and present complicated factual subjects such as government policies and company sales manuals.

Increasingly the readers themselves were also getting in on the act. Manga fans had grown to such an extent that conventions, hosting hundreds of thousands of visitors, were being held where *dōjinshi* were traded. Many of these *dōjinshi* use the characters from the creator's favourite manga in new adventures and spins-offs from the original plots. So accurately are these manga drawn and so professionally are they put together that they are often difficult to tell from the real thing.

Even though such publications flagrantly ignore Japanese copyright laws – not to mention depicting star characters in sexually compromising positions their official creators would never dream of placing them in – the *dōjinshi* scene has been allowed to flourish for a couple of reasons. Japan is largely a consensus-based society where direct confrontation is avoided – lawsuits are usually the very last, rather than the first resort of disgruntled citizens and corporations.

Manga publishers and artists are also wary of alienating the most enthusiastic and, to a large extent, influential sector of their readership with heavy-handed tactics. Besides, these über-fans are not only serving up good ideas that manga publishers may capitalize on but also feeding the talent pool needed for the industry. Hence artists of the calibre of Rumiko Takahashi and the collective **CLAMP** got their breaks in the industry by working on *dōjinshi*. The series *Haibane Renmei* also started life as a *dōjinshi* by **Yoshitoshi Abe**, as did Takahashi Okazaki's *Afro Samurai*.

DIY manga

Fans who self-publish their own *dōjinshi* manga are known as *dōjinshika*. The word is made up of *dōjin*, which literally means "same person" but actually refers to a group of people who share a common interest, and *shi*, a contraction of *zasshi* or "magazine". Although there are plenty of individual *dōjinshika* artists, many such fanzines are put together by a group of people known as a *dōjinshi* circle.

Rather than original ideas, the vast majority of *dōjinshi* are based on established manga and are highly personal riffs on favourite characters much like fan fiction based on the Harry Potter books and the like. The rarer original works are often the output of artists, both amateur and professional, who are unable, or choose not, to go through regular publishing channels. *Dōjinshi* are traded in shops (there are manga stores in Japan devoted to selling them), over the Internet and at comic book conventions such as the Comiket (www.comiket.co.jp) in Tokyo.

To get an idea of the scale of the *dōjinshi* market, Comiket, which is held twice a year, regularly attracts thirty five thousand *dōjinshi* circles and upwards of five hundred thousand visitors over its three-day run. Cruising the aisles of the convention (or any other outlet for *dōjinshi* for that matter), it appears what fans like most is to see their favourite characters get it on – which means many *dōjinshi* are sexually explicit, even pornographic. Original artists have also been known to dabble in a bit of *ero-dōjinshi* (erotic *dōjinshi*) to have some fun and get around the censorship rules that established publishers must follow.

Haibane Renmei

dir Tomokazu Tokoro, 2002, 13 x 30m

Inspired by Haruki Murakami's novel *Hard-Boiled Wonderland and the End of the World*, the artist Yoshitoshi Abe first started working on this haunting fable in a *dōjinshi*. The title translates as "Charcoal Feather Federation", a reference to the stunted wings that sprout from the backs of the main characters, who inhabit the strange world that Rakka inexplicably falls into. Soon Rakka is growing her own wings and gains a halo, but her unsettling experiences lead her to believe that she's neither an angel nor in heaven. Fans have speculated that the *haibane* are children who died young or even committed suicide. The sepia-toned colours of the production design give the anime a highly distinctive look.

A global phenomenon

In the last couple of decades manga, like anime, have become a global phenomenon. In the US, Frederik L. Schodt's *Manga! Manga! The World of Japanese Comics* in 1983, was the first English-language book on the subject and contained translations of episodes from four manga, including Tezuka's *Phoenix* and Riyoko Ikeda's *Rose of Versailles*. More translations followed, but the growth of sales in the US was small scale until the breakout hit of Kazuo Koike and Goseki Kojima's *Lone Wolf and Cub* in 1987. Its success was aided by the gritty covers, designed by Frank Miller of *Sin City* and *300* fame.

In 1988, Marvel Epic started releasing colourized and "flipped" (i.e. images were reordered to be read in Western fashion from left to right, front to back) editions of Katsuhiro's Ōtomo's *Akira* (see

Canon). It would be another twelve years though before the series was published in the US as it was originally intended in a monochrome edition faithfully rendered by **Dark Horse** comics. By this point overseas fans wanted authenticity, having been educated in the unique stylistic conventions of manga and their interest piqued by a rising tide of anime movies and series.

Today, manga is the **fastest growing book category** in the US, claiming almost two thirds of a market worth $330 million. Major bookstores devote shelves to the latest translations which hit the market at a rate of up to thirty new titles per week. So popular have manga become that many overseas artists are producing their own manga-style comics and books: in the UK both Shakespeare and the Bible have been given a manga-style makeover, while in the US manga publisher Seven Seas Entertainment has asked its Western artists to draw in the left-to-right format.

In 2006 the Japanese foreign minister, Taro Aso, an unabashed manga fan, mentioned during his announcement of the International Manga Award about receiving a Polish version of Rumiko Takahashi's *Inuyasha* from his visiting Polish counterpart. The award's first winner, Lee Chi Ching, comes from Hong Kong, while runners-up hail from Australia and Malaysia.

Future challenges

The Japanese government's adoption of manga and anime as the nation's pop-cultural ambassadors is timely, for at home there are signs that the industry is faltering and in need of new readers. The Research Institute for Publication's figures show that in 2006, domestic sales of manga fell 4.2 percent from 2005 to ¥481 billion. The market has been contracting for at least a decade – by some accounts by up to twenty percent – and all the indications are that the trend will continue as Japan's population shrinks and potential readers shift their attentions to contemporary media such as the internet and mobile phone services.

Responding to such changes in the domestic market, publishers are offering manga that are downloadable to mobile phones in chapters costing around ¥50 each. Known as *keitai* manga (*keitai* is the Japanese for mobile phone) this new format offers stories frame by frame, with the ability to pan across an image. Readers can control the speed at which they watch, turn speech bubbles on and off and, for a more

courtesy of FUNimation Entertainment

Floppy of hair and black of lung, Ginko is the hero of "green" anime *Mushi-shi* stimulating read, the phone will vibrate at key moments. Hundreds of titles are available covering old favourites such as Leiji Matsumoto's *Ginga Tetsudō 999* to stories developed specifically for release via *keitai*.

The yet-to-peak overseas appetite for Japanese pop culture, fuelled by its touting by trendsetters such as Tyler Brûlé's *Monocle* magazine that runs a manga with each issue, and a generation of kids raised on Playstation and Nintendo, is also likely to keep manga (and anime) from sinking. Recent hits include Hiromu Arakawa's *Fullmetal Alchemist* (see Canon), *Monster* by Naoki Urasawa (see below), *Mushi-shi* by Yuki Urushibara (see below), and *Death Note* by writer Tsugumi Ōba and artist Takeshi Obata, a manga turned into an anime series and a couple of live-action films.

Manga's unique graphic style of presentation also continues to influence and inspire a generation of creative types working mainly outside the medium, from video game designers such as Kazuhiko Aoki (the *Final Fantasy* series) to contemporary artists including Yoshitomo Nara, Chiho Aoshima and Takeshi Murakami, who formulated the concept of **superflat** (see p.246).

Mushi-shi

dir Hiroshi Nagahama, 2005–06, 26 x 30m

The supernatural genre is given a New Age twist in this popular manga and anime series, ranking high in a poll of fans conducted for the Japan Media Arts Festival. The anime does a good job of replicating the ethereal, nature-bound world of Urushibara's manga with its floppy-haired and eternally chain-smoking hero Ginko. Each episode features a separate case for the itinerant expert in the primal energy forms known as *mushi*.

From manga to anime

It's back to Tezuka again to examine some of the issues that arise when turning manga into anime. Tezuka's Astro Boy (or Tetsuwan Atomu as he is known in Japan) wasn't the first manga character to come to animated life – you need to go back to Suiho Tagawa's **Norakuro** and Ryuichi Yokoyama's Fuku-chan to find examples of that; both characters appeared in propaganda films in the run-up to and during World War II. However, Astro Boy was the first manga character to appear in a long-running, regular TV series. This gave his creator ample opportunity to fiddle with all aspects of the original manga, from character design to plot points that he was not happy with.

The *Dragon Ball Z* gang: a good long fight sure helps an anime catch up with its manga original
courtesy of FUNimation Entertainment

One of the main reasons for some of the changes was the fact that the anime *Astro Boy* was aimed at a far wider TV audience, many of whom would be unfamiliar with the original manga. Complex stories needed to be simplified to fit the half-hour format. To increase the possibilities of overseas sales, direct references to Japan and Japanese culture were minimized. For example, as Schodt points out in his book *The Astro Boy Essays*, Tezuka "deliberately tried to anticipate the feelings of foreigners and to avoid any imagery that they might regard as too 'Oriental' or 'exotic'". Churches appear, rather than Buddhist temples or Shinto shrines, and English was used for details such as the contract in which Dr Tenma sells Atom to the circus.

For Tezuka's subsequent anime *Kimba the White Lion* (see Canon), the overarching theme from the manga of a noble creature battling his base animal nature was largely neutered by the demands of his US co-producers who didn't want American kids exposed to the brutal realities of the jungle. Even for the second series, which was not picked up by US network TV, Tezuka largely avoided showing Kimba eating meat.

The different drawing style sometimes required for the TV series would also influence that of the manga – fans, after all, wanted to see their heroes looking the same both in print and on TV. Once marketing of character goods came into the equation – as was certainly the case with Astro Boy, whose licensed image would appear on everything from candy to the shirt sleeves of the professional Sankei Atoms baseball team – it was the TV version that, like it or not, became set in stone.

Filling in story gaps

Astro Boy's weekly production schedule also revealed another problem that has consistently dogged manga being adapted into anime – the outpacing of the TV episodes over production of the manga. As a solution, new stories are created to pad out an anime series until the manga catches up with it.

Alternatively the anime may simply extend the action of particular scenes – witness the seemingly never-ending fights between characters in the *Dragon Ball* and *Dragon Ball Z* series or the 84 filler episodes (136–220) of *Naruto* that bridged the gap between the end of volume 27 of the *Naruto* manga and the start of volume 28, covered in the series *Naruto: Shippūden*.

Another common approach is to allow the story arcs between manga and anime to differ. Examples of this include *Akira*, which was originally serialized in *Young Magazine* from 1982 and 1990, the story concluding long after Katsuhiro Ōtomo had finished his anime, and Miyazaki's manga of *Nausicaä of the Valley of the Wind*, which wound up in 1994, a decade after the movie. Neither have the same ending as their respective movies.

Once a manga has been completed, studios – eager to milk a committed fan base – will often put out a final OAV (DVD release only) matching the manga ending. Famous examples of this are *Rurouni Kenshin* (see p.218) and *Hellsing*. The real manga ending of *Rurouni Kenshin*

One of *Hellsing*'s creatures of the night: you might need to be a blood-sucking immortal to keep up with the long-running saga

courtesy of FUNimation Entertainment

was animated in the sequel OAV *Samurai X Reflection*. The new OAV series *Hellsing Ultimate*, which began in 2006, has started from the beginning, re-animating the same material as the first TV version in preparation for finally animating the later manga content. Particularly frustrating for fans was the fact that the trailer for the original *Hellsing* TV series in 2001 contained footage of the Major, the main villain of the later manga, who then does not appear in the first series at all – earning him the nickname "Major Not Appearing in This Anime". Fans had to wait seven years for him to show up in *Hellsing Ultimate*.

Manga artists

Some *mangaka* such as Tezuka, Ōtomo and Leiji Matsumoto have proved themselves to be talented anime-makers. A few animators have also found that they, understandably, have a propensity to be excellent manga artists: the most famous example is Hayao Miyazaki, who penned *Nausicaä of the Valley of the Wind* (see Canon) as a manga before he made the movie of the same name. Below is a brief review of the major artists whose manga have been turned into anime by others.

CLAMP

The creative powerhouse that is CLAMP started as an all-female twelve-member *dōjinshi* circle in 1989, producing their versions of the soccer team manga *Captain Tsubasa*. CLAMP's speciality has been magical girl sagas with several of their works, including *Card Captor Sakura*, *Chobits*, *Tsubasa Reservoir Chronicles* and *X* (also known as *X/1999*), having made the leap into anime series and movies. Their particular talent has been their ability to create stories and characters (invariably with beautiful looks) that appeal to both young men and women.

CLAMP has a habit of recycling particular characters under different names in different dramas, much as Tezuka did in his manga. The group currently numbers four members– Mokona, Tsubaki Nekoi, Satsuki Igarashi and Ageha Ōkawa, who, under her real name of Nanase Ōkawa, acts as the screenwriter for many of the series made from their work. For more information on CLAMP, check out their website at www.clamp-net.com.

From books to anime

Apart from manga, Japanese and world literature have provided a rich seam for anime to mine for source material. *Night on the Galactic Railroad* (*Ginga Testudō no Yoru*, see Canon) was based on the classic Japanese children's book of 1927 and made into an anime feature by Gisaburo Sugii in 1985. A couple of years later the same director gave an elegant anime makeover to what is considered to be the world's first novel, *The Tale of Genji* (*Genji Monogatari*).

Animated Classics of Japanese Literature (1986) is a 37-episode TV series, directed by Fumio Kurokawa, based on stories by Lafcadio Hearn (*Ghost Story*), Yukio Mishima (*The Sound of Waves*), and Natsume Sōseki (*Botchan*). In 1982, Rintarō directed a TV movie version of Sōseki's comic novel *I Am a Cat*, told from a feline point of view.

In 1974 Isao Takahata and Hayao Miyazaki collaborated on *Heidi*, a 52-week long adaptation of Johanna Spyri's classic of children's literature. The success of this format led to the commissioning by Nippon Animation of its World Masterpiece Theater series of shows that ran from 1975. Other noteworthy shows directed by Takahata in this series included Lucy Maude Montgomery's *Anne of Green Gables* and *3000 Leagues in Search of Mother* (*Haha o Tazunete Sanzenri*), partly based on the novel *Cuore* (*Heart*) by Edmondo de Amicis.

Both directors share a love of literature that has provided inspiration for many of their projects at Studio Ghibli, including *Grave of the Fireflies* (see Canon), *Kiki's Delivery Service* (see Canon), and *Howl's Moving Castle* (see Canon). The tradition has continued with Gorō Miyazaki's *Tales from Earthsea*, based on Ursula Le Guin's *Earthsea,* series of fantasy novels.

Chobits

dir Morio Asaka, 2002, 26 x 25m

CLAMP's venture into the territory of *seinen* manga (it was originally serialized in *Young*, the same magazine in which *Akira* and *Ghost in the Shell* premiered) ended up producing a computer story that was far from your average boy-falls-for-cute-humanoid-computer tale. Chii, the *persocom* in question, turns out to have some rather special powers, tipping the anime's notional genre closer to a contemporary reworking of the magical girl genre which it parodies. There's also a reference to *Maison Ikkoku*, with the lead male character Hideki spending part of the story living in a Tokyo boarding house swotting for his school exams.

X: The Movie

dir Rintarō, 2000, 100m

Made before CLAMP finished penning their millennium angst manga of the same name, this visually jaw-dropping movie benefits from veteran director Rintarō's assured sense of style, but suffers from a barely comprehensible plot. It's an end-of-the-world saga, sprinkled with Shinto mysticism, in which the Dragons of the Heaven confront the Dragons of Earth with Tokyo as the battleground. Endless flurries of petals and feathers fall from the sky as CLAMP's trademark pretty boys and girls fly across the city leaving destruction in their wake.

Machiko Hasegawa

Affectionately known as the "grandmother of manga", Hasegawa (1920–92) deserves recognition not only for being a pioneering female *mangaka*, working in what was then a male-dominated industry from the age of 14, but also for creating *Sazae-san,* a four-panel comic strip that ran for 25 years in the *Asahi Shimbun* (*Asahi Newspaper*) from 1949. These comic tales of Tokyo housewife and mother Sazae Isono made their TV debut in 1969 and are still on air, making it the world's longest-running animated series.

Sazae-san has always been Japanese TV's highest rated anime, with a consistent audience share of 25 percent, far outstripping even the likes of more recent hits such as *Pokémon*. If you're in Tokyo and would like to find out more about the artist, drop by the Machiko Hasegawa Art Museum (1-30-6 Sakura-Shinmachi, Setagaya-ku; Tues–Sun 10am–5.30pm; ¥600; www.hasegawamachiko.jp).

Riyoko Ikeda

Considered one of the group of female *mangaka* who helped define the distinctively florid style of *shōjo* manga, Riyoko Ikeda, born in Ōsaka in 1947, is most famous for *Rose of Versailles*. Serialized from 1972 to 1973 in the *shōjo* magazine *Margaret*, it has sold over fifteen million copies in its ten *tankōbon* volumes and was adapted into a successful stage show for the all-female theatre troupe Takarazuka (see p.249) in 1974 that has become a cherished part of their repertoire. The first two volumes were also the first English-translated manga to be made commercially available in North America in 1983.

Only one other of Ikeda's manga *Oniisama e…* (*Brother, Dear Brother*), has been made into an anime. Its controversial subject matter – the feverish goings-on at an elite girls' school spanning the gamut from incest and bullying to drug addiction and suicide – caused the dubbed version of the series to be pulled from the schedules in France and Italy before the end of its 26-episode run – apparently the TV channels had thought they were buying a cartoon show suitable for children's hour. Riyoko Ikeda's official site is www.ikeda-riyoko-pro.com.

Rose of Versailles

Versailles no Bara

dir Tadao Nagahama & Osamu Dezaki, 1979, 41 x 30m

Set in eighteenth-century France, *Rose of Versailles* is a genre-defining *shōjo* show (see Canon) that was a refreshing change of pace from the predominant space-saga anime of the 1970s. Born a girl, but brought up as a boy, Oscar Françoise de Jarjayes is a fencing prodigy who becomes Marie Antoinette's chief protector. The blossoming friendship between the two and their doomed love affairs form the backbone for a powerful and complex story that skilfully weaves in real events and historical figures.

Shōtarō Ishinomori

Born Shōtarō Onodera, Ishinomori (1938–98) is best known for the series *Cyborg 009* and the live-action *tokusatsu* ("special effects") series *Kamen Rider*. He changed his surname a couple of times (also being known as Ishimori), his career having started in the mid-1950s when he was talent spotted by Osamu Tezuka and asked to assist with the production of *Astro Boy*. The team of superpower heroes who are the stars of *Cyborg 009* set the blueprint for many similar manga, anime and live-action Japanese shows to come. Ishinomori's rounded drawing style, richly imagined characters and metaphorical plots were influenced by his mentor Tezuka. His work is highlighted in the Manga Museum in Ishinomaki (see p.281).

Cyborg 009

dir Yugo Serikawa, 1966, 64m

Tōei Animation's first sci-fi anime introduced Joe Shimamura, a.k.a. Cyborg 009, whose smashed body is restored with a host of super-hero attributes. Leading a multinational cast of eight similar cyborgs, Joe battles with Black Ghost, leader of the nasty Merchants of Death. Made using limited animation techniques, *Cyborg 009* looks crude compared to Tōei's earlier theatrical releases. A sequel, *Cyborg 009: Monster War*, followed in 1967 and in 1980 there was *Cyborg 009: Legend of the Super Galaxy*. There have also been three TV series based on the manga, the most recent, a rather soulless 2D digital animation, in 2001.

Takao Saitō

Hailing from Ōsaka and born in 1936, Takao Saitō is best known as the creator of *Golgo 13*, a graphically realistic series for which he has won several awards. As a young *mangaka* in Tokyo in 1964, Saitō drew a four-volume manga about James Bond, a character to whom the amoral assassin hero of *Golgo 13*, Duke Togo, is most frequently compared. (The series' title being Togo's code name.) In 2008 *Golgo 13* got a new lease of life with his first appearance in a TV anime series.

Although Saitō is considered one of the defining artists of *gekiga* manga, he's also turned his talents to science-fiction type stories, too. His 1970s manga *Barom One* formed the basis for a 2002 anime series about two teenage boys, who have the ability to turn into the monster-battling robot of the title. Saitō's official website is www.saito-pro.co.jp.

Golgo 13: The Professional

dir Osamu Dezaki, 1983, 94m

This is a guilty pleasure if ever there was one. For all its snazzy effects – including split-screen action and freeze frames mimicking the graphic style of Saitō's drawings – *Golgo 13* can't escape its cheesy characterization and plotting. The unstoppable anti-hero assassin Duke Togo (a.k.a. Golgo 13) strides through the action dispatching snarling, drooling villains and nubile beauties with the stony personality of a brick wall. He would return in 1998's straight-to-video *Golgo 13: Queen Bee*, a visually more polished product, in which Duke's target is Sonia, a ruthless Central American rebel leader and cocaine racketeer, who also happens to be a sex-mad babe.

Masamune Shirow

Among the cadre of artists who got their break through the *dōjinshi* scene is Masamune Shirow, born Masanori Ōta in Kōbe in 1961. His first major work, published in 1985, was the sci-fi manga *Appleseed*. It went on to win an award and has served as the basis for several anime productions, as has his *Ghost in the Shell* (see Canon), which brought Shirow, who specializes in cyberpunk, police-military state type storylines, even more fame. Despite this, the artist shies away from revealing his face in the media and continues to work in Kōbe, at a distance from Tokyo's manga publishers and anime studios.

Other Shirow works to be made into anime include *Dominion* (1988), another police-versus-rogue-android tale, and *Black Magic M66*, based on his original *dōjinshi* and the only anime that the artist has been fully involved in the production of. Recently he's worked on the original story line for Production I.G's twentieth anniversary project *Ghost Hound*, and their 2008 sci-fi suspense series *Real Drive*.

Appleseed

dir Shinji Aramaki, 2004, 105m

State-of-the-art CGI is used for this all-guns-blasting take on Masamune Shirow's manga, set in a far-from-perfect future where humans battle a genetically altered species called Bioroids. The kick-ass heroine Deunan is backed up by former lover Briareos who, following massive battle injuries, has become a rabbit-eared cyborg. The original 1988 adaptation by Gainax had a better script, but this is far fancier eye candy. The follow-up *Appleseed: ExMachina,* also directed by Aramaki and produced by John Woo, was released in 2007 and features even more polished CGI animation.

Rumiko Takahashi

Manga such as *Urusei Yatsura*, *Maison Ikkoku*, *Ranma 1/2* and *Inuyasha*, and their popular anime spin-offs, have made creator Rumiko Takahashi one of the wealthiest women in the business. Born in 1957 in Niigata, Takahashi started her career by joining a manga school run by Kazuo Koike, the artist responsible for *Lone Wolf and Cub* and *Crying Freeman*, who encouraged her to produce her first *dōjinshi* works.

Takahashi's professional life began in 1978 with *Urusei Yatsura* (see Canon), and she's hardly looked back since. Drawing in the *shōnen* manga style, she takes a free-flowing approach to genres, a prime example being *Ranma 1/2* which is equal parts kung fu, romance and sitcom. One of the best websites on Takahashi is the fan-run Runik World (www.furinkan.com/takahashi).

Ranma 1/2

Ranma Nibun-no-ichi

dir Tomomi Mochizuki *et al*, 1989–92, 161 x 25m

Ranma Saotome and his martial arts master father fall into a magical pool. Forever after, whenever Ranma is splashed with cold water he turns into a girl while his dad becomes a panda. Such gender/species-swapping confusion provides the bulk of the comedy in what is otherwise a very drawn-out romance between Ranma and the feisty Akane Tendo. Once you've got the basics of the plot down it hardly matters in which order you watch the episodes or various movies in a series that replays many of the setups of Takahashi's earlier success *Urusei Yatsura*.

Inuyasha

dir Masashi Ikeda, Yasunao Aoki, 2000–04, 167 x 30m

More action-packed than Takahashi's usual output, this epic, and famously inconclusive, TV series plus four feature-length movies, is based on the artist's longest running manga serial – 56 volumes as of its conclusion in June 2008. It's about Kagome, a schoolgirl who trips back and forth in time through a wormhole, from modern Japan to a mystical, feudal past where she teams up with the half-demon Inuyasha on a quest for the widely scattered shards of the precious Jewel of Four Souls. If you're looking for some kind of closure, the second movie at least provides a glimpse into the possible future lives of the main characters.

Naoki Urasawa

Manga's contemporary star is Naoki Urasawa, born in 1960. His breakout hit was *Yawara! A Fashionable Judo Girl*, serialized in *Big Comic Spirits* (as much as his work has been since) from 1987 to 1993 and made into an anime series in 1989. Follow-ups include *Master Keaton* created with writer **Hokusei Katsushika**, the sci-fi mystery *20th Century Boys* currently being adapted into a live-action trilogy of movies, and – his most famous work overseas – *Monster*, an eighteen-volume psychological thriller set in Germany and created between 1994 and 2001.

Aspects of *Monster* were inspired by several of Tezuka's manga including *Black Jack*, *Adolf* and *MW*. It's a measure of Urasawa's talent that he was permitted by Tezuka's estate to use an *Astro Boy* episode entitled "The World's Strongest Robot" as the basis for his currently ongoing series *Pluto*. This film, a noirish sci-fi thriller only features the robot boy in a cameo role, the lead character instead being Gesicht, a robot detective. *Pluto* won a prize at the 2005 **Japan Media Arts Festival** and also the Tezuka Osamu Cultural Prize, which Urasawa had received once before for *Monster*.

Master Keaton

dir Masayuki Kojima, 1998–99, 39 x 25m

Imagine Sherlock Holmes with a dash of James Bond and Indiana Jones and you have *Master Keaton*. As an investigator for insurance agents Lloyd's of London, the half-British, half-Japanese Taichi Keaton-Hiraga is called upon to solve a variety of cases around the world, many of which form the self-contained episodes of this sophisticated series. The globetrotting locations and cerebral story lines, often involving the hero's skills as a historian and amateur archaeologist, lift *Master Keaton* well above the average anime series.

Monster

dir Masayuki Kojima, 2004, 74 x 24m

What this cracking thriller lacks in flashy visuals it more than makes up for in its painstakingly faithful adaptation of the original award-winning manga. When Japanese brain surgeon Kenzo Tenma puts his career on the line to save the life of a young boy, little does he realize that that same boy will grow up to be a cold-blooded sociopath – the monster of the title. With the police seeking to pin a series of murders on Tenma, it's up to the doctor to track down his nemesis.

Mitsuteru Yokoyama

With his manga *Tetsujin 28-gō* (*Iron Man No 28*) and *Maho Tsukai Sally* (*Little Witch Sally*), Mitsuteru Yokoyama (1934–2004) was the forefather of the giant robot and

Japan Media Arts Festival

Japan's Agency of Cultural Affairs has held the Japan Media Arts Festival (plaza.bunka.go.jp/english) each year since 1997. The festival, which focuses on the Japanese contemporary art scene, awards prizes in four categories, including ones for animation (both long and short form) and manga. Past anime winners have included *Princess Mononoke*, *Millennium Actress* and *The Girl Who Leapt Through Time* for anime and *The Manga Classics of Japan*, *Mushi-shi* and *A Spirit of the Sun* for manga. Jury members are highly esteemed practitioners, critics and scholars within the respective industries. The festival's official prizewinners often throw up some intriguing discoveries, particularly when it comes to experimental short anime and less mainstream manga works, but there were no surprises when, for the festival's tenth anniversary in 2006, fans were polled for their top ten anime and top ten manga of all time:

Top 10 Manga

1. Slam Dunk
2. JoJo's Bizarre Adventure
3. Dragon Ball
4. Full Metal Alchemist
5. Doraemon
6. Phoenix
7. Black Jack
8. Nausicaä of the Valley of the Wind
9. Mushi-shi
10. Death Note

Top 10 Anime

1. Neon Genesis Evangelion
2. Nausicaä of the Valley of the Wind
3. Laputa: Castle in the Sky
4. Mobile Suit Gundam
5. Lupin III: The Castle of Cagliostro
6. Mushi-shi
7. Ghost in the Shell: Stand Alone Complex
8. My Neighbour Totoro
9. Full Metal Alchemist
10. Ghost in the Shell

magical girl anime genres. *Tetsujin 28 gō* first appeared as a manga series in 1956 and was hot on the heels of *Astro Boy* in being made into a TV series in 1963. Yokoyama's *Giant Robo* also got the anime treatment in the early 1990s in a retro-looking style that was homage to the 1960s series. His magnum opus, the sixty-volume *Sangokushi* (based on the Chinese fable that also formed the basis of the popular 1970s live-action TV series *The Water Margin*), was turned into an anime series in 1991.

Gigantor

Tetsujin 28-go

dir Yonehiko Watanabe, Tadao Wakabayashi, 1963, 52 x 30m

"Quicker than quick, stronger than strong!" was the tag line for the US version of this classic kids' anime, based on Mitsuteru Yokoyama's manga. Set in a stylishly retro 2000, its heroes are the plucky boy detective Jimmy Sparks (Shōtarō Kaneda in the Japanese original) and his radio-controlled robot (Tetsujin 28), which he uses to battle the usual cast of deranged villains. A big hit in the US and Australia, the original black-and-white show (of which only 52 of the original 96 Japanese episodes were translated into English), has had several revivals, the most interesting of which is 2004's *Tetsujin 28*, which returns the action to the immediate post-World War II setting of the original manga.

decoding anime

just what does it all mean?

Like an intergalactic magpie, anime zooms at light speed from the distant past to the far future, touching on everything from bicycle races to blood-sucking vampires.

It's an art form that can bring to life the imaginary worlds of science fiction, fantasy and horror, as well as everyday tales of romance or sporting drama.

Many anime straddle genre boundaries, gaining their power and popularity from multi-layered themes and influences. References to Japanese culture and lifestyle, such as religion, school and even other anime, are also an integral aspect of many shows. It's time to decode anime...

Science fiction

The birth of anime's most popular genre dates back to *Astro Boy* sparking to animated life in 1963. This was the pre-digital effects era, the time of the original *Godzilla* movie, which demonstrates how ill-equipped Japanese live-action cinema was at creating believable sci-fi adventures. In anime, however, for a fraction of the cost literally anything is possible – and it can all look fantastic.

The trickle of sci-fi shows that commenced in the 1960s with *Gigantor* and *Gatchaman*, had swelled to a flood by the 1970s, in the wake of mega hits such as *Mazinger Z* and *Space Battleship Yamato*. As the world went crazy over *Star Wars*, the 1980s witnessed a flood of sci-fi anime onto the small screen, including the *Mobile Suit Gundam* and *Macross* franchises and the start of the epic series *Legend of Galactic Heroes*. The era also produced some of the medium's most enduring big screen classics – *Akira*, *Nausicaä of the Valley of the Wind* and *Wings of Honneamise*.

Today, the most interesting contemporary sci-fi anime are perhaps those that mull over the impact that advanced technology has on daily life, such as *Patlabor*, *Ghost in the Shell*, *Serial Experiments Lain* and *Dennō Coil*. However, barring the occasional invigorating reboot, such as with *Neon Genesis Evangelion* or *Cowboy Bebop*, sci-fi anime has been stuck in a rut since the 1970s, shows regularly regurgitating a clichéd set of character types, plots and mecha.

The evolution of robots

One area in which science fiction anime has excelled is in its depiction of robot technology, collectively known as **mecha** (an abbreviation of "mechanical"). The Japanese affinity for such robotic devices predates anime by several centuries. During the Edo period (1603–1867), small mechanical dolls known as *karakuri* were used by feudal lords to serve tea and entertain guests. Their modern-day equivalent are pet robots such as Sony's Aibo dog and the baby harp seal Paro.

In anime, robots have been honed and reworked countless times over a half century to become far more sophisticated and multifaceted than a simple mechanical doll or animal. Go Nagai's *Mazinger Z* introduced the idea of a **pilotable robot** – which is really a sophisticated version of a tank or fighter plane. A comic version of such a mecha is the robotic hospital bed of *Roujin Z*, controlled by an old man – a refreshing change from the angst-ridden teenagers who, since

Mazinger Z, have been typecast in the driving seat.

Over time a subtle distinction has evolved between "real" and "super" robots – the operation of the former typically being grounded in proven science. **Real robots** break down and require repairs, or need to have their ammunition replaced, a good example being those in the *Patlabor* series and movies (see Canon), used for construction and policing duties.

Super robots, like superheroes, are invariably giant sized and often

Anime demographics

Target audiences for anime tend to follow those of the manga or game source material that most likely preceded them. First come shows and movies for young children (or *kodomo* in Japanese) such as *Pokémon*, *Doraemon* and *My Neighbour Totoro*. Despite anime's reputation for targeting teens and adults with its material, it's such kids' shows that are the most prolific and keep the medium financially afloat.

Next come *shōnen* (boys) and *shōjo* (girls) shows, designed to appeal to teenagers up to the brink of adulthood. A typical *shōnen* show is likely to be heavy on robotic technology, such as those in the *Gundam* franchise, or fighting, like *Naruto*. A *shōjo* show will focus more on fantasy and romance, like *Rose of Versailles* or *Sailor Moon*, and is often distinguished by a more florid art style and a cast of uniformly beautiful doe-eyed characters. Occasionally a show, such as *Escaflowne*, is deliberately designed to have crossover appeal to both boys and girls, so contains elements of both genres.

Seinen anime, such as *Ghost in the Shell*, *Patlabor* or *Zipang*, aimed at young men of college age are more common than their female counterpart (*josei*), but the latter do exist – in the form of shows such as *Hataraki Man* (2006) about a hard-working young female editor at a magazine.

Japan stands out in the range and volume of anime it produces for adults. Subjects vary from straight dramas such as *Only Yesterday* to complex psychological thriller, like *Perfect Blue* and the X-rated horror of *Urotsukidōji* (*Legend of the Overfiend*). At the very adult end of the scale there is everything from straight heterosexual porn, known as hentai, to shows designed to appeal to more esoteric tastes, such as yaoi (for women into homosexual love stories). There is even lolicon, which caters to the unpleasant fantasies of those who lust after skimpily dressed schoolgirls (see p.223).

have special powers which, by the convention established in *Mazinger Z*, are activated by the screeched voice command of the pilot (i.e. *"Rocket Punch!"* or *"Lightning Kick!")*. The original super robot was Mitsuteru Yokoyama's *Tetsujin 28-gō*, a.k.a. *Gigantor* (see p.198) – a radio-controlled rather than piloted model.

Robots that look human (or **androids**), such as Astro Boy, can go by several other generic names in anime – such as "persocoms" in *Chobits*, "boomers" in *Bubblegum Crisis* and *jinzō ningen* (artificial humans) in *Dragonball*. In the *Appleseed* movies **bio-androids**, built from soft protein-based components rather than metal and plastic, are also integral to the plot. Straddling the boundary between robots and humans are **cyborgs**, such as Motoko Kusanagi and her colleague Batou in *Ghost in the Shell*, which are part-human, part-machine.

Legend of Galactic Heroes

Ginga Eiyû Densetsu

dir Noburo Ishiguro, 1988–97, 110 x 25m

Anime's *War and Peace* – notably a work without an alien life form or transforming robots in sight – is based on the eighteen-novel opus by Yoshiki Tanaka. First released as a series of home videos, its growing popularity secured it a TV slot. With a cast of hundreds and impressive space battles, the series follows the fortunes of Reinhardt von Lohengramm and Yang Wen-Li, idealistic and driven young soldiers on rival sides in the 150-year-old war between the Galactic Empire and the Free Planets Alliance. Messy politics and tragedy of conflict both feature large in this ambitious show, which spawned five movies that are all prequels or side stories to the main action.

Armitage III: Poly-Matrix

dir Hiroyuki Ochi, 90m, 1997

Blade Runner is the main inspiration for this sci-fi conspiracy thriller set in the Martian city of St Lowell, where the neon burns bright, it's forever raining and a serial killer is on the loose terminating super-advanced robots who pass for humans. Compiled from a 1994 four-episode video series, this movie version signed up Kiefer Sutherland to voice broad-shouldered cop Ross Sylibus and Elizabeth Berkley (of *Showgirls* notoriety) for robo-heroine Naomi Armitage, a kick-ass cop dressed like a cheap hooker. Scripted by Chiaki Konaka, the writer of *Serial Experiments Lain* (see Canon), it comes off like an adult-rated version of *Astro Boy*.

Dennō Coil

dir Mitsuo Iso, 2007, 26 x 30m

Set in the fictional city of Daikoku in 2026, Dennō Coil imagines a world where virtual reality (or, as the series has it, "augmented reality" – AR) has become part of daily life. Yūko Okonogi and her chums in the Coil Cyber Detective Agency use AR spectacles and other technology to investigate mysterious goings-on in the virtual world, eventually uncovering a grand conspiracy. Although it bears some similarities to Serial Experiments Lain (see Canon), Dennō Coil marries imaginative ideas about near-future technology with appealing characterization and distinctive animation.

Kaiba

dir Masaki Yuasa, 2008, 12 x 25m

This hyper-surreal sci-fi love story comes from the feverish imagination of Masaki Yuasa, director of the disturbingly out there *Cat Soup* and wonderful *Mind Game* (see Canon). Adopting the retro 1960s graphic style of Osamu Tezuka, *Kaiba* is set in a world where memories have become commodities to be recorded, stored and traded. The system allows the rich to switch their ageing bodies for younger models while hanging on to their own set of memories, but it is also wide open to exploitation with memories being stolen and illegally altered. The plot follows a man possibly called Warp, who wakes with a hole in his chest and no memory of who he is, as he travels across a corrupted universe searching for his true identity. Premiered on the Japanese cable channel Wowow, the official website is www.wowow.co.jp/anime/kaiba. An excellent fan site is Chast to It! (kaiba.and-hearts.net).

Fantasy and fables

Anime is an ideal medium for fantasy and it would be easy to count many science-fiction and horror/supernatural shows as falling within this genre. Fantasy can also include alternative history scenarios, such as *Jin-Roh* (see Canon), and fairy/folk tales like *Little Norse Prince* (see Canon). If any distinctions are to be made, then it would be between fantasies that draw on Asian traditions and beliefs, and those that reference stories from other parts of the world.

One of the most popular sources for **Oriental-influenced anime** has been *Xiyouji*, or *Journey to the West*, by Wu Cheng'en, a classic of sixteenth-century Chinese literature. It's also commonly known outside Japan as *Monkey*; British and Australian readers of a certain age are likely to recall the live-action TV series of the same name screened in a dubbed version in the late 1970s.

Xiyouji is based on historical events from the sixth century and is about the adventures of a young priest who travels to and from India in search of Buddhist sutras. In a self-contained prequel to the main action of the book, the monkey king Son Goku is introduced. After attaining great powers, Son Goku is trapped under a mountain by Buddha for five

Religious influences

Shinto is Japan's indigenous religion and all the Japanese by default belong to it. Around half the population also claim to be practising **Buddhists,** while around one million are **Christian**. References to all three religions turn up in anime, as well as to the teachings of the Chinese scholar Confucius – though these are more of an ethical code than a religion.

Shinto is an animist religion that believes in hundreds of *kami* (gods) who are part of nature; see *Spirited Away* (Canon). As the *kami* favour harmony and cooperation a tolerance of other religions is unproblematic, allowing the combination of Shinto's nature worship with the worship of an almighty deity, such as that in Christianity, or with the philosophical moral code of Buddhism. The cycle of birth, life, death and rebirth found in Buddhism underlies several of Osamu Tezuka's anime, most notably the *Phoenix* series.

Religious ideas are so deeply ingrained in daily life in Japan that, while many people might not regularly practise any faith, they find it quite natural to pray at a shrine or temple during annual festivals or on a sightseeing trip. Festivals with a religious basis happen regularly and many Shinto customs are common, from those involved in marriage ceremonies to the ritual purification of building plots and new cars. For example, in *My Neighbour Totoro* the Kusakabe family make a short prayer at the forest shrine and in *Pom Poko* developers seek a blessing on the ground before beginning construction.

Judaeo-Christian beliefs and iconography, including the cross, the sephiroth of the Kabbalah and the Lance of Longinus (thrust into the crucified Jesus by a Roman soldier), are plundered in *Neon Genesis Evangelion* and used as window-dressing to the main action. In Greek *evangelion* means gospel, so the show's title can be "translated" as the Gospel of the New Beginning. Although references to Shinto and Buddhism are avoided in *Astro Boy*, Christianity shows up in several episodes, including most controversially the "Eyes of Christ", in which a priest is murdered in his church. Before dying he scratches a clue to the identity of his killers on the eye of a statue of Jesus.

hundred years until he's released by the questing priest whom he agrees to serve thereafter.

First partially adapted in Noburo Ōfujis 1926 short *Saiyuki Songoku Monogatari*, the story is not only the basis for Tōei's 1960 movie *Saiyuki* (known outside of Japan as *Alakazam the Great*, see p.10), but also several later anime, including the *Dragon Ball* series and the *Gensōmaden Saiyūki* videos and TV series made by **Studio Pierrot** from 2000 to 2002. The story was given a sci-fi spin in Leiji Matsumoto's *Starzinger* in 1978 and even used as a device by Rintarō in his film biography *Tezuka Osamu Story: I am Son-Goku* (1989). Elements of *Xiyouji* can be traced in the pirate adventure series *One Piece* (1998) and have been parodied in episodes of, among others, *Love Hina*, *Naruto* and *Ranma 1/2*.

All the early Tōei films dip into the well of Oriental legend for their inspiration, including *Hakujaden* (*Panda and the Magic Serpent*) and *Little Prince and the Eight-Headed Dragon*, as well as the 1979 production *Tarō the Dragon Boy* (see Canon). Hayao Miyazaki's *My Neighbour Totoro*, *Princess Mononoke* and *Spirited Away* also reference Japanese folk traditions, particularly the many spirits of the Shinto religion, as do *Ranma 1/2* and *Inuyasha*, both based on manga by Rumiko Takashi.

Little Prince and the Eight-Headed Dragon

Wanpaku Ōji no Orochi Taiji

dir Yugo Serikawa, 1963, 86m

Based on mythical episodes from the *Nihon Shoki* – one of the oldest books of Japanese history – this strikingly beautiful early Tōei Animation feature saw the studio establish a distinctive visual style of clean-lined, brightly coloured characters under the direction of master animator and children's book illustrator Yasuji Mori. The Little Prince of the title is Susano'o who, in the company of talking rabbit Akahana, goes in search of his beloved, but deceased mother Izanami. Having overcome fiery warriors and giant fish on his travels, the climax comes when brave Susano'o, astride a flying horse borrowed from Greek legend, battles the eight-headed dragon to save Princess Kushinada– an ending that was apparently the idea of young Hayao Miyazaki.

Pokémon

Pocket Monsters

dir Kunihiko Yuyama, 1997–present, over 550 episodes x 25m

In the late 1990s the world of kids' anime was conquered by Ash Ketchum (or Satoshi as he is known in the Japanese original), his vivid yellow pal Pikachu and an army of nearly five hundred other pocket monsters. Powered along by a multi-million dollar ad campaign, nothing stood in the colourful, imaginative series' way, not even an infamous early episode in which strobe lighting effects caused scores of Japanese kids to be hospitalized with seizures. Apart from the regular series, there have been ten movies, rousing higher quality animated adventures, and numerous shorts and TV specials. The official website is www.pokemon.com.

Naruto

dir Hayato Date, 2002–07, 220 x 25m

At the start of this phenomenally popular series, Naruto – he of the orange tracksuit, black headband and spiky blonde hair – is an unruly orphan boy, with the demonic spirit of a nine-tailed fox sealed inside him at birth.

Joining the village ninja school, he channels his energies into becoming the *hokage* – top ninja – training with star pupil Sasuke and plucky *kunoichi* (girl ninja) Sakura. Apart from great fight scenes and plenty of cool ninja combat techniques, the show's strengths are its ongoing narrative and the maturing of Naruto into a skilful team player.

Summer with Coo

Kappa no Coo to Natsuyasumi

dir Keichi Hara, 2007, 138m

Winner of the Grand Prize in the 2007 Japan Media Arts Festival, this gently humorous and thought-provoking children's film combines the heart-warming charm of Spielberg's *ET* with the environmental concerns of the best of Miyazaki's films. Schoolboy Koichi brings home an intriguing fossil from the local river only for it to come to life as a baby water sprite (or *kappa*). He calls it Coo and together they go on an adventure to the Tono valley, the crucible of Japanese folklore, where Coo hopes to find his family roots.

Japanese folk tales

Japanese mythology and folk tales have provided rich pickings for anime since its inception. There's even been a series called *Japanese Folk Tales* (*Manga Nihon Mukashi-banashi*) which ran for 1467 episodes from 1975 to 1994. Folklore characters include the pot-bellied raccoon-like *tanuki*, stars of Isao Takahata's *Pom Poko*, who have the ability to change into other creatures or objects; the long-nosed goblin *tengu* who turns up in *Tarō the Dragon Boy*; and the *kappa* water-sprite star of *Summer with Coo* (see above).

The tale of the fisherman **Urashima Tarō,** who is transported to the underwater Dragon Kingdom by a turtle he has saved, is one of the more commonly referenced fables. Urashima falls for the kingdom's princess and stays for what he thinks is a couple of years, but on returning to the real world he finds that hundreds of years have passed and all the people he once knew have died. First appearing in anime form in 1925 in Hakuzan Kimura's *Dreamy Urashima*, the story most famously formed the basis for *Urusei Yatsura 2: Beautiful Dreamer* (see Canon). Faye Valentine in *Cowboy Bebop* (see Canon) experiences her own Urashima Tarō moment on recovering the memory of her traumatic past; likewise the space-travelling heroes of *Gunbuster* (see Canon) also find their lives radically out of time with their earthly counterparts.

In the **Momotarō** stories, an old childless couple find a baby boy inside a giant peach, so name him Momotarō (Peach Tarō). He grows up to be a brave and adventurous lad who battles and overcomes the demons plaguing his village together

Two Momotarōs: 1942's *Momotarō: Eagle of the Sea* and, below, 1928's *Momotarō is the Greatest*

with three friends – a dog, monkey and pheasant. Momotarō has been a favourite subject for anime from the medium's inception; he starred in a couple of World War II propaganda films and has even appeared in female form in *Princess Minky Momo,* also known as *Magical Princess Gigi*.

The Bamboo Cutter's Tale (*Taketori Monogatari*) starts similarly to the story of Momotarō, with an old childless couple finding a golden-haired baby girl inside a stalk of bamboo. They adopt the child, naming her Princess Kaguya, an alternative name by which the story is known. As an adult, Kaguya reveals that she is originally from the moon, which is where she eventually returns, but not before capturing the heart of the emperor. He has his army march to the summit of Mount Fuji to burn Kaguya's last letter to him in the hope that the smoke from the message will reach the moon, thus providing a legendary explanation for Fuji's volcanic activity. The tale influenced the plots of the *Inuyasha* movie *The Castle Beyond the Looking Glass* (*Kagami no Naka no Mugenjō*) and *Sailor Moon S: The Movie: Hearts in Ice* (*Gekijōban Bishōjo Senshi Sailor Moon S*).

Another celestial maiden, the *tennyo,* pops up in the tale of **Hagoromo** along with her magical feathered cloak (the *hagoromo*). A fisherman finds the *tennyo*'s lost cloak, but when she comes looking for it he refuses to give it back unless she marries him. Years later, the *tennyo,* having discovered the cloak's whereabouts from her

children, returns to her own world. The story provided the basis for *Ceres: Celestial Legend* (*Ayashi no Ceres*).

One fable referenced in *My Neighbour Totoro* (see Canon), when Satsuki draws her sister Mei as a crab waiting for seeds to grow, is that of the **Monkey and the Crab**. A hungry monkey swaps a persimmon tree seed for a rice ball from a crab. The seed eventually grows into a fruit-bearing tree, and the cheeky monkey climbs the tree to eat the persimmons, refusing to share them with the crab. The crab grabs the monkey's tail in his pincers and only lets him go once he has some fruit and three hairs from the tail – which explains why there are hairs on crab claws.

Western-influenced fantasy

For fantasy inspiration from outside of Japan, anime creators have travelled broadly. Greek mythology provided the basis for the movie feature *Arion* and TV series *Ulysses 31*, a space-based reworking of Homer's *Odyssey*, while Tezuka's *Arabian Nights* draws on Sheherazade's classic tale. The Norse goddess Verthandi served as the inspiration for Belldandy in the series *Oh My Goddess!* The Dungeons & Dragons-type fantasies of role-playing games have also proved popular, first making their mark in *Record of Lodoss War* and later in the more light-hearted *Slayers* and fantasy-meets-mecha of *Escaflowne*. The medieval fantasy series *Berserk* (1997) ditches elves in favour of gory swordfights and the trappings of the occult.

Although witchcraft can have a very dark edge in anime, the concept of a kind-hearted, pretty witch, as popularized in the live-action show *Bewitched*, led to *Little Witch Sally* in 1966. This series is credited with kicking off the sub-genre of **magical girl shows** which also draw on some of the Alice in Wonderland-type ideas that Tezuka played around with in *Marvelous Melmo* (1971), in which a ten-year-old uses magic pills to alter her age back and forth between adult and child.

Magical girl shows have since become an anime staple. In the 1990s the *Sailor Moon* franchise tweaked the format, presenting a *team* of magical girls, while *Card Captor Sakura* tapped into the potential for spin-off products with a heroine in pursuit of a series of magical cards. *Magic Users' Club* (*Mahō Sukai Tai*, 1996), which depicts an after-school club practising witch-craft, pointy hats and all, is notable for including one unabashedly camp gay *bishōnen*, Aburatsubō, who rides his flying broom sidesaddle. Other than this, magical boys in the Harry Potter mould are a less common anime archetype, although brothers Edward and Alphonse Elric in *Fullmetal Alchemist* (see Canon) certainly qualify.

When not raiding the Japanese folklore cupboard, Hayao Miyazaki has favoured European fantasy for inspiration. *Kiki's Delivery Service* can be counted as part of the magical girl sub-genre while *Howl's Moving Castle* has a dandyish wizard as its hero. *Porco Rosso* casts a pig-faced pilot in the lead role and *Castle in the Sky* references Jonathan Swift's *Gulliver's Travels*. Miyazaki's latest movie *Gake no ue no Ponyo*, while set in Japan, is partly based on the Hans Christian Anderson story *The Little Mermaid*.

Escaflowne

Tenku no Escaflowne

dir Kazuki Akane, 1996, series 26 x 25m

Also known as *Vision of Escaflowne*, this cliché-packed fantasy series, with a spunky schoolgirl heroine and the giant mecha of the title, was designed to appeal to both teenage boys and

Edward and Alphonse Elric in *Fullmetal Alchemist:* the anime equivalent of Harry Potter and his friends?

courtesy of FUNimation Entertainment

A vision of *Escaflowne*

girls – in which it succeeded admirably. A mysterious force transports high-school athlete Hitomi to the strange world of Gaea, where she teams up with boy-prince Van Fanel and others in their quest against the evil forces of Zaibach. *Escaflowne: The Movie* (2000, 98m) is a re-imagining of the series with new artwork, character design and an interesting switch in the personalities of Hitomi and Van.

Record of Lodoss War

Lodoss to Senki

dir Akinori Nagaoka, 1990, 13 x 30m

Dwarfs, elves and goblins all feature in this Dungeons & Dragons-inspired anime, which follows valiant knight Parn as he battles against the evil sorceress Karla, instigator of the eternal wars of the kingdom of Lodoss. Despite the largely pedestrian level of animation used for the straight-to-video format, the creators succeed in conjuring up an engaging yarn and memorable characters that have a loyal following among older anime fans.

Sailor Moon

Bishōjo Senshi Sailor Moon

dir Junichi Satō et al, 1992–97, 200 x 25m

Credited with turning on a generation of young girls to anime, this series – which ran for five seasons as well as six movies and short features – pits five "magical girls", dressed in sailor-style school uniforms (common in Japan), against a host of demons in a complex interplanetary saga embracing comedy, romance and tragedy. Several androgynous male characters, and the butch-femme Sailor Scouts Uranus and Neptune from season three, added an intriguing layer of sexual ambiguity to the affair, even though much of this would have flown over the heads of the target market, starry-eyed with the sailors' pretty outfits and demon-busting accessories.

R.O.D.
Read or Die

dir Kōji Masunari, 2001, 90m

This stylishly handled fantasy mixed elements of *Mission Impossible* with Jasper Fford's *Thursday Next* novels. Bespectacled, bookish Yomiko Readman is the unlikely superhero in this fun alternative history fantasy about clones of obscure historic figures (including French entomologist Jean-Henri Fabre, the fifteenth-century Zen priest Ikkyu and pioneering aviator Otto Lilienthal) creating global havoc. The British Library's Special Ops Division assigns Readman, a.k.a. The Paper, along with fellow agents Deep and Drake Anderson to the case. A short series with different characters followed this initial DVD release.

Horror and the supernatural

Japan's pantheon of supernatural spirits, ghosts and monsters (or *yōkai*) has bequeathed anime a rich brew of potentially scary material. The *yuki-onna*, or ghostly snow woman, for example, shows up in *Tarō the Dragon Boy*; the shape-shifting fox character of Shippo in *Inuyasha* is inspired by Shinto's fox spirit or *Kitsune-rei* – there's also a demonic nine-tailed fox spirit sealed within the body of boy ninja *Naruto*; and fanged *oni*, or demons, are just one of the traditional foes in the *Spirit Warrior* series (also known as *Peacock King*).

Back in the 1960s, the folklore demon designs of Tezuka's *Dororo* established traditional horror as a legitimate area for manga and anime, inspiring many imitators. *Ayakashi Classic Japanese Horror* and its sequel *Mononoke* are interesting, mildly experimental works essaying traditional Japanese ghost stories in the style of *ukiyo-e* prints.

Contemporary Tokyo has proved a popular setting for horror anime including two exemplars of the **urban gothic style** – *Wicked City* and *Demon City Shinjuku* – as well as *X: The Movie* and the similar *Karas*. *Le Portrait de Petit Cossette* brings goth Loli-style horror to an antique shop in a Tokyo shopping mall, while souped-up 3D spirits haunt the streets of Tokyo in *Kakurenbo: Hide and Seek* (although the scenery design, especially of the temple, is inspired by Hong Kong's Kowloon). Futuristic Neo-Tokyo is the location for *Akira*, which includes one of anime's most skin-crawling scenes, in which Tetsuo transforms into a hideously expanding blob of fleshy tissues and mechanized hardware.

Akira is a good example of how horror infiltrates other genres such as fantasy and sci-fi, where plots involving hideous monsters, alien or otherwise, are a dime a dozen. Zombies with mercury in their veins instead of blood add a chilling touch to the historical drama *Le Chevalier*

Beware the death gods!

Shinigami (death gods) seem to be all the rage in anime and manga, dragging their weary bones through *Bleach*, *Death Note*, *Yu Yu Hakusho* and *Descendants of Darkness* (*Yami no Matsuei*) and, most recently, *Soul Eater*. They have also featured in *Princess Mononoke* and *Naruto* and are referenced in *Black Jack*, *Hellsing* and *Gundam Wing*. Although they sound like an ancient Shinto deity, *Shinigami* are, in fact, a relatively recent addition to Japanese popular culture, first imported as an idea from Europe during the latter half of the nineteenth century, where they turned up in popular comic theatrical monologues known as *rakugo*.

courtesy of FUNimation Entertainment

Battlers of death gods: the cast of *Yu Yu Hakusho*

D'Eon (see p.218), while the concept of rape by tentacle came to hideous life in the infamous *Urotsukidōji* series of video nasties (also known as *Legend of the Overfiend*).

When in doubt, anime makers fall back on Dracula-style **vampires**, a staple of the horror genre. They've turned up everywhere from the fog-bound streets of London in *Hellsing* (2001) to a US air base in Japan during the Vietnam War in *Blood: The Last Vampire*, and even thousands of years in the future in *Vampire Hunter D* (1985).

Despite these considerable efforts, anime horror that is genuinely frightening remains elusive, mainly because the medium's flat two dimensions tend to dull the visceral impact of flowing rivers of blood and gore. This explains the preference of filmmakers to adapt horror manga into live-action features – *Death*

Note being a good example. Horror that works best in anime tends to be more cerebral and subtle, as in the psychological chillers *Perfect Blue* (see Canon) and *Paranoia Agent* (see Canon), or the paranormal thrillers *Boogiepop Phantom* and *Ghost Hound*. Alternatively, it can arise from the depiction of terrifying real events, such as those in *Barefoot Gen* (see Canon).

Blood: The Last Vampire

Buraddo Za Rasuto Vanpaia

dir Hiroyuki Kitakubo, 2000, 48m

In Japan's first fully digital anime, produced by Production I.G, half-vampire schoolgirl Saya hunts down Chiropterans – monsters disguised as humans – slaying them with her samurai sword. Designed as a multimedia project, with appeal to foreign markets (hence the mainly English dialogue), it's a visually dazzling, highly atmospheric feature that leaves you wanting more. This follows in the series *Blood+* (2005), directed by Junichi Fujisaku, which brings the action forward from 1966 to 2005. After suffering a mental breakdown in 1972, a softer-faced but no less deadly Saya is on a global hunt for the Chiropterans whose proliferation is explicitly linked to the Vietnam War.

Kakurenbo: Hide and Seek

dir Shuhei Morita, 2005, 25m

A highly impressive debut for a handful of animators working outside the studio system. Hikora joins seven other kids wearing fox masks in a game of *otokoyo* (hide and seek) on the dimly lit streets of Tokyo. He's searching for his sister Sorincha who has gone missing, like all other children who have played this game at night. Much care was taken to make this 3D computer-graphic anime have a hand-drawn quality. Eerie music and silence add to the tension. Morita has since teamed up with Katsuhiro Ōtomo to direct the DVD sci-fi series *Freedom*.

Boogiepop Phantom

Bugipoppu wa Warawanai: Boogiepop Phantom

dir Takashi Watanabe, 2000, 12 x 30m

With its eerily off-kilter world, shot as if through a brown fog, this is an original Japanese take on horror in the spirit of the live-action movie *The Ring*. A serial killer on the loose, an androgynous phantom, and creepy paranormal events plague an ensemble of teenagers. Some go missing, others lose their minds. Motorbike-riding Nagi Kirima, haunted by the murder of her father five years earlier, sets out to investigate. Each episode of the complex story is told from one character's point of view, the solution to the puzzle made more obscure by out-of-sequence events and flips back and forth in time.

Super deformed

Although the anime norm of huge eyes would be seen as a deformity in real life, in the anime world **super deformity** (or **SD**) refers to a drawing style that morphs regularly proportioned characters into squashed-down or comically exaggerated versions of their former selves. The typical look is an oversized head atop stunted torso and limbs.

SD most often happens in comedies as a visual emphasis of a character's sudden change of emotions, be it a rush of anger, a pang of hunger or the fluttering butterflies of love. Such SD versions of characters typically only last for a few seconds but occasionally there are comedy shows where that look is the norm, for example *Petit Eva~Evangelion@school,* a parody of *Neon Genesis Evangelion*. The most famous SD series is *SD Gundam* which has spawned fourteen anime spoofs since 1989. SD drawing shouldn't be confused with chibi characters who are small and cute and often out of proportion all the time, an example being the nine-year-old *Chibi Maruko-chan*.

Comedy and satire

Like their foreign counterparts, Japan's first animators quickly realized how well their chosen medium suited comedy routines by creating humorous short cartoons largely aimed at entertaining kids. Osamu Tezuka, who loved to insert slapstick comedy and one-off gags in his manga and anime, pioneered adult anime humour in *Arabian Nights* and *Cleopatra*. Both these movies deviate into silly and surreal moments for comic effect, often switching back and forth at random with straight characterization and more cartoony-style images – a style aped to the max in later years by shows such as *His and Her Circumstances* and *Excel Saga*.

Sitcoms have been a standard of the medium for several decades. There are romantically themed shows such as *Maison Ikkoku*, or those with a sci-fi setting like *Urusei Yatsura*, *Tenchi Muyo!* (1992–99) and *Irresponsible Captain Tylor* (1992), with its lazybones hero blundering his way to success in space. There are comedies set in high school such as *Azumanga Daioh* (2002) and those in fantasy-land like *Dragon Half* (1993) where heroine Mink's mum is a dragon and her dad is a knight. Children's anime continues to play up the comedy – be it the slapstick shtick of the Keystone kittens in *Puss 'n Boots* or the bumbling villains Jessie and James in *Pokémon*.

More subtle humour is provided by satires such as *The Melancholy of Haruhi Suzumiya*, with its deadpan, sarcastic take on the supernatural, or *Welcome to the NHK* (2007), which marries housebound social introverts to the weirder shores of nerdiness. Hana the transvestite tramp in *Tokyo Godfathers* is among anime's most hilarious characters.

A lot of anime humour can also be self-referential, the stereotypes and clichés of other shows providing fertile source material for **lampoons and parodies**, such as *Excel Saga* and the bread-baking show *Yakitate!! Japan* (see p.230). Forming a mini-genre within this are anime about anime, kicking off with the famous Gainax spoof *Otaku no Video* and culminating more recently in *Anime Runner Kuromi* (2001) a comedy about life in an anime company, and the geek-fest *Genshiken* (2004). To get all the jokes and punning references in any of these requires a lifetime's diligent study of anime and Japanese pop culture.

Excel Saga

Ekuseru Sāga

dir Shinichi Watanabe, 1999–2000, 26 x 30m

Hyperactive Excel and consumptive Hyatt are agents for the secret organization Across, headed by cool megalomanic Il Palazzo. They're on a mission to conquer the corrupt world, if only Excel can keep hunger at bay and avoid snacking on her pet pooch Menchi. In zany episodes that lampoon everything from dating games and giant robot shows to the post-apocalyptic battles of *Fist of the North Star*, they cross paths with Nabeshin, the Afro-haired alter ego of director

courtesy of FUNimation Entertainment

Screwball comedy meets science fiction in the long-running *Tenchi Muyo!*

It's nerd versus nerd in *Otaku no Video*, as the anime industry takes the mickey out of itself

Watanabe and the original manga's author Kōshi Rikudō. Turn on the DVD's vid notes feature to clue into the parodies and puns in this quack experimental anime.

Welcome to the NHK
NHK ni Yōkoso!

dir Yusuke Yamamoto, 2006, 24 x 30m

Although it's often wickedly funny there are some serious underlying issues driving the plot of *Welcome to the NHK*, including depression, addiction to lolicon porn, internet suicide clubs and acute social withdrawal syndrome (or *hikikomori* in Japanese) from which the university dropout hero Tatsuhiro suffers. To Tatsuhiro's rescue comes Kaoru, his neighbour and old schoolfriend turned computer programming otaku, and the mysterious girl Misaki who appoints herself as Tatsuhiro's amateur shrink.

Otaku no Video

dir Takeshi Mori, 1991, 95m

Anime's *Spinal Tap* sees the folks at Gainax affectionately parody their own rise from a bunch of geeks selling garage kits (home-made model kits) to "ota-kings" of the anime industry. The lead characters Ken Kubo and Tanaka are based on Gainax founders Hiroyuki Yamaga and Toshio Okada and references are made to a host of classic seventies anime including *Mobile Suit Gundam* and *Space Battleship Yamato*. The animation is intercut with hilarious live-action mockumentary interviews with all kinds of otaku, not just those obsessed with anime.

Historical dramas

Samurai dramas have always been a safe bet for Japanese TV and cinema so it's not surprising that anime has also ventured into this territory. Usually it has been in terms of fantastical ninja-fixated films and series such as *Ninja Scroll* (see Canon) and *Samurai Deeper Kyō* (2002), which have scant relation to actual historical events and personages. Then there are the likes of *Samurai Champloo* (see Canon) and *Afro Samurai* that remix the past with the streetwise elements of the present to appeal to modern audiences.

Straight historical dramas in the Merchant–Ivory mould are a much rarer breed. Heian era (794–1195) courtly life is the focus of *Tale of Genji* while *The Sensualist* is faithfully based on an Edo-era story by seventeenth-century poet Ihara Saikaku. *Rurouni Kenshin* and the follow-up video series *Samurai X* (see Canon) are mainly serious dramas set in the turbulent quasi-civil war years of mid-nineteenth-century Japan, when factions supporting the emperor sought to topple the shogun.

The traumas of **World War II** feature as part of the arc of twentieth-century Japanese history as refracted through the parallel timeline of Japanese cinema in *Millennium Actress*. More real wartime events provide the material for *Barefoot Gen, Grave of the Fireflies, The Cockpit* (1994), *Rail of the Star* (1993) and *Nagasaki 1945: The Angelus Bell* (2005).

Historical dramas set **overseas** are an eclectic bunch, in which the facts of history are equally open to creative interpretation. The basics of Cleopatra's legend just about remain discernible in Tezuka's irreverent version. Marie Antoinette fares better in *Rose of Versailles* – at least from the point of view of fact – and still ends up on a scaffold. The unfortunate queen's predecessors – King Louis XV and his consort Maria – feature in *Le Chevalier D'Eon,* very loosely based on the real historical figure Chevalier D'Eon.

Each episode of the Japanese version of the Franco-Japanese co-

courtesy of FUNimation Entertainment

Romance in the old-fashioned way: *Le Chevalier D'Eon*

production *Mysterious Cities of Gold* (see p.241), set mainly in sixteenth-century Central and South America, included codas on the historical contexts and facts behind the series. Although most of it is pure fantasy, the Victorian settings of London and Manchester in *Steamboy* (see Canon) feel right enough, as they do in the *Upstairs, Downstairs*-style romance of *Emma* which captures London circa 1885 with meticulous detail.

Rurouni Kenshin

dir Kazuhiro Furuhashi, Hatsuki Tsuji, 1996, 95 x 25m

Highly popular series charting the adventures of mysterious ex-assassin Kenshin Himura, as he settles first as a boarder into a Tokyo *dōjō* (martial arts school) run by the orphaned teenage girl Kaoru Kamiya, and later as he returns to Kyoto to assist the government in hunting down a band of anti-establishment rebels. The action-packed series has a very different look and tone to the highly rated *Samurai X* videos (see Canon), the characters appearing more cartoonish, the violence being far less bloody, and the humour, such as Kaoru's lack of skill in the kitchen, played up to the hilt.

Zipang

dir Kazuhiro Furuhashi, 2004, 26 x 25m

The basic premise of this fascinating series – that a contemporary Japanese naval destroyer ends up in the thick of the Battle of the Midway after slipping through a time warp – is pure sci-fi. However, meticulous attention to the facts of the Pacific War make this a very credible historical series. Despite the wartime setting, it is light on action and heavy on tactical manoeuvres and philosophical debate over whether the contemporary Japanese should intervene or let history take its course. Military buffs will also thrill to the precise level of detail given to the computer-generated battleships, including a re-creation of the famous *Yamato*.

Emma

dir Tsuneo Kobayashi, 2005, 12 x 25m

Not to be confused with Jane Austen's novel, this romantic tale of poor Yorkshire lass Emma, maid to the kindly governess Ms Stownar, is an entertaining breath of fresh air, a historical drama played straight and made with heart. Emma starts a romance with wealthy William Jones but in class-bound Victorian society their liaison seems doomed. Complicating matters is Hakim Atawari, an Indian prince and friend of William's, who also falls for Emma's charms. Based on the manga by Kaoru Mori that is said to have ignited the breakout success of maid cafés from the cosplay culture.

Le Chevalier D'Eon

dir Kazuhiro Furuhashi, 2006–07, 24 x 30m

Based on the historical fantasy novel by Tow Ubukata, this is one of Production I.G's more engaging TV projects and an interesting step in the evolution of *shōjo* anime (see box on p.201). Like *Rose of Versailles* the story, set in eighteenth-century France, is packed with real historical characters. The most fascinating among them is D'Eon de Beaumont, the chevalier of the title – a diplomat, soldier and spy for King Louis XV, who frequently dressed as a woman. Political scheming, fast-moving sword fights and the supernatural are the other eclectic ingredients of this exotic-looking cocktail.

Crime, action and adventure

Assassins, spies, cops and robbers, as well as a diverse assortment of other action-orientated character, have all found a home in anime. One of the medium's most successful schemers, the rakish criminal **Lupin III**, has planned heists and charmed women around the globe in an ongoing series of adventures since 1971, the most famous of which is *Castle of Cagliostro* (see Canon).

The action is more hard-boiled in the hit-man **thrillers** *Golgo 13: The Professional* and its follow-up *Golgo 13: Queen Bee* but no less cheesy than in *Licensed by Royalty* in which the crime-fighting secret agents Rowe Rickenbacker and Jack Hofner are named after the makes of guitar favoured by John Lennon and Paul McCartney.

Geopolitical issues plucked from the headlines of Pakistan and Russia are the background for the more serious *Yugo the Negotiator*. The Cold War posturings that form the basis of *Silent Service* are also no laughing matter. Generally less provocative, but just as contemporary in presenting its mystery or adventure of the week is *Master Keaton*.

For those who prefer their **murder mysteries** strictly old school, there have been anime adaptations of several Agatha Christie novels in the series *Hercule Poirot and Miss Marple* (2004), while the faintest shades of Dashiell Hammett and the private-eye format hang over the movie *Domain of Murder* (1992). *Conan the Boy Detective* (*Meitantei Conan*), also known as *Case Closed* in the US, is a very popular mystery TV series and string of movies (twelve as of 2008) about a sixteen-year-old Sherlock

The way of the warrior

Japan's warrior caste, the **samurai**, date back to the ninth century, when feudal lords began to maintain private armies. Gradually, they evolved into an elite group of hereditary warriors, their lives governed by an unwritten code of behaviour which came to be known as *bushidō*, the way of the warrior. Though practice was often far from the ideal, *bushidō* encouraged rigorous self-discipline, the observance of strict laws of etiquette and, most importantly, unquestioning loyalty.

According to this code, the samurai, his wife and children were expected to die willingly to protect the life and honour of their feudal lord. If they failed in this duty, or were about to be taken prisoner on a battlefield, then suicide was the only fitting response. The traditional, and excruciatingly painful, method of ritual suicide was disembowelment with a sword or dagger (*seppuku*), though in later years an accomplice would stand by to cut off the victim's head.

By the mid-seventeenth century a distinct class system was entrenched in Japan in which samurai were deemed "the masters of the four classes" – above farmers, artisans and merchants. They alone were permitted to carry swords, and even had the right to kill any member of the lower orders for disrespectful behaviour, real or imagined – a privilege known as *kirisute-gomen*, literally "cut, throw away, pardon".

In over two hundred years of peaceful rule under Tokugawa shoguns, many samurai found themselves out of work as their lords were dispossessed and fiefdoms redistributed. Many became ronin, or masterless samurai, whose lives were romanticized in such films as Akira Kurosawa's *The Seven Samurai*, given an anime treatment in *Samurai 7*. Even though the events of the series *Rurouni Kenshin* take place after the abolition of the caste system, the ethical code and behaviour of samurai are its foundation.

Holmes-style detective, who, due to the kind of weird circumstances that are common in anime finds himself transformed into a seven-year-old. Straight cop shows range from the bland, soap-opera antics of *You're Under Arrest* (1994) to the ridiculous stereotyping and setups of *Mad Bull 34* (1990).

Silent Service

Chinmoku no Kantai

dir Ryosuke Takahashi, 1995, 100m

Those who favour military and diplomatic intrigue over action eye candy will enjoy this taut thriller based on an award-winning manga by Kaiji Kawaguchi. Set on, and under, the high seas the plot recalls *The Hunt for Red October*, with its focus on the Cold War politics of an earlier era. On its maiden voyage, Captain Shiro Kaieda and his crew take over the top-secret nuclear submarine the *Sea Bat*, renaming it the independent nation of Yamato. The US military who developed the sub along with the Japanese try to recapture

It was Colonel Mustard, in the library, with the revolver: *Conan the Boy Detective* closes another case.

courtesy of FUNimation Entertainment

Family life

Romantic and comedy-style sitcom shows, as well as a goodly selection of other anime genres, provide a glimpse of average Japanese **family life**. In city-bound stories, characters often live in tiny, humble-looking low-rise flats, or *aparto*. In the suburbs or countryside they may be fortunate enough to have a whole house such as the Moriboshi's in *Urusei Yatsura* or the family in *My Neighbours the Yamadas*. What will be typical to both is that the rooms have *tatami* (woven grass mat) flooring and that characters will always be seen removing their shoes in the doorway (or *genkan*) and donning slippers before entering the main house.

Other typical features of a Japanese home include sliding screen doors and windows (*fusuma*) usually covered with traditional paper. In the corner of the main room will be a *tokanoma*, or alcove, for displaying some seasonal plant or work of art. There may also be a small shrine to honour deceased relatives. Kitchens are rarely grandiose – for a beautifully detailed example of one see *Whispers of the Heart* – and often families will gather together there or around a low table, sat cross-legged on cushions, in the living room to share a meal. When it is bedtime, futon mattresses are rolled out directly on to the tatami from closets.

Bathtime has its own set of rituals and setup. Japanese wash themselves outside the bath and use the tub's clean water to soak. It's not unusual for members of the opposite sex to bathe together – there are examples of this in both *My Neighbour Totoro* and *Grave of the Fireflies*.

it but the cool-headed captain outsmarts them at each strategic move.

Yugo the Negotiator

dir Seiji Kishi, Shinya Hanai, 2004, 13 x 25m

Master negotiator Yugo Beppu brings his brilliant analytical and diplomatic skills to bear on hostage crises and other tense situations around the world. This series focuses on two of his cases, the first set in Pakistan, the second in Siberia. Each was animated by different production teams so there are noticeable differences in their art styles. Based on the manga by Shinji Makari and Shu Akana the action in this cerebrally appealing show is downplayed in favour of a detailed examination of culture, politics and psychological manipulation.

Romance and daily drama

A few Tōei features of the late 1950s and 1960s featured a boy wooing a girl as part of their plot (see *Hakujuden* and *Puss 'n Boots*), but **romance-themed anime** truly began to blossom in the 1970s as *shōjo* manga (comics aimed at young girls) went mass market. A ground-breaking series was *Candy Candy* (1976) about an unfortunate orphan girl called Candice whose search for love seems forever thwarted by circumstance out of her control.

Lovers not quite getting together provided the ongoing drama – along with the thrills of baseball – in *Touch* (1985), a hit sports drama (see p.231/below). The courtships of unlikely suitors in series such as *Maison*

The meaning of moe

Are you experiencing warm, parental-type feelings towards the wide-eyed innocent little girls and submissive maids of anime? If so, you may be coming down with a dose of **moe**.

Pronounced *mow-eh* and written with the kanji that means "to sprout or bud", the word's origin has also been linked to the verb *moeru* meaning to burn, as in burn with passion, and to the names of certain anime characters such as Hotaru Tomoe in *Sailor Moon*. In Japanese contemporary slang, however, moe commonly refers to a particular style of anime character that typically, but not exclusively, is a young, innocent, emotionally naïve girl.

Moe waifs have been cropping up in anime for decades, some pinpointing their birth back to Clarisse in *Castle of Cagliostro* (see Canon), others linking it into the general love of *kawaii* (cute) characters, both human and animal, that seems to be an inseparable component of popular Japanese culture. The non-sexual nature of the fetish is usually agreed on.

This said, the distance between moe and the unambivalent **lolicon** anime is dangerously close. Referring to the title of Vladimir Nabokov's novel about the sexual infatuation of a middle-aged man for a twelve-year-old girl, lolicon (a shortening of Lolita complex) anime panders to such perverted sexual tastes. The pederast's version of lolicon is **shotacon**, an abbreviation for Shōtarō complex, named after the boy hero of *Testugin 28-gō* (*Gigantor*).

Ikkoku (1986) and *Kimagure Orange Road* (1987) were equally drawn out, although eventually consummated. A twisted form of romance is the focus of *Revolutionary Girl Utena* (see Canon), a show that prepared the way to the same-sex liaisons of yuri and yaoi anime – see below, while the crazy antics and visuals of *His and Her Circumstances* are icing on the cake of this series, main theme of the budding love affair of Sōichirō and Yukino which, yet again, is unresolved by the series end.

courtesy of FUNimation Entertainment

Negima: one of anime's wackiest takes on the high-school sitcom

Studio Ghibli's movies often incorporate romance. This is most notable in *Whispers of the Heart* and *Only Yesterday*, but love affairs also fuel the plots of *Porco Rosso* and *Howl's Moving Castle*. Old-fashioned romance is the driving force of the Victorian servant girl drama *Emma*. The pangs of teenage first love are also essayed in **Makoto Shinkai**'s trilogy of shorts *5 Centimeters per Second* (see Canon) Naoyoshi Shiotani's two-part DVD *Tokyo Marble Chocolate* (2007), which views a relationship from both the boy's and the girl's point of view, the twenty-first century re-imagining of Shakespeare's star-crossed lovers in

Anime goes to school

The Japanese take education very seriously and although mandatory schooling starts from the age of six, it's not unusual for children to attend daily kindergarten from much earlier, particularly if their parents are intent on having them accepted at prestigious institutions later in life.

Although compulsory schooling ends after middle school (grades 7 to 9), the vast majority of students continue through grades 10 to 12 in high school. This is where the competition for educational success becomes most intense, as students prepare for their *nyugakushiken* university and college entrance exams. Often, as well as regular school, they will attend *juku* (cram schools) after hours. The stress of the system has been the background to several anime including *Serial Experiments: Lain* and *Boogiepop Phantom*.

It's not all played seriously in anime, as high school-set sitcoms such as *Urusei Yatsura*, *Azumanga Daioh* and *His and Her Circumstances* show. More bizarre school situations are the focus of *Cromartie High* (*Sakigatte!! Cromartie Koko*, 2004), in which the classrooms are packed with teenage delinquents as well as a gorilla and a robot boy. In *Ōran High School Host Club* (2006), students from an elite boys school play male hosts at a women's bar on the side, while in *Revolutionary Girl Utena* lessons never seem to get in the way of the duelling, hormonally charged student body.

Anime studio **Shaft** (www.shaft-web.co.jp) has carved out a niche producing some of the wackiest of recent high-school-set sitcoms, including *Pani Poni Dash*, *Negima* and *Sayonara Zetsubō Sensei*.

courtesy of FUNimation Entertainment

Your schooldays probably had little in common with life at *Ōran High School*

© Gonzo Digimation Holdings

Shakespeare gets anime-ted in *Romeo x Juliet*

Romeo x Juliet (2007), set in the floating city of Neo-Verona.

His and Her Circumstances

Kareshi Kanojo no Jijō

dir Hideaki Anno, Kazuya Tsurumaki, 1998, 26 x 30m

Funny and charming, this wacky sitcom charts the budding romance of high-school darling Yukino Miyazawa with rival overachiever and heart-throb Sōichirō Arima. While both appear to be perfect to their classmates, Yukino is actually vain, self-obsessed and a slob, while Sōichirō is a mess of social anxieties. A wide range of drawing styles and visual tricks are used, including paper cutouts and pop-up information commenting on the characters' actions, all to great effect. However, clashes with the broadcaster and the original manga's author Masami Tsuda led to Anno walking from the series after episode 18, with a subsequent deterioration of quality thereafter.

Maison Ikkoku

dir Kazuo Yamazaki, 1986–88; 96 x 25m

Another popular manga by Rumiko Takahashi provided the basis for this charming, if dated, romantic sitcom that foregoes the fantasy and sci-fi trappings of her other series to concentrate on the extended courtship of student Yusaku Godai and Kyoko Otonashi, the pretty young widow who's the caretaker of the boarding house he lives in. Along for the ride are the house's colourful cast of characters who like nothing better than either to gossip about each other or throw parties and outings. For full details of the series see the excellent fan site furinkan.com/maison.

Human Crossing

Ningen Kōsaten

dir Akira Kumeichi, Kazunari Kumi, 2003, 13 x 24m

This interesting series uses simple, unflashy animation to tell a series of self-contained modern-day dramas zoning in on individuals' feelings and relationships as they reach moments of self-realization or crossroads in their lives. Episodes include ones about a workaholic father attempting to reconnect with his alienated son; siblings having to look after an ageing father that neither of them particularly cares for; and a bullied primary school boy who is encouraged by a strange old man to stand up for himself.

Romeo x Juliet

dir Fumitoshi Oizaki, 2007, 24 x 25m

Japan has a folklore and literary tradition of doomed young lovers who enter into suicide pacts – which has obvious parallels to Shakespeare's play about the fateful attraction between the offspring of rival families. Like its previous makeover of *Seven Samurai*, Gonzo gives *Romeo and Juliet* a stylish sci-fi spin that preserves little of the original story beyond characters' names and its tragic denouement. Juliet, for example, is transformed from virginal waif into a kick-ass vigilante swordswoman, the last member of the Capulets, who disguises herself as a boy to evade the Montagues.

The Melancholy of Haruhi Suzumiya

dir Tatsuya Ishihara, 2006, 14 x 30m

If you're going to do moe (see box on p.223), this series, whose popularity spread like a viral disease through the global fan community, is the one to watch. Bossy little madam Haruhi Suzumiya is an ADD-afflicted teen who doesn't realize she's (whisper it!) God. Fortunately she's unwittingly gathered around her a group of equally powerful (yet undercover) fellow students who conspire to stop her destroying the world each time she gets bored. Deadpan wit and catchy dance routines ensue in this multi-layered satire on the magical girl/school sitcom genres.

Erotica and pornography

Although he played it principally for laughs, little could Osamu Tezuka realize what kind of genie he'd be letting out of the bottle when he introduced anime erotica to the world in *Arabian Nights*. What started out as a bit of fun, and one that was reasonably tasteful, has ended up in the worst perversions of lolicon and tits-and-tentacles porn.

Like its live-action counterpart, anime porn (generally known as hentai in Japanese) broke into the big time with the development of **home video.** It's proved a lucrative sideline for the industry with titles such as *Urotsukidoji* (*Legend of the Overfiend*) and the *Cream Lemon* series among anime's best sellers. *La Blue Girl* (1992) stands out for bothering to include a plot, and one that contains some ridiculous twists. The schoolgirl heroine, the scion of an ancient clan of sex-specialist ninjas, discovers that her long-lost father is in fact the king of the tentacle demons, who fell in love with, and married, her mother.

For all its commercial success, anime porn still stumbles over the same obstacle as that laid before its horror brethren – a distinct lack of realism. The most sophisticated examples of erotic anime at least acknowledge this: *Tragedy of Belladona* and *The Sensualist* (*Ihara Saikaku: Koshoku Ichidai Otoko*, 1990) both use copious amounts of sexual symbolism, painting very pretty animated pictures of suggestively blooming flowers, caressing tendrils of hair or intermingling sinuous lines that evoke body parts. One culturally unique symbol of sexual arousal is the **bloody nose**. This often pops up in anime for comedy effect, such as when Ataru Moroboshi in *Urusei Yatsura* gets turned on by a woman, or in the case of Ōta in the *Patlabor* series, who thrills to big guns.

Romantic manga tales of boys in love with each other have also led to the sub-genre of **yaoi anime**. A contraction of "*yamanshi, ochinashi, iminashi*" ("no climax, no punchline, no meaning"), the term has shed its negative origins to be embraced chiefly by female fans, who are said to yearn for the purity and beauty of such relationships – which in their anime versions rarely end on a positive note. Examples include the cop show *Fake* (1996) and the emotionally intense sci-fi drama *Ai no Kusabe* (*Ties of Love*, 1992). A good website to find out more is Boys on Boys on Film (www.boysonboysonfilm.com).

The all-female equivalent of yaoi is **yuri,** said to derive from the lesbian term *yurizoku* (meaning "lily tribe"). Although few, if any, anime

Hentai or just etchi?

Sometimes you'll hear the term *etchi* (the Japanese pronunciation of the letter H) used interchangeably with hentai, or to describe sexually provocative material that could be anything along the spectrum from a saucy clip of jiggling breasts, as in *Gunbusters* or *The Melancholy of Haruhi Suzumiya*, to soft-porn offerings.

The pixelation effect

Until recently, Japanese obscenity laws frowned on clear depictions of genitalia and pubic hair. The result of this is that anime porn and erotica have either fallen back on the pixelation or blurring of the sexual organs, a technique used in live-action Japanese porn, or come up with some interesting variations of their own. A strategic placing of a symbolic substitute, such as the hilt of a sword across the groin of a warrior, is one way of conveying an erect member without causing the Japanese censor to reach for his scissors. Another hackneyed technique is to introduce randy monsters with orifice-invading tentacles.

are intentionally made specifically for a lesbian audience there are plenty of hentai with lesbian scenes, as well as titles such as *Revolutionary Girl Utena,* that have an unmistakable Sapphic theme.

Tragedy of Belladona

Kanashimi no Belladona

dir Eiichi Yamamoto, 1973, 89m

This erotically charged reworking of the story of Joan of Arc, based on the nineteenth-century novel *La Sorcière* by Jules Michelet, imaginatively breaks up full animation with still frame images. Mega-eyelashed Jeanne's marriage to wimpy Jean is barely a day old when she is brutally raped by the local lord, triggering a carnal enslavement to the devil and the eventual wrath of the townsfolk. The acid-trip illustrations by Kuni Fukai and animation by Gisaburō Sugii are weirdly beautiful, revealing influences from artists such as Gustav Klimt, Egon Schiele and Marc Chagall.

Urotsukidōji

Legend of the Overfiend & Legend of the Demon Womb

dir Hideki Takayama, 1987–91, 108m & 88m

Responsible for introducing the concept of tentacle rape to an unsuspecting but, if sales are anything to go by, appreciative global audience, this ripe slice of erotic horror is a bona fide shocker. Originally released as a five-part video series, the episodes were edited together in the UK into two movies: *Legend of the Overfiend* and *Legend of the Demon Womb*. The perplexingly complex plot starts with half-man, half-beast Amanojaku on a quest to locate the Chojin (the Overfiend), who can unite his kind with the worlds of humans and demons – then goes rapidly downhill.

Sports, martial arts and contests

The competitive drama of sports featured in some of Japan's earliest anime, but these almost always involved cute animals aping humans in shorts such as *Animal Olympics* (1928) and *Animal Great Baseball Battle* (1949). In the 1960s, as TV anime chanced subject matter beyond sci-fi and fantasy, sports involving actual people were first broached with motor-racing in *Speed Racer* (1967) and baseball in *Star of the Giants* (*Kyojin no Hoshi*; 1968). The success of this latter series, in which Hyuma Hoshi rises up the ranks of the real-life team the Yomuri Giants, firmly established the sports genre and many of its key stylistic elements.

The plots of most sports-themed anime are practically indistinguishable. They typically involve an underdog protagonist struggling and eventually succeeding in their chosen sporting area after facing many obstacles including illness and death of loved ones. A tough but inspiring coach and an equally driven and sometimes unscrupulous opponent are also stock characters.

Baseball-themed stories have remained a staple, one of the most

Anime and food

Food crops up a lot in anime, from the simple quest to grow rice in *Tarō the Dragon Boy* to the inedible concoctions that are Lum's alien version of cooking in *Urusei Yatsura*. As in real-life Japan, anime mums and big sisters seem to be forever preparing rice balls (*onigiri*) and lunch boxes (*bentō*) for their husbands and children. For a quick snack you'll often see characters slurping up bowls of *rāmen* (noodles) while at anime festivals there are always stalls selling *okonomiyaki* – a kind of batter, meat and seafood pancake – or *takoyaki* – battered octopus balls.

Yakitate!! Japan (*Freshly Baked!! Japan*; 2004–06) is a jaunty comedy series about boy-baker genius Kazuma Azuma and his dream of creating the perfect Japanese bread (or "Ja-pan", *pan* being the Japanese word for bread). The show is packed with similar puns and parodies of other anime, from *Black Jack* to *Mobile Suit Gundam*. The story arc mimics the conventions of sports anime, with Azuma striving to win in a series of international competitions. It also manages to pack in plenty of information about different styles of baking.

famous being *Touch* (1985) based on the manga by **Mitsuru Adachi**, who also turned to softball and boxing to spice up his high-school comedy romance *Slow Step* (1991). An all-girl baseball team training to compete against the boys in Japan's prestigious National High School Baseball Championship was the twist in *Princess Nine* (1998).

A much-loved **boxing**-themed series from 1970 in Japan is *Tomorrow's Joe* (*Ashita no Joe*; 1970) which follows the genre's conventions down the line with its bad boy made good hero Joe Yabuki. Its director **Osamu Dezaki** (see p.153) would also work on the **tennis** saga *Aim for the Ace* (*Ace o Nerae*, 1973) a series that *Gunbuster* parodied. Tennis racquets were dusted off again in 2001 for *Prince of Tennis* (*Tennis no Ojisama*). Other sports given the anime treatment include baseball in *Slam Dunk* (1994), soccer in *Captain Tsubasa* (1983), and long-distance cycle racing in *Nasu: Summer in Andalucia* (2003).

Martial arts are also a popular inspiration for anime, ranging from the fantasy-style brawling of *Streetfighter II* (1994) and *Fist of the North Star* (1984–87) to more realistic depictions in shows such as *Yawara!* (1989), which substituted judo for tennis in an *Aim for the Ace* format with the heroine aiming for a chance to compete in the 1992 Barcelona Olympics. Life imitated art when sixteen-year-old Ryoko Tamara won a silver medal at the actual Olympic contest, securing the media nickname of Yawara-chan in the process.

It's not all about physical battles. The mental challenges of table-top games are the focus of the dark and violent *Akagi* (2005), in which a thirteen-year-old master of mahjong takes on players in Japan's criminal underworld, as well as the charming *Hikaru-no-Go* (2001), which injects humour and suspense into the world of go, a board game that's a highly sophisticated variation of chequers.

Hikaru-no-Go

dir Shin Nishizawa, Jun Kamiya, Tetsuya Endo, 2001–03, 75 x 23m

Dusting off his grandfather's old go board, schoolboy Hikaru Shindo discovers he's released the tenth-century spirit of master go player Fujiwara no Sai, who won't rest until he's had the chance to play the game's "divine move". Sai persuades a reluctant Hikaru to be his proxy, teaching both the boy and the audience all about the ancient chequers-like game in the process, at the same time as he catches up with twenty-first-century life. It's a very entertaining series with nicely fleshed-out characters including Hikaru's contemporary rivals Akira Toya, the overachieving son of bad-boy player Tetsuo Kaga.

Nasu: Summer in Andalusia

Nasu: Andalusia no Natsu

dir Kitaro Kosaka, 2003, 47m

One of the few anime to be screened at the Cannes Film Festival, *Nasu* is about professional cyclist Pepe who's competing in the Vuelta, a Tour de France-style race across Spain. As a lowly support member of his team, Pepe is facing the sack as the race approaches his home town in the scorched heights of Andalusia, on the very same day his older brother and former fiancée are set to marry. Kosaka, who worked as an animation director at Studio Ghibli, applies the dynamic drawing style of the original manga to heighten the thrill of the climactic race. A sequel, *Nasu: A Migratory Bird with Suitcase* (*Nasu: Suitcase no Wataridori*), was released in 2007.

6

anime impact

beyond Japan – and beyond animation?

Anime has proved itself to be one of the most potent weapons in Japan's "soft power" arsenal. Originally shaped by animation from the US and elsewhere, its images, ideas and stories are now avidly lapped up and emulated abroad. Some anime-inspired shows have even been reworked back in Japan.

This chapter travels along these cross-cultural highways, with pit stops to check out the increasing synergy between anime and computer games, as well as the medium's impact on contemporary art, fashion and theatre.

"Americanime"

From the US to Japan

North America's appetite for anime has caused consternation among some commentators, who believe that producers are now pandering to what this audience wants, rather than hanging on to what is uniquely Japanese about their product – hence diluting its unique selling point. But ever since anime's pioneering days, Japanese animators have taken their cues from across the Pacific.

Tezuka and many of his contemporaries idolized Walt Disney and Max Fleischer and it shows in their drawings, which reflect the simplified lines, enlarged eyes and expressive features of famous American cartoon characters such as Felix the Cat, Betty Boop and Mickey Mouse. Tōei Animation's earliest features also mimicked the Disney formula, albeit with a distinct sensibility when it came to their source material – the use of Asian, rather than European, folk tales.

As the TV anime industry took off in the 1960s, the genre's influences broadened from American animation to American live-action shows such as *Bewitched* and *I Dream of Jeannie*, both of which were hugely popular in Japan and sparked the development of the "magical girl" genre (see p.208). *Star Trek* would also be an inspiration to a generation of anime producers in the 1970s, inter-galactic quests forming the basis of *Space Cruiser Yamato* and other similar series.

Japan's success at making animation on the cheap encouraged US animation studios to subcontract work there, just as Japan does today to more cost-effective studios in South Korea, China and Southeast Asia. Most notably, Rankin/Bass, founded as Videocraft International in the 1960s, engaged **Tadahito Mochinaga** at MOM films to make many of their stop-motion features, including their perennial Christmas favourite *Rudolph the Red-Nosed Reindeer* (1964). Several of Rankin/Bass's cel-animation features, such as *The Hobbit* (1977), *The Return of the King* (1980) and *The Last Unicorn* (1981) were animated by **Topcraft**, founded by ex-Tōei animator Toru Hara in 1972. The skills built up on such projects secured Topcraft the job of animating Miyazaki's *Nausicaä of the Valley of the Wind*. Many Topcraft staff subsequently joined the newly formed Studio Ghibli – the only Japanese studio dedicated to making full animation to the quality of that still produced by Disney.

Subcontracting animation to Japan is still common, recent examples including *Highlander: Search for Vengeance*, made by Madhouse for Hong Kong/US studio IMAGI, and *Batman: Gotham Knight*, made by Studio 4°C, Production I.G and Madhouse for Warner Bros. Tōei are also collaborating with Disney

Anime aesthetics

Manga are drawn in a wide variety of styles, and the anime that are based on them typically reflect this. However, there are certain common design points that have cemented the idea in the public's eye of an overall "anime look". Here are some of the key elements.

• **Big eyes** Copied from US cartoons by the likes of Tezuka and co in the early days of manga and anime, this has become a convention and is typically used to give a character a cute, appealing quality. Characters with small or oriental-looking eyes tend to be less sympathetic, unless there's a decision to make all the characters look more realistically Japanese.

• **Wacky, windblown hair** Anime characters have the wildest hairdos, frequently in totally unnatural colours. This helps to make a character easily recognizable: in *Akira*, for example, where most characters have the regular dark Japanese hair colour, note how identifying different characters requires more attention. Another common feature of hair is how frequently it appears to be ruffled by and flowing with the wind. This effect is used to enhance the realism of the animation and add atmosphere.

• **Sweats and blushes** If an anime character finds themselves in a stressful or embarrassing situation, a couple of things can happen. One is that their faces bristle with big drops of sweat. Second – and this usually involves one or both halves of a couple having romantic feelings for each other – is that their cheeks blush red.

• **Abstract patterns and effects** The speed lines that are used to suggest rapid action in manga, for instance, are often carried through to anime, as are the swirly patterns and sudden appearance of flowers or twinkles in romantic situations and *shōjo*-based shows.

• **Pillow moments** Keep an eye out in anime for the brief cutaway shots from the main action of a story, focusing in on a static or nature-related detail in the scene. Such so-called "pillow moments" are used to add atmosphere and/or a moment of stillness, and are not necessarily a consequence of limited animation.

to make animations for Disney's Japanese satellite TV channel, while Madhouse produce a Japanese version of *Lilo and Stitch*, set in Okinawa.

From Japan to the US

The growing popularity of Japanese pop culture, and anime in particular, in the US in the 1980s and 1990s has dramatically shifted the artistic relationship in Japan's favour. Entranced by anime's distinctive look, US animators began to pay homage in their own works.

Blossom, Bubbles, and Buttercup – a.k.a. the *Powerpuff Girls*, created by Craig McCracken in 1998 for Hanna-Barbera – owe their cute looks and super-powers partly to anime such as *Sailor Moon*, as well as to the live-action Japanese show *Super Sentai* with its cast of colour-coded superheroes fighting a variety of villains and monsters. Proving that the pop-cultural superhighway continues to flow in both directions, in 2006 came the debut of *Demashita! Powerpuff Girls Z*, an anime based on the US series.

Animation director on the *Powerpuff Girls* movie was Genndy Tartakovsky, a Russian-born, US-based animator who also openly acknowledges his artistic debt to anime. This is most obvious in his show *Samurai Jack* (2001–04) which, apart from samurai and martial arts films, also displays stylistic influences from classic anime such as **Tōei**'s 1963 feature *Little Prince and the Eight Headed Dragon*. The series also explicitly references *Lone Wolf and Cub* by having the hit manga's main characters (Ogami Itto and Daigoro) cameo in one episode.

Hollywood's most famous anime fans are Andy and Larry Wachowski, who, off the back of their anime-inspired *Matrix* trilogy, commissioned *The Animatrix*. Comprised of nine animated shorts, of which seven were directed by Japanese animators, it became one of the biggest selling anime DVDs ever. Fellow cinema über-geek **Quentin Tarantino**, a big fan of *Ghost in the Shell* and *Blood*, commissioned Production I.G to make *The Origin of O-Ren* sequence of *Kill Bill: Vol. 1*.

While the anime roots of US shows such as *Avatar: The Last Airbender* are clear, the creative relationship between the two countries has become so intertwined that for some projects it's difficult to pinpoint on which side of the Pacific the initial inspiration comes from. The hip-hop-infused *Afro Samurai* started life as a *dōjinshi* manga in 1999, but it was American money and the

Anime goes live

Just as sophisticated CGI effects have made it possible to render faithful adaptations of US comics such as *Batman*, *Spiderman* and *X-Men*, so too are anime being given the live- action treatment – although just how "live" such movies are, given the level of special effects used, is a moot point.

Tezuka Osamu's grizzly 1960s manga and anime *Dororo*, about a cursed warrior and his accomplice, a young female thief, was made into a live-action movie in 2007, as was *Mushi-shi*, directed by no lesser a figure than Katsuhiro Ōtomo. Hideaki Anno has directed a live-action version of Go Nagai's *Cutie Honey*. In 2009 Japanese indie movie maker Takeshi Mikii presented his take on *Yatterman* (www.yatterman-movie.com), a hit kids' TV show from the late 1970s, in Tatsunoko Production's *Time Bokan* series, famous for its giant dog-shaped robot.

Following the success of the live-action *Transformers* in 2007, Hollywood is also getting in on the act. The Wachowski brothers' latest project is *Speed Racer* (speedracerthemovie.warnerbros.com), which mixes live-action and spectacular CGI effects to re-create the iconic 1960s anime. *Dragonball*, directed by James Wong and scheduled for release in 2009 brings to life Goku, anime's favourite martial arts fighter.

Possible upcoming projects include a live-action *Robotech* (made by Tobey Maguire's production company), while Leonardo di Caprio has his sights set on a live-action *Akira*. The motorcycle-tyre-burning action will be shifted to New-Manhattan and six volumes of Ōtomo's manga will be covered in two films, the first scheduled for a summer 2009 release. Steven Spielberg's Dreamworks have also licensed the rights to make a live-action version of *Ghost in the Shell*.

star power of **Samuel L. Jackson** that got the Gonzo-animated show premiered on Spike TV in the US before it hit screens in Japan.

The angelic gothic-Lolita-styled heroine of the English-language manga *Princess Ai* is the co-creation of manga-loving rock diva Courtney Love, who worked with TOKYOPOP's CEO Stuart Levy (under his pseudonym DJ Milky) and Japanese manga artists Ai Yazawa and Misaho Kujiradō on the concept. *Princess Ai* is now being adapted into a series combining animation with live action by Japanese studio Satelight (www.satelight.co.jp).

Lasseter on Miyazaki

John Lasseter, founder of Pixar, makers of the CG animation mega-hits *Toy Story*, *Finding Nemo*, *The Incredibles* and *Ratatouille*, is a huge fan of Studio Ghibli films and in particular those of Hayao Miyazaki. On the Disney-issued US DVDs of Studio Ghibli's films he usually pops up to provide an introduction and is sometimes seen with Miyazaki himself. Here's what he had to say about how Miyazaki's work has influenced his:

"At Pixar, when we have a problem and we can't seem to solve it, we often take a laser disc of one of Miyazaki's films and look at a scene in our screening room for a shot of inspiration and it always works! We come away amazed and inspired. *Toy Story* owes a huge debt of gratitude to the films of Miyazaki."

The Animatrix

dir Kōji Morimoto, Shinichirō Watanabe, Yoshiaki Kawajiri, Mahiro Maeda, Takeshi Koike, Peter Chung, Andy Jones, 2002, 102m

Want to know how computers got the upper hand and humans ended up becoming the batteries that power the Matrix? The visually dazzling two-part short *Second Renaissance*, directed by Mahiro Maeda, explains all and is a highlight of this compendium of nine stylistically different animated shorts – all inspired by *The Matrix* and directed by some of the established and rising stars of anime. Four of the segments were written by the brothers Wachowski. The DVD includes a short documentary on the history of anime; the official website is www.intothematrix.com.

Afro Samurai

Afuro Samurai

dir Fuminori Kizaki, Jamie Simone, 2006, 5 x 25m

Knowingly hip and ultra violent, this short-run series was produced by Samuel L. Jackson, who also provides the voice of the lead character, a badass dude with a mother of an Afro. It's an example of how the US popularity of anime is influencing the artistic direction of the medium. These samurai may use mobile phones and groove away to the hip-hop score of RZA, but they can still wield a sword to gory effect when it counts – which is pretty much most of the time. A condensed movie version was released in 2007, and a second series is planned. For more details see www.afrosamurai.com.

Japanese warriors go hip-hop, with a little help from Samuel L. Jackson, in *Afro Samurai*

European influences

Great **Russian animators**, such as Lev Atamatov and Youri Norstein, are hugely respected in Japan. At the start of his career at Tōei in the early 1960s, a frustrated Hayao Miyazaki considered throwing in the towel. It was seeing Atamatov's beautiful 1957 feature *The Snow Queen*, based on the Hans Christian Anderson story, that restored his faith in the power of animation as an art form.

The Snow Queen also directly influenced aspects of Isao Takahata's *The Little Norse Prince* (see Canon), as well as later shows of his such as *Heidi*. Norstein and Alexander Petrov were among the non-Japanese animators invited to contribute segments to *Winter Days* (*Fuyu no Hi*, 2003), an arty compilation film on which Takahata also worked.

When Miyazaki and Isao Takahata left Tōei in 1971 to join the studio A-Pro, one of the first projects they tried (unsuccessfully) to make was

The gaijin are coming

With the Japanese government now sponsoring the International Manga Award for overseas artists working in the medium, it's clear that a Japanese passport is no longer essential for those wanting to create manga. However, in anime the situation is not so simple. Its arbiters are not so laissez faire: the *Anime Encyclopedia*'s authors Jonathan Clements and Helen McCarthy class anime as being "animation from Japan, with a high number of Japanese creatives working in the upper echelons of production: director, writer, designer, key animators and music."

Even so, anime studios are far from shy about gathering overseas funding for their shows, or directly harnessing the talents of *gaijin* (non-Japanese) creatives. This has most commonly been in the area of music and occasionally voice acting for releases primarily aimed at the overseas market. Characters' designs for Madhouse's 1999 series *Reign: The Conqueror* (also known as *Alexander*) were provided by Korean-American Peter Chung, who was later one of the *gaijin* contributing a segment to *The Animatrix*.

In 2007 TV Asahi started screening the kids' anime *Hatarakizzu Maihamu-gumi* (*Master Hamsters*), about five young rodents who transform into a carpenter, a firefighter, a doctor, a pastry chef and a racing driver for a variety of missions. Made by Tōei, the show's creator and producer is Gyarmath Bogdan, who grew up watching subtitled anime in his native Romania.

Tekkon Kinkreet (see Canon), directed by Michael Arias, has a screenplay by Anthony Weintraub and music by the British electronic group Plaid. Arias first came to Japan from the US to develop software used in *Princess Mononoke* (and in nearly every Studio Ghibli feature since) to give 3D CG animation the appearance of traditional 2D cel animation. He also acted as producer on the Studio 4°C segments of *The Animatrix*.

an adaptation of the popular Swedish children's book *Pippi Longstocking*. Miyazaki visited Sweden and later went to the Alps, Italy and elsewhere in Europe while working on other *World Masterpiece Theater* (see p.16) shows with Takahata. Miyazaki films such as *Castle in the Sky*, *Kiki's Delivery Service* and *Porco Rosso*, dip into this well of European inspiration.

The characters, plots and sci-fi machinery of Gerry and Sylvia Anderson puppet shows such as *Thunderbirds* and *Captain Scarlet* hailing from the UK in the 1960s impacted on the team-of-five hero concept of series such as *Skyers 5* (1967 & 1971), *Zero Tester* (1973) and *Gatchaman*, not to mention being more directly replicated in *Thunderbirds 2086* (1982). In the 1970s, *Marine Boy* was the UK's principal exposure to anime, although few of its tea-time fans knew it as such.

Meanwhile, across **continental Europe** anime was becoming a staple of childrens' television via straight imports such as Go Nagai's robot show *Grandizer*, better known to its French and Spanish fans as *Goldorak*, and shows including *Maya the Bee*, *Ulysses 31*, *The Mysterious Cities of Gold*, *Sherlock Hound* and *Dogtanian and the Three Muskerhounds*, all joint works between studios in Japan and TV production houses, respectively, in Germany, France, Italy and Spain. France, in particular, with its strong culture of comics (what they call *bande dessinée*) has a high regard for anime and co-productions continue to this day. One of the latest is the Rintarō-directed film *Yona Yona Penguin*, a mix of 3D and 2D animation made jointly by Japan's Madhouse and France's Denis Friedman Productions.

In one of the most left-field of European co-productions, the **Vatican**, via the Italian national broadcaster RAI, requested in 1984 that Osamu Tezuka make an anime version of Bible stories. Tezuka had already drawn a manga version of Old Testament parables and worked for a couple of years on a pilot featuring Noah. The 26-episode series *In the Beginning*, first broadcast in 1992, was completed by Osamu Dezaki after Tezuka's premature death.

Ulysses 31

Uchū Densetsu Ulysses 31

dir Bernard Deyriès, Tadao Nagahama, 1981–82, 26 x 24m

Homer's *Odyssey* gets run through the anime mill and re-emerges in this imaginative French-Japanese co-production that was a hit across Europe. The setting is now outer space in the thirty-first century, where intergalactic hero Ulysses is forced to kill the Cyclops on the planet of Troy in order to rescue his son, thus upsetting the gods and initiating the series' long quest for the Kingdom of Hades. Alongside the cast of Greek original characters are Ulysses' new companions on the spaceship *Odyssey*: Yumi, a blue-skinned alien girl, and the nail-eating mini-robot Nono.

Mysterious Cities of Gold

Taiyō no Ko Esuteban

dir Edouard David, Bernard Deyriès, Kenichi Maruyama, Kenichi Murakami, 1982–83, 39 x 25m

DiC Entertainment teamed up with Studio Pierrot to make this adventure series that combined historical fantasy, sci-fi and a dash of education. It's 1532 and young mariner Estaban sails to the New World in search of treasure and his lost father. There he encounters not only Central and South American

The Ghibli Museum library collection

Hayao Miyazaki and Isao Takahata wear their love of European animation and storytelling on their sleeves. As a way of introducing the Japanese public to some of the European arthouse gems that have inspired them, Studio Ghibli has created the **Ghibli Museum Library Collection** (www.ghibli-museum.jp/library) to distribute foreign animation in Japan, both theatrically and on DVD. Among the titles so far released are Aleksandr Petrov's *My Love*; Michel Ocelot's *Azur et Asmar*; Paul Grimault's *Le Roi et l'Oiseau* and Lev Atamatov's *The Snow Queen*.

tribes such as the Inca, Mayans and Olmecs but also the lost technologically advanced empire of Mu. Each of the episodes screened in Japan concluded with a mini live-action documentary about the various historical themes covered in the series.

Heidi

Alps no Shōjo Heidi

dir Isao Takahata, 1974, 52 x 25m

Based on Johanna Spyri's much-loved children's book, *Heidi* is about an eight-year-old orphan who shuttles between her grandpa's house in the Alps and her aunt's home in Frankfurt where she befriends the disabled Klara. Takahata's enchanting production proved so successful on its initial broadcast in Japan that it trumped *Space Ship Yamato* in the TV ratings and created a boom in Japanese tourism to the Swiss Alps. In its wake followed the annual *World Masterpiece Theatre* series of children's classics.

Sherlock Hound

Meitantei Holmes

dir Hayao Miyazaki, Kyosuke Mikuriya, 1984–85, 26 x 25m

Conan Doyle's characters are depicted as dogs in this fun series, a co-production between Tokyo Movie Shinsha and Italian TV station RAI. Bearing the unmistakable touch of Miyazaki, there are car-chases and aerial scenes. Mrs Hudson, who in the original stories is a dowdy middle-aged housekeeper, is transformed into one of Miyazaki's spunky young heroines. Miyazaki directed the first six episodes in 1981 before a copyright dispute with Conan Doyle's estate put the series on hold until 1984, by which time he'd moved on to new projects.

The Asian connection

South Korea is the third largest producer of animation worldwide (after the US and Japan), a position achieved because of patronage of its industry by, among others, anime studios. This was despite Korea banning all Japanese cultural products, including anime, until as recently as 1998, because of anti-Japanese feelings following World War II.

Ways around the ban included dubbing anime into Korean and stripping it of all Japanese references before being broadcast, or just making a Korean copy of the original; for example, the giant robot anime *Mazinger Z* served as the template for the incredibly similar Korean show *Robot Taekwon V*. After the ban was lifted, more direct cooperation was possible, to the point where today there's something of a boom in such projects. *Winter Sonata*, a Korean live-action soap opera that was a huge success in Japan, is being made into an anime.

Seoul-based DR Movie (www.drmovie.biz) is partly owned by **Madhouse** and has worked with them, **Production I.G**, gonzo and Studio Ghibli on a variety of projects. These include *Spirited Away*; *Metropolis*; the ill-received *Reign: The Conquerer*, a 1999 sci-fi reworking of the life of Alexander the Great, for which Korean-born American animator **Peter Chung** (who made the anime-influenced series and movie *Aeon Flux* as well as a segment of *The Animatrix*) provided the main character designs; and *Robotech: The Shadow Chronicles*, the 2007 instalment of the popular franchise (see Canon). To find out more about South Korean animation go to www.koreacontent.org, the website of the Korea Culture & Content Agency (KOCCA).

China holds the title of producing Asia's first (and only the world's third) feature-length cartoon, *Princess Iron Fan*, directed by brothers Wan Guchang and Wan Laiming in Japanese-controlled Shanghai in 1941. This achievement spurred the Japanese military government into sponsoring a home-grown feature to restore honour. It also inspired Osamu Tezuka, who saw the film when he was a teenager and went on to adapt its source material – the classical Chinese novel *Journey to the West* (see p.203) – in manga and anime form.

In the immediate post-war years, and then after the Cultural Revolution, Japanese stop-motion animators **Tadahito Mochinaga** and **Kihachiro Kawamoto** both worked with China's premier animation studio, the Shanghai Animation Film

Studio. Cheap labour means that many anime are now partly made in China: Tezuka Productions has a studio in Beijing, for example.

Hong Kong's re-absorption back into China has provided access to the former British colony's powerhouse film community. The most notable results of this are the CG productions by **IMAGI** (www.imagi.com.hk) of two anime classics: *Gatchaman* and *Astro Boy*.

This first co-production between **India** and Japan had long been the dream of Japanese documentary filmmaker **Yugo Sako**. It took a whole decade to bring his anime version of the sacred Hindu text *Ramayana* to the screen, because of the need to assuage religious sensitivities and train up an army of local animators. Sako hired India's most respected animator Ram Mohan to co-direct and design the film's key art.

Highlander: Search for Vengeance

dir Yoshiaki Kawajiri, 2007, 80m

Animated in Japan by Madhouse, with funding from Hong Kong/US company IMAGI, this is part of a new breed of anime, such as *Afro Samurai* and *Vampire Hunter D Bloodlust* (also directed by Kawajiri), that have been made specifically with English-speaking markets in mind. Kawajiri brings his usual sex-and-violence panache to this gorgeously animated film about the immortal Colin McCloud, out for revenge against fellow Roman immortal Marcus Octavius for killing his wife millennia ago. Sadly, the script is packed with cheesy lines and trite plotting.

The Prince of Light: The Legend of Ramayana

Rāmayāna: Rāma-Ōji Densetsu

dir Ram Mohan, Yugo Sako, 1998, 96m

Also known simply as *Ramayana*, this Indian/Japanese co-production cherry-picks some of the most exciting and anime-worthy episodes from the epic Hindu legend. Brave Prince Ram is joined by his faithful brother Lakshman and the monkey god Hanuman on a quest to rescue his wife, the beautiful Sita, from the demon king Ravan. The visuals are an appealing blend of anime and Indian artistic styles. The website is www.princeoflightmovie.com.

Kihachiro Kawamoto Film Works

Kihachiro Kawamoto Sakuhinshu

dir Kihachiro Kawamoto, 2002, 151m

Kihachiro Kawamoto is one of the leading stop-motion animators in Japan. This showcase collection of eleven of his beautifully atmospheric works includes *To Shoot Without Shooting* (1988) a co-production with Shanghai Animation Film Studio about a Chinese archer striving to improve his skill, and the Brothers Grimm-style fairy tale *Briar Rose* (1990), made with Trnka Studios in Prague, where Kawamoto first learned his stop-motion craft.

Toys and video games

The commercial synergy between anime, toys and other merchandising dates back to the days of Suihō Tagawa's manga character Norakuro, the star of several pre-World War II shorts (see p.5). Tezuka cashed in on *Astro Boy*'s TV success with licensing deals that saw the boy robot's image used on a host of merchandise, quite apart from the predictable toy copies. Decades later, the world is awash with products based on anime, from Pokémon video games to cuddly copies of Totoro.

One anime toy blockbuster has been **transforming robots**. They had been around a while, featuring for example in the original *Macross* series (see Canon), before the US toy giant Hasbro provided scripts and toy designs that resulted in the original *Transformers* series in 1985, animated by Tōei. This US-Japanese co-production would become one of the most successful anime franchises of all time, as well as a goldmine for transforming-robot toy sales. Two decades down the line the appeal of the basic concept remains strong, its popularity boosted by the CGI/live-action feature *Transformers*, directed by Michael Bay in 2007.

As **computer games** took off in the 1980s, many anime studios and their staff seized the opportunity to put their skills to use in another medium. In turn, computer-game hits such as *Super Mario Brothers*, *Streetfighter II* and *Pokémon* were an inspiration for anime. Tie-in concepts proliferated in much the same symbiotic way that robot shows had grown hand in hand with a blitz in robot toys.

Now there are even shows such as *.Hack// Sign,* which is an anime about an online role-playing game, that has a real-world game tie-in. It's got to the point where it's becoming nearly as common for an anime to be originally based on a computer game idea as a manga.

With far better financial rewards on offer within the gaming industry, the flow of creative talent is heading that way rather than towards anime studios, where pay has traditionally been poor. The inevitable result has been a series of business deals that have seen gaming companies either taking over or acquiring stakes in anime studios, such as Namco teaming up with Bandai, and Takara's buyout of Tatsunoko.

Final Fantasy: The Spirits Within

dir Sakaguchi Hironobu, 2001, 106m

Can this really be called anime? It has its roots in the Japanese video role-playing game and is directed by the game's creator Hironobu

Sakaguchi. However, it was made in Hawaii with US money and a production cast stacked with non-Japanese talent, technically making it an American rather than Japanese product. Breaking ground with state-of-the-art CGI animation, the movie nonetheless bombed at the box office, losing over $120million, proving that Sakaguchi should have stuck to game design. However, all that CGI development work would pay off in the improved visuals of subsequent computer games and other effects-enhanced Hollywood epics.

.Hack // Sign

dir Kōichi Mashimo, 2002, 26 x 25m

Those into online role-playing games (RPGs) will enjoy this leisurely paced series more than most; character development is emphasized over action. Pronounced Dot Hack Sign, it's about a online RPG called *The World* that sucks in the kids that play it, refusing to let them log out. Developed by Bandai and CyberConnect2, the series is part of a package that includes a PlayStation 2 game, a series of straight-to-video anime, a manga and a novel. Its success ensured several follow-up series including 2006's *.hack//ROOTS.*

Anime, art and fashion

The popular arts of anime and manga are increasingly being taken seriously by high art institutions and granted major exhibitions, such as *Little Boy: The Arts of Japan's Exploding Subcultures* in New York in 2005. Tezuka's artwork has been the subject of several exhibitions, both in and out of Japan, and in 2007, when the dreamlike and beautifully detailed background art of Kazuo Oga for Studio Ghibli's films was displayed in Tokyo's Museum of Contemporary Art, over 200,000 people attended during its 66 days.

The curator of the *Little Boy* exhibition was **Takeshi Murakami**, one of Japan's most respected and successful contemporary artists. Born in 1962, Murakami is a child of the anime age, inspired by series such as Leiji Matsumoto's *Galaxy Express 999* and Gainax's DAIKON shorts. His *Time Bokan* series reworks the familiar image from the same-named anime of the atomic mushroom cloud crossed with a skull and serves as an ironic critique on Japanese culture's determination to find something cute about the ultimate war symbol.

Murakami is not the only contemporary Japanese artist who dips into the anime/manga well for inspiration: works by Yoshitomo Nara and Chiho Aoshima share similar pop cultural inspiration. In 2008 Hisashi Tenmyouya's painting *RX-78-2 Kabuki-mono 2005 Version*, featuring a mobile suit robot from *Mobile Suit Gundam* on a background of gold leaf, was sold at an auction in Hong Kong for HK$4.8 million ($615,000).

In 2000 Murakami drew up a manifesto coining the word **superflat** to describe art such as his, inspired

The "Magnetic Rose" section of *Memories*, directed by Kōji Morimoto

by the two-dimensional style and prettified images of anime and the fetishized objects of a generation of otaku or obsessive fans (see p.271). The concept struck a chord, and has been used to categorize the more avant-garde style of some artists working within anime, such as **Kōji Morimoto** of Studio 4°C (who directed the "Magnetic Rose" section of *Memories* and a segment of *The Animatrix*, as well as supervising the animation of *Mind Game* and *Tekkon Kinkreet*).

Murakami's anime-inspired designs grace a range of Louis Vuitton products, evidence not just of the artist's Andy Warhol-like philosophy of art as a commodity, but also of how anime both influences and is influenced by **fashion**. Key characters in series such as *Rozen*

Maiden (2002) and *Le Portrait de Petit Cossette* adopt the Japanese street look called **Gothic Lolita**, influenced by Victorian-era fashion, the campy costumes of Japanese rock bands and froufrou of the 1980s New Romantic genre of music. In turn, the anime reinterpretation is reflected in cosplay costumes (see p.269).

Le Portrait de Petit Cossette

Cossette no Shozo

dir Akiyuki Shinbo, 2004, 3 x 38m

So what if little Cossette's fashions are all wrong for late eighteenth-century France? The girl whose spirit returns to claim the soul of her murderer now living inside sensitive twenty-first-century art student Eiri has a Goth Loli look straight from the streets of Harajuku, Tokyo's teen-fashion Mecca. The plot of this three-part series is loopy but rich on suspenseful atmosphere and trippy eye-candy visuals that frequently turn as surreal as a Salvador Dalí painting.

AMVs

Original anime has been created for music videos such as French group Daft Punk's collaboration with Leiji Matsumoto and Studio Ghibli's clip for the Japanese pop duo Chage and Aska. Britney Spears also hijacked many images from the *Ghost in the Shell* franchise for the animated clip for her song "Break the Ice". However, by far the most common anime music videos (AMVs) are those created by fans who have spliced together clips of their favourite anime to accompany a particular piece of music.

Although making an AMV from media you own for private consumption is considered okay, distributing it via YouTube and other similar file-sharing sites plunges creators into the legally grey area of copyright violation. Despite this, you'll find thousands of AMVs on the internet, and AMV competitions are held at many anime conventions. Copyright holders often hold off prosecution for the same reasons that dōjinshi manga are tolerated (see p.183), namely that AMVs can be seen as a form of unpaid promotion for their properties and to avoid a backlash from the most committed of anime fans. This said, music rights holders have been more aggressive in pursuing their copyright, forcing some hosting sites to remove offending AMVs.

If you want to find out more, **Anime Music Video.org** (www.animemusicvideos.org) offers plenty of tips on making AMVs, details on AMV contests and a good selection of links to other sites with information on this area.

Stage musicals

The profound impact of the **Takarazuka Revue** (kageki.hankyu.co.jp) on the development of *shōjo* (girls) manga and anime is well documented. Osamu Tezuka grew up in Takarazuka, the town in which railway magnate Ichizō Kobayashi founded an all-female theatrical company in 1914. His mother was a huge fan of Takarazuka's lavish, Broadway-style shows and apart from taking her son to see them, often had actress friends babysit him. This early exposure to the razzle-dazzle of showbiz and Takarazuka's cross-dressing heroes led to the creation of *Princess Knight*, Tezuka's seminal *shōjo* manga, and later anime, in which the heroine is disguised as a prince.

Princess Knight's success established the genre, and many of the conventions,

Tezuka's *Black Jack*: perhaps not the first thing you'd think of turning into a stage musical. Then again...

of girls' manga – eventually leading to one of its most beloved creations, the French Revolution-set, cross-dressing saga *Rose of Versailles*. The manga was adapted by Takarazuka to become one of their signature shows, five years before the anime version appeared. The theatre company has also mounted productions of other Tezuka manga that were turned into anime, including *Black Jack* and *Phoenix*.

Thousands of young girls apply annually to join the company at the age of sixteen and become a Takarasienne. After a year's studying together they are divided into those who will perform the male roles (*otokoyaku*) and those who remain female (*musumeyaku*). *Otokoyaku* cut their hair short and act like men, even speaking in the masculine form of Japanese, both on and off stage.

Takarazuka's success with stage versions of anime and manga have prompted other producers to take a punt on this material. Among the shows out there yet to make it to Broadway or the West End are ones based on *The Prince of Tennis, Sailor Moon, Naruto,* the basketball saga *Slam Dunk* and even the supernatural chiller *Bleach,* which has spawned an incredible five (and counting) rock musicals since 2005.

7

Anime information

where to go next

Once you've caught the anime bug, you'll want to dig deeper into the fascinating history, context and meanings of the medium. This chapter is your roadmap for further exploration, pinpointing the prime locations for watching or buying anime and associated memorabilia, as well as the pick of the books, magazines and websites to read.

Taking it to the next level, there's also the lowdown on the major fan conventions (cons), cosplay, and places you'll want to visit should you make it to Japan, the ultimate anime destination.

Audiovisual: TV, VOD and rental

It's no secret that the majority of anime fans download their favourite shows online – legally or otherwise. It's a change that is surely coming to all kinds of TV and film content, as digital delivery of media becomes standardized around the world. Signs of the times include the Sony-owned satellite channel **Animax** (www.animax-asia.com), a round-the-clock network dedicated to anime, which operates across much of Asia, and in parts of Europe and Africa and Latin America. One of its newer services is Animax Mobile, streaming anime to mobile phones in either full episodes or bite-sized portions of between five and seven minutes; so far the service is available in Australia, Canada, Hong Kong and Taiwan. Peer-to-peer (P2P) applications, such as **BitTorrent** (see box opposite), are also getting into the online digital entertainment business, distributing anime both for free and for a fee, as are Microsoft through their game console **Xbox** (www.x-box.com) to which you can download anime directly.

However, anime on either network or cable TV is far from dead. Popular shows, both new releases and classics, are always being picked up for transmission. Practically all channels have online sites and on some of them it's possible to watch **video on demand** (VOD), either for free (supported by ads) or for a rental fee. Similar VOD services are also being offered by the major DVD **rental** sites such as Netflix in the US, and Lovefilm .com in the UK, as well as through Amazon Unboxed and Mac's iTunes TV service.

A warning before you dive in. So far, it has been common for VOD to have **digital rights management** (DRM) encryption which bars digital downloads being copied. There have been instances where DRM videos have errors and have stopped allowing playback. Also, as of the time of research, Mac users can only use iTunes as their download service – Amazon Unboxed, Netflix, and all other forms of DRM videos are tied to Microsoft Windows and will not play on Macs or on the iPhone. DRM protection may eventually disappear from video, as it is doing for music downloads. The situation is in flux, so it pays to do some online research before deciding which way to view anime is best for you.

The US and Canada

The first click on the remote for most US-based anime fans is the adult-oriented cartoon channel **Adult Swim** (www.adultswim.com), sharing space with the **Cartoon Network** (www.cartoonnetwork.com), the cable home of anime hits such as *Pokémon* and *Naruto*. Some of its programming, including anime, is available free via **Adult Swim Video**, an ad-supported streaming VOD site. Note that Adult Swim channels outside of the US tend not to screen as much anime.

More anime programming can be found on the cable channels **IFC** (www.ifc.com), **Imaginasian** (www.iatv.tv) and **Starz Edge** (www.starz.com). *Digimon* and *Hello Kitty* screen on **Toon Disney** (psc.disney.go.com/abcnetworks/toondisney/index.html). **G4TechTV** (www.g4techtv.ca) provides fans in **Canada** with their anime fix. For comprehensive weekly listings of what's showing on all these channels and more, go to www.animenewsnetwork.com.

A couple of the major anime licensing companies that have moved into programming are ADV, with their **Anime Network** (www.theanimenet-

BitTorrent

There's no denying the impact that **BitTorrent** (www.bittorrent.com) and other peer-to-peer (P2P) file-sharing systems have had, and are continuing to have, on anime distribution (see box overleaf). BitTorrent is a protocol designed for transferring files that enables users to connect to each other directly to send and receive portions of the file. To use BitTorrent you first have to download the free program from the company's website. You then search the web for a "torrent file" of the anime – or any other video, game or piece of music you're after – which, when found, causes the program to download from other online users of BitTorrent.

Because of its role in enabling piracy of media content, BitTorrent was initially hounded by the film and music industries. However, its runaway success established the business conditions for a legitimate company that officially licenses content from rights holders to be distributed via BitTorrent's own website. Go there and you'll find anime that you can either watch for free, rent or buy for as little as $1.99 per episode. The same is true for similar services such as **Vuze** (www.vuze.com) and **iTunes** (www.apple.com/itunes), the only download option so far to offer VOD media playable on either Macs or personal computers.

work.com), which also screens non-ADV licensed shows and **Funimation** with **Funimation Channel** (www.funimationchannel.com).

Joining a **DVD rental service** such as **Netflix** (www.netflix.com), **Blockbuster** (www.blockbuster.com), the dedicated **Rent Anime.com** (www.rentanime.com), or **Zip** (www.zip.ca) in Canada, is a good idea to gain access to vast libraries of anime beyond the financial reach of all but the wealthiest and most committed of fans.

The UK

Anime Central (www.animecentral.com) offers a substantial wedge of anime programming from the evening to the early morning daily on Sky Channel 199. Other cable channels hosting anime include **Rockworld TV** (www.rockworld.tv) and **Jetix**

Fansubs and illegal downloads

A fansub, short for fan subtitled, is when a fan or group of fans subtitle an anime into English or another language, for distribution among themselves and the wider public. It's a practice that dates from the early days of video technology when relatively little anime was licensed for distribution overseas and fans wanting to see the show that their Japanese counterparts were raving about had few options other than to take matters into their own hands.

Fansubbing is illegal but was largely tolerated partly because there was only a limited number of copies that could be made of a subtitled video tape. It was also useful to rights holders in that it spread a taste for anime among a foreign audience with the side benefit of providing cost-free test-marketing of which titles were the most popular – identifying the prime candidates to be legitimately subtitled and distributed. There was also a very loosely interpreted code of ethics among fansubbers: that producing fansubs was not a commercial enterprise (therefore the service should be free to all users) and a title would be withdrawn from distribution once a legitimately licensed version became available.

The dawn of the broadband digital age, however, has turned fansubbing into the industry's Pandora's box. What started as a handful of fans sharing a subtitled video has grown into literally millions of digitized packets of anime whizzing their way around the world courtesy of file-sharing P2P progams such as BitTorrent. Via this protocol alone, it's believed that six million copies of illegal, English-subtitled Japanese ani-

(www.jetix.co.uk). You might occasionally catch anime on the **Film Four** (www.filmfour.com) and **Sci-Fi** (www.scifi.co.uk) channels as well as terrestrial channels such as the BBC.

Among several major online DVD rental sites is **LoveFilm.com** (www.lovefilm.com) which has over 600 anime titles on its books, some available for immediate download.

Australia

In Australia, the main DVD rental site is **Bigpond Movies** (www.bigpondmovies.com) which carries over two thousand anime titles.

Anime often shows up on the terrestrial channel SBS and Animax's VOD channel is available on the 3 mobile phone network (www.three.com.au).

mated videos are downloaded each week, according to a report presented in February 2008 by the Japanese government's Task Force on Media Content Business and Japanese Brands. Currently the tiniest percentage of this traffic is actually being paid for.

All this is having serious financial repercussions on the current business model of anime. With DVD sales plummeting, it just doesn't make sense for overseas distributors to pay the kind of fees they once did to Japanese rights holders for titles that consumers are already downloading, illegally, for free via the internet. Those large fees coupled with low sales volumes means that DVDs have also tended to be priced at a point beyond the pocket of the average fan, which – in a vicious circle – sends fans back to the internet, searching for files of the very latest anime from Japan that typically would take months for overseas distributors to get onto the market.

With the writing on the wall for DVDs, anime studios in Japan and licensors in the US and elsewhere are dipping their toes into VOD. GDH, the parent company of Gonzo have inked deals with YouTube, BOST TV and Crunchyroll to offer a couple of their anime on a pay-what-you want basis, known as "open-pricing". Others are making some of their shows available at reasonable prices, generally around $1.99 per episode. It's likely that free, advertising-supported anime VOD will also be another route trialled. Fansubs are never going to disappear entirely, but for fans who would prefer not to break the law to see a subtitled or dubbed show the options are continually widening.

Bootleg alert

It is a sad fact that many fans fall foul of **bootleg copies** of anime DVDs and CDs bought over the internet. Taiwan and Hong Kong, in particular, pour out truck loads of illegal merchandise with amazing speed, and in packaging which looks completely professional, sometimes even more so than the legal packaging. Many fans run across these for sale online and, mistaking them for the real thing, order boxes of their favourite series which arrive only to turn out to have subtitles written by people who barely know English. Suspect DVDs can usually be spotted by a few telltale characteristics:

- they are coded Region All instead of region 1 or region 2
- they have no English dub track
- they have English and Chinese subtitles
- the Japanese logo appears larger than the English logo in the art.

Bootleg CDs are almost impossible to detect since they intentionally duplicate the packaging of the official releases; the only way to tell is to look up the company that put out the original and make sure its name is on a CD before you buy it, since the bootleggers have their own corporate names that they put on their CDs in place of the official ones. The vast majority of Japanese anime soundtracks for sale at conventions, in US stores and online are these bootlegs which are also usually much cheaper than legal Japanese discs, averaging $15 each instead of $25–35.

The only way to be 100 percent certain of getting legal CDs is to order through a reputable company such as Right Stuf or, for CDs released in Japan, from reliable internet shops, notably CDJapan, AnimeNation (www.animenation.com) and Amazon.jp.

portable digital media

DVD sales are declining, under attack not just from next generation portable media such as Blu-ray but also online downloads. Anime is particularly hard hit with distributors in flux as this guide is written. **Geneon**, one the largest anime companies in the US, shut up shop in 2007 and another big gun ADV has undergone realignment of its business both in the US and UK.

Still, for the time being, DVDs remain the best way for a committed fan to collect their favourite anime. Savvy licensees are rising to the rising to the challenge by offering value added packages including credible extras and professional packaging. Also, don't throw out that VCR yet – some shows that were released originally on **video** back in the 1980s and 1990s have either yet to surface on DVD or are never going to anyway. Start hunting for rarities on eBay and via specialist anime shopping sites.

The **US and Canada** have the largest number of anime distributors. These include: **ADV Films** (www.advfilms.com); **Animeigo** (www.animeigo.com); **Bandai Entertainment** (www.Bandai-ent.com); **Bandai Visual** (www.bandaivisual.us); **Central Park Media** (www.centralparkmedia.com) which has both the *US Manga Corp* and *Anime Today* labels; **Discotek** (www.discotekmedia.com); **Disney** (disney.go.com/disneyvideos/animatedfilms) for most of Studio Ghibli's movies including those by Hayao Miyazaki and Isao Takahata; **Funimation** (www.funimation.com); **Manga** (www.manga.com); **Media Blasters** (www.media-blasters.com); **Right Stuf** (www.rightstuf.com); **Sony Pictures** (www.sonypictures.com) and **Viz Media** (www.viz.com). Right Stuf is a fan favourite place to buy DVDs from all sources since they often have the best prices and occasionally hold fire sales of older material.

In the **UK,** ADV Films has struck a deal to have its titles sold via **Lace Digital Media** (www.lacedigitalmediasales.com). There's also **Bandai** (www.bandai.co.uk), **Manga** (www.manga.com), **Optimum Releasing** (www.optimumreleasing.com) which handles all the Studio Ghibli titles plus a few other feature-film anime, and **MVM Entertainment** (www.mvm-films.com) which supplies all anime DVDs currently available in the UK and runs the shopping site Anime-on-Line (www.anime-on-line.com). In **Australia** the anime market is dominated by **Madman** (www.madman.com.au).

For titles not yet licensed to your region or for the truly devoted fan who wants to round out their collection with special editions and series that will never be carried overseas, the obvious place to shop is **Japan** – which thanks to the internet is just a few keystrokes away. **CDJapan** (www.cdjapan.co.jp) has a massive catalogue, including not just anime DVDs (for which you'll need a DVD player capable of playing region 2 discs) but also manga, CDs, toys and other anime-related merchandise. Additional sources for Asian-release DVDs, books and other merchandise are **Yes Asia** (us.yesasia.com/en/index.aspx) and **Amazon Japan** (www.amazon.co.jp).

Books

A small library can be filled with the ever-growing list of books about anime, manga and other manifestations of Japanese popular culture. Titles range from jaunty "how-to" tutorials on the basics of animation to barely penetrable academic dissertations on the most arcane byways of the medium. California-based **Stone Bridge Press** (www.stonebridge.com) have become something of a specialist publisher in this niche. If it's Japanese culture in general that you wish to read more about, a good starting point is the international website of Japanese publishing powerhouse **Kodansha** (www.kodansha-intl.com).

General

Anime Classics ZETTAI!

100 Must-See Japanese Animation Masterpieces

Brian Camp and Julie Davis (Stone Bridge Press, 2007)

A valiant attempt to whittle down the multitude of titles out there to the bare essentials. The authors' selection for their top hundred titles leans heavily towards sci-fi and the licensed shows and films popular among North American fandom. There are some very curious omissions, but each title included gets a very thorough, easy-to-read review, including interesting notes on its art style, thematic contents, and any adult elements that you might not want your kids exposed to.

The Anime Companion Vols 1–2

Gilles Poitras (Stone Bridge Press, 1999 & 2000)

Poitras pulls off the tricky task of making this glossary/mini-encyclopedia, covering the myriad aspects of Japanese society and culture encountered in anime, not only thorough and accurate but also entertaining. Entries deal with Japanese history, geography, literature, landmarks and modern-day culture, and are enlivened with the author's personal asides. Volume 2 is improved with the addition of Japanese text for each entry.

The Anime Encyclopedia

Jonathan Clements and Helen McCarthy (Stone Bridge Press, 2006)

Written by two of the most seasoned pros in anime journalism, the second edition of this nearly 900-page reference work, with over 3000 entries, is so comprehensive that it should be considered every fan's bible. Unlike the actual Bible, it's very witty, never short of an opinion and refreshingly critical. The authors' attacks on some of anime's sacred cows, multitude of lazy rehashes and downright duds is balanced by their love and enthusiasm for the medium's gems and insight into its history and development, related in a series of scholarly yet highly readable essays peppered throughout the book.

Anime Essentials

Gilles Poitras (Stone Bridge Press, 2001)

Showing its age with reviews of anime that largely predate the DVD explosion of titles, this concise guide nonetheless covers all the relevant ground, serving as a basic introduction to those new to the medium.

Anime Interviews

The First Five Years of Animerica Anime and Manga Monthly (1992–97)

Ed. Trish Ledoux (Viz Media, 1997)

Back in the day when *Animerica* was a proper magazine and not a free little pamphlet (available at Borders and Waldenbooks in the US) that mainly acts as publicity for Viz Media's products, it carried a series of interviews with major figures in the anime universe. The cream of them are collected in this book edited by the magazine's former editor.

Cruising the Anime City

An Otaku Guide to Neo Tokyo

Patrick Macias and Tomohiro Machiyama (Stone Bridge Press, 2004)

In a set-up that could only be replicated in the wackiest of anime, Mexican-American ex-pat otaku commentator Macias and Japanese movie critic and journo Machiyama prove ideal guides to the pop-cultural byways of Japan's capital. Whatever you're after, be it capsule toys (*gachapon*) of *Evachara* or manga rarities, these guys know where to find it.

The Science of Anime

Mecha-Noids and AI-Super-Bots

Lois H. Gresh & Robert Weinberg (Thunder's Mouth Press, 2005)

Having tackled the scientific side of *Star Trek* and superheroes, Gresh and Weinberg take on anime, covering everything from piloted mecha, such as in *Mobile Suit Gundam*, to the artificial intelligence of *Ghost in the Machine* and the question of whether humans are evolving as a species. It's a thought-provoking, easy read that might make you reconsider how close real life is to anime.

Wrong About Japan

Peter Carey (Alfred Knopf, 2004)

If only we all had Booker Prize-winning Australian authors such as Carey as our fathers! He kindly treats his anime-obsessed twelve-year-old son to a trip to Tokyo, and thoughtfully arranges interviews with such luminaries as Yoshiyuki Tomino and Hayao Miyazaki. While little more than an erudite travel feature in book form, Carey's befuddled opinions about anime's cultural impact will strike a chord with many other parents wondering about their offspring's obsession.

Artists and directors

The Astro Boy Essays

Frederik L. Schodt (Stone Bridge Press, 2007)

Schodt frequently interpreted for Osamu Tezuka and counted him as a mentor and friend, so is highly qualified to write this quasi-biography of the artist's most famous creation. In the process, he recounts the compelling and revealing lifestory of the great

Tezuka himself, a highly complex character who both loved and despised his iconic little robot boy.

Hayao Miyazaki
Master of Japanese Animation

Helen McCarthy (Stone Bridge Press, 1999)

Revised in 2002, this is clearly a work of love for McCarthy who goes into great detail on all aspects of each of Miyazaki's directorial efforts from *Castle of Cagliostro* to *Princess Mononoke*. As complete a portrait in English as we're likely to get of this workaholic, genius animator who has done more to shape global perceptions of Japanese animation for the better than practically anyone else.

Mobile Suit Gundam
Awakening, Escalation, Confrontation

Yoshiyuki Tomino (Stone Bridge Press, 2004)

As translated by the prolific Fred L. Schodt, this novelization of the original *Mobile Suit Gundam* series by its creator Tomino explores in more detail the future space federation in the grip of war and the various characters caught up in it.

Stray Dog of Anime
The Films of Mamoru Oshii

Brian Ruh (Palgrave Macmillan, 2004)

American academic Ruh provides a highly readable and thought-provoking account of the influences and circumstances that have shaped the works of one of animes most distinctive and visionary creators.

Japanese cinema and pop culture

The Encyclopedia of Japanese Pop Culture

Mark Schilling (Weatherhill, 1997)

Forget sumo, samurai and ikebana. Godzilla, pop idols, instant ramen and anime stars such as Doraemon are really where Japan's culture's at. Schilling's book is an indispensable, spot-on guide to what fires the Japanese imagination and opens up their wallets.

A Hundred Years of Japanese Films

Donald Richie (Kodansha, 2002)

A potted history of Japanese cinema from one of the foremost authorities on the subject. It includes a short section on the history and development of anime.

The Midnight Eye Guide to New Japanese Film

Tom Mes & Jasper Sharp (Stone Bridge Press, 2007)

A spin-off from the excellent website devoted to Japanese film, this punchily written guide puts anime in context with its live-action brethren and includes profiles of anime's leading talents including Hayao Miyazaki.

Critical analysis

Anime Explosion

Patrick Drazen (Stone Bridge Press, 2003)

If you suspect there's more to some of the anime you watch than can be taken at face value this highly accessible study confirms it. Anime is interpreted from a number of fascinating perspectives including the supernatural, war, religion and sexual politics. Thirteen chapters take on key films and directors in more detail.

Anime From Akira to Howl's Moving Castle

Susan J. Napier (Palgrave Macmillan, 2005)

Although it's peppered with academic jargon, Napier's thoughtful and deeply researched work remains a good introduction to anime that fans will find accessible. It includes chapters on some of the key works of Studio Ghibli.

Cinema Anime

Ed. Steven T. Brown (Palgrave Macmillan, 2006)

Eight scholarly essays by leading academics in the field including Susan Napier on Satoshi Kon's anime, Antonia Levi on how anime and manga are becoming Americanized, and Brian Ruh deconstructing *FLCL*.

JapanAmerica

Roland Kelts (Palgrave Macmillan, 2006)

Marvellously readable, personalized account which picks apart the roots of contemporary US fascination with anime and how that is impacting on the industry back in Japan. Kelts, half-Japanese, half-American and living in both countries, makes many intelligent observations while digging up some fascinating tales such as how *Gatchaman* first morphed into *Battle of the Planets*.

Little Boy

Ed. Takashi Murakami (Yale University Press, 2005)

As it's out of print, you'll need to head to your nearest library to search out this gorgeously illustrated accompaniment to the *Little Boy: The Arts of Japan's Exploding Subculture* exhibition put on by the Japan Society in New York in 2005 and curated by Takashi Murakami. Apart from the visuals, the book includes several intelligent essays about Japanese pop culture and the influence of manga and anime on contemporary art in the country.

100 Anime

Philip Brophy (BFI Publishing, 2005)

An eclectic selection of reviews that covers neither the medium's top hundred titles nor a representative cross section. Brophy's pop-cultural analysis veers wildly from sublime insight to meaningless academic babble, fulfilling his self-stated mission to leave the reader "disorientated yet seduced".

Samurai From Outer Space

Understanding Japanese Animation

Antonia Levi (Open Court, 1996)

Sprightly cultural context from a Japanese history professor who's also an anime fan. It tackles topics such as the birth of fandom in the US, and the nature and role of heroes, villains, robots and women in anime – although it's based on information over a decade old now. Footnotes provide useful background on aspects of Japanese culture and history.

Watching Anime, Reading Manga
25 Years of Essays and Reviews

Fred Patten (Stone Bridge Press, 2004)

Few American observers have been immersed in the world of anime and manga for as long as fan-turned-critic Fred Patten. This collection of his writing includes sections on fandom, the business of anime, specific artists and movies. It's a bit repetitious but Patten's easy-going style and boundless enthusiasm make it a pleasurable and enlightening read. His scholarly appraisal of the Simba vs Kimba affair (see p.70) is definitive.

Anime art

If you're into anime for the art, then there's a number of books published that kindly freeze-frame and reproduce images from some of the classic films and series. Apart from titles on many of Miyazaki's films for Studio Ghibli, there are "Art of" books for, among others, *Akira*, *Full Metal Alchemist*, *Inuyasha*, *Naruto* and *Robotech: The Shadow Chronicles*.

Anime Art

Keith Sparrow (Collins Design, 2005)

If you fancy yourself as an animator, then pick up this easy-to-follow book by a prolific storyboard artist and comic book collector. Sparrow shows exactly how to create animations and includes several step-by-step projects that can easily be followed.

Anime Poster Art

Tomokazu Nagai et al. (Cocoro Books, 2003)

Drool over the lovely poster art and graphics in this collection of 160 full-colour reproductions, including images from programmes and flyers. Movies and series featured include *Akira*, *Space Battle Ship Yamato* and many of Studio Ghibli's films.

Manga

Apart from the books about the medium of manga listed below, take a look at the sites of the following publishers for the actual manga that are the basis and inspiration for many anime:

Dark Horse Comics: www.darkhorse.com
Del Rey: www.delreymanga.com
Digital Manga Publishing: www.dmpbooks.com
Kodansha: www.kodanclub.com
Tokyo Pop: www.tokyopop.com
Viz Media: www.viz.com

Dreamland Japan
Writings on Modern Manga

Frederik L. Schodt (Stone Bridge Press, 1996)

The follow-up to *Manga! Manga!* sees the dean of US manga scholars further elucidate the history and development of Japanese comic books through a series of highly readable essays, profiling the top publications and artists, with a chapter on Osamu Tezuka.

Manga! Manga! The World of Japanese Comics

Frederik L. Schodt (Kodansha, 1983)

American manga enthusiast Schodt inspired future generations of fellow US fans when he wrote this first English survey of manga. Still in print and relevant over twenty years later, it's a classic and includes translated samples from Tezuka's *Phoenix*, Matsumoto's *Ghost Warrior*, Ikeda's *Rose of Versailles* and Nakazawa's *Barefoot Gen*.

Manga: Sixty Years of Japanese Comics

Paul Gravett (Laurence King, 2004)

Gorgeously illustrated full-colour work with insightful essays on manga's history and impact by a leading British writer on comic book culture.

Manga: The Complete Guide

Jason Thompson (Del Rey, 2007)

Concise reviews of over nine hundred manga series are supplemented by meatier background features on various genres and artists. For parents anxious about what their kids are reading, the appropriate age rating for each manga helps sort the harmless from the hentai.

Rough Guide to Manga

Jason S. Yadao (Rough Guides, 2008)

A companion guide to this book, with in-depth reviews of fifty essential manga plus a comprehensive history of the medium and its greatest exponents.

Tezuka: The Marvel of Manga

Ed. Philip Brophy (National Gallery of Victoria, 2006)

Produced in conjunction with the exhibition of the same name first held in Melbourne in 2006, this beautiful little book has translated essays by Japanese manga scholars as well as the never dull but sometimes obscure commentary of curator Brophy.

Magazines and journals

In Japan the major anime magazines – *Animage* (www.tokuma.co.jp/animage) and *Newtype* (pc.webnt.jp) – have been around for decades and have a devoted readership. Elsewhere, anime magazines are rarely as long lasting, their purpose as news and publicity vehicles having largely been usurped by more frequently updated websites.

All the magazines listed below are published in the US. In the UK both **Neo** (www.neomag.co.uk) and **SFX Magazine** (www.sfx.co.uk) have features on anime. In Australia there's the relatively new quarterly **Animavericks** (www.animavericks.com) and the free quarterly **Anime Update**, produced by Madman Entertainment, available at DVD stores and inside the company's DVDs. South Africa has the bi-monthly **Otaku** (www.otakumag.

co.za), which covers all aspects of Japanese pop culture; its website offers links to sources of anime across the country.

Anime Insider

www.wizarduniverse.com/magazine/anime

With a price point that's easy on the pocket of fans, this nicely designed monthly US publication has found a niche. Although the content is driven by what American anime companies are releasing, it's strong on features and putting anime in the context of Japanese pop culture, with sections on what's going on in the worlds of manga, music, video games and life in Japan in general.

Mechademia

www.mechademia.org/about

Published by the University of Minnesota Press, this readable and very prettily designed academic journal takes a serious critical look at aspects of the anime and manga universe. Each edition is organized around a particular theme: volume 1 focused on the mediums' "emerging worlds", with features on anime fandom in the US and the superflat art style inspired by manga and anime.

Otaku USA

www.otakuusamagazine.com

The bi-monthly *Otaku USA* aims to capitalize on American youth's obsession for all things connected with pop Japan culture: anime, manga, games, films, toys, j-pop, cosplay, snack foods, whatever. With über-otaku Patrick Macias at the helm, it has in-built street-cred. It has a relatively high price but does come with posters and a DVD of various anime episodes and previews.

Protoculture Addicts

www.protoculture.ca/Proto/index.htm

This Canadian-based magazine celebrated its twentieth anniversary in December 2007, an unparalleled milestone for an anime publication outside of Japan. These days it's owned by the website Anime News Network but retains a distinctive voice through its in-depth features and critical reviews. Many past editions can be downloaded as e-books.

Websites

There are thousands of fan and professionally created anime websites documenting every niche and byway of the medium. Research into them all would run the risk of a person ending up like Lain from *Serial Experiments Lain* (see Canon), trapped in the internet for life. Preceding chapters of this book reference specific websites on individual movies, people and topics. The following cover more general ground.

General info

Akadot.com

www.akadot.com
Online magazine featuring industry news, reviews of the latest titles, in-depth articles about major developments in the anime/manga community, and interviews.

Animated Divots

www.animated-divots.com
Includes a comprehensive chronology of animation from around the world.

Anime.com

www.anime.com
Monthly online magazine site carrying mainly reviews of DVDs, manga, books, and toys – not just about anime but also related Japanese culture and animation from other countries.

Anime Academy

www.animeacademy.com
Cutely designed site that takes the form of a higher-ed school with lectures on various anime topics, a library of reviews, a student lounge with forums and even a campus shop.

Anime News Network

www.animenewsnetwork.com
ANN has established itself as the premier source of up-to-the-moment news and information through its amazingly comprehensive online encyclopedia and spunkily opinionated reviews and columns, among the best of which are Justin Sevakis' *Buried Treasure/Garbage*, spotlighting his personal highs and lows in anime. They also run regular TV podcasts.

Anime on DVD

www.animeondvd.com
There's an incredible amount of detail here on all DVD and Blu-ray format releases (mainly for the North American region) since 1997. The reviews are especially thorough, often having separate consideration of the audio tracks, quality of video transfer, packaging, menu interface and extras.

AnimeResearch.com

www.animeresearch.com
Anime scholar and author Brian Ruh gathers together links to the growing body of academic research into the medium.

Animation World

mag.awn.com
Well-produced and authoritative online magazine that covers all aspects of animation, not just that from Japan. It includes regular anime reviews, reports from the cons and high-level industry background and features.

Anipike.com

www.anipike.com
Contemporary incarnation of Anime Web Turnpike founded back in 1995, thus making it one of the longest running anime websites going. It provides a comprehensive index of links to anime fan sites.

ComiPress

comipress.com
There's plenty of interest for anime fans in this site that reports on manga news and trends

from around the world with a natural focus on Japan and the US markets.

Gilles' Service to Fans Page

www.koyagi.com

When not writing books on anime, Gilles Poitras is a librarian, so it's no surprise that his personal site is a mine of useful links and references.

Glen Johnson's 60s Anime

home.alphalink.com.au/~roglen/index.htm

From *The Amazing Three* to *8th Man*, the major anime series exports of the 1960s are present and correct at this Australian fan's site.

Internet Movie Database

www.imdb.com

First stop for many film fans searching out cast and production details, this comprehensive site also includes information on many anime series, although it's far from infallible.

JAI

www.jai2.com/Welcome.htm

Personal site of manga expert Fred L. Schodt which apart from introducing his own works has some interesting features tucked away, including a long interview with publicity-shy artist Masamune Shirow.

Philip Brophy

www.philipbrophy.com

Buried in the site of Australian pop-cultural artist, writer and musician Brophy are several of his inimitable features on anime, as well as links to his various books and details of the anime/manga-related exhibitions he's curated.

Midnight Eye

www.midnighteyec.com

The best website on Japanese cinema by a mile includes erudite reviews of major anime feature releases as well as older classics, interviews with the major directors (think Hayao Miyazaki and Satoshi Kon) and general features.

Online Bibliography of Anime and Manga Research

corneredangel.com/amwess/

If you're preparing a class paper on anime or want to dig deeper into the vast body of academic research, fan-written works and media articles on the medium, this comprehensive listing of writings on all aspects of anime, manga and fandom is a good starting point.

Otaku News

www.otakunews.com

Good UK-based fan site, that also has a US edition and includes interesting features and news snippets on Japanese pop culture in general.

rec.arts.anime.misc

groups.google.com/group/rec.arts.anime.misc/topics

Follow discussion threads by fans on all aspects of anime. Click through to links for rec.arts groups specifically for animation and manga fans.

Tezuka in English

tezukainenglish.com

The official Tezuka Productions site (en.tezuka.co.jp/home.html) is a mine of information on the great artist and his works, but navigation is tricky to say the least. Harvard history grad Ada Palmer provides an easy route in via her meticulously researched and beautifully presented site. There's so much to admire here, including in-depth essays on Takarazuka and Rock Holmes, the most versatile star in Tezuka's repertory of characters, and links to Tezuka-related topics elsewhere on the web.

Blogs and podcasts

Anime News Network (see above) also offer regular podcasts of its TV shows.

Anime Today

www.rightstuf.com/rssite/animeToday

Well-produced podcast magazine shows, including interviews, reviews and features on the anime and manga world, are broadcast roughly every couple of weeks on this segment of the Right Stuf website.

Anime TV

www.goanimetv.com

Video podcast review show, presented in an MTV style, on anime releases both on DVD and televised on network and cable.

Anime World Order Podcast

animeworldorder.blogspot.com

Lively, opinionated and pretty informed chat, rants and reviews from motormouth Daryl Surat and chums.

Anipages Daily

www.pelleas.net/aniTOP

Benjamin Ettinger's goldmine of a site showcases his incredible level of knowledge and erudition on anime, going further and deeper than practically anyone else out there. Check it out for reviews of all the Tōei features, profiles of key animators and raves about many quality anime from other parts of the world, too.

Conversations on Ghibli

www.ghiblicon.blogspot.com

Minneapolis-based artist Daniel Thomas MacInnes's blog isn't just about Ghibli but musings on anime in general. It includes intelligent reviews of both Ghibli and non-Ghibli films and series.

An Eternal Thought in the Mind of Godzilla

www.patrickmacias.blogs.com

Dispatches from the bleeding edge of all that is cool/crazy/nerdy and plain bizarre about Japan from the self-styled otaku's otaku Macias, author of august tomes including *Japanese Schoolgirl Inferno: Tokyo Teen Fashion Subculture Handbook* and *Cruising the Anime City*.

Frames Per Second

www.fpsmagazine.com/blog/labels/anime.php

The anime blog at online animation magazine *Frames Per Second* is worth checking out for titbits of info and views from a range of contributors. The mag itself also has worthwhile interviews, reviews and other features.

Memorabilia and more

Watching and reading about anime sometimes just isn't enough. Producers have long understood this urge to dive into a fantasy world and helpfully – both for fans and corporate profits – have secured merchandising deals that launched a gazillion robot and spaceship toys or computer games based on anime. For those who aspire to live the full anime lifestyle, from wearing T-shirts emblazoned with Astro Boy to decorating their homes with posters, plushies and character-printed pillows, there's an Everest-sized mountain of merchandise out there to conquer.

As ever, the internet acts as an enabler. A starting point for serious toy collectors would be a resource such as **Chogokin.net** (www.chogokin.net), providing links to many other specialist sites such as Collection DX (www.collectiondx.com), which runs news, reviews and podcasts on the world of Japanese toys and games and anime.

For all the hottest merchandise direct from **Japan,** try Hobby Link Japan (www.hlj.com) and J-List Japan (www.jlist.com), which stocks everything from miniature Tokyo Towers and sweet snack foods to more – ahem – personal items such as a Hello Kitty vibrator and hardcore *yaoi* anime and manga.

In the US, apart from the aforementioned sites of various anime distributors such as The Right Stuf, there are Action HQ.com (www.actionhq.com) and Image Anime (www.imageanime.com), the site of a popular New York-based store.

UK sites of interest include Mecha Production Facility (www.mech-a.com); Tokyo Toys (www.tokyotoys.com) and Forbidden Planet (forbiddenplanet.com/fp), which has eight stores across the country. A useful starting point for information on where to buy anime merchandise in Australia is the Australian Anime Shopping Guide (members.iimetro.com.au/~mwhitley/cas.htm), although it hasn't been updated since 2006.

Fan conventions

Overseas fans of anime and manga have been gathering for conventions (cons) since the 1970s. In the last decade the number and size of

Cosplay

Short for "costume play", **cosplay** (*ko-su-pu-re* in Japanese) is when fans dress up as their favourite character from anime, manga, video games or Japanese rock (J-rock) bands. Not a uniquely Japanese phenomena – fans of *Star Trek* and *The Rocky Horror Picture Show* have been frocking up at screenings and conventions worldwide for decades – cosplay is a great example of how the interaction of Japanese and US pop cultures has formed something new.

Legend has it that the word was coined by Japanese journalist Nobuyuki Takahashi in 1984 when he wrote a feature about US fans dressing up for a masquerade (costume fashion/skit show) at a sci-fi convention in LA. Since then the term has caught on around the world and it's now inconceivable for an anime convention anywhere not to have a substantial cosplay element to it, both in terms of competitions and masquerade balls, and informally in fans simply gathering to compare costumes. In Tokyo's Harajuku and Akihabara districts on a Sunday afternoon, devoted cosplayers take their shows to the streets.

Anyone can – and does – cosplay, with practically any character or show fair game. As in all dressing up, there are those who indulge in "crossplay", i.e. men dressing as female characters and vice versa, a tradition that honours similar role reversals in anime such as *Princess Knight*, *Rose of Versailles* and *Ranma 1/2*. Although there are shops that cater to cosplayers, many devotees make their own. A good starting point is a book like Gerry Poulos' *Cosplay* (Stone Bridge Press, 2006) or a website such as **Cosplay.com** (www.cosplay.com). For a comprehensive list of links to a wide range of sites related to cosplay and convention masquerades, go to www.nyx.net/%7Ewsantoso/cosplay.html.

For those who want to take their cosplay to the ultimate level there's the **World Cosplay Summit** (www.tv-aichi.co.jp/wcs/e/) held annually since 2003 by the Aichi Broadcasting Company in Nagoya with participants from up to fourteen countries.

these cons has grown in proportion to anime's fan base to the point where the headline event, LA's Anime Expo, attracts in excess of forty thousand fans and is more akin to a giant trade fair. Distributors and studios now frequently use cons as a platform from which to launch new products, make major announcements on future releases and premiere anime.

Cons are a brilliant way to connect with fellow fans and to meet and listen to some of the people involved in the industry, including voice actors, anime directors, producers and character designers, who often show up as con guests. Screenings happen practically nonstop over several days. There are often discussion panels and various competitions, including cosplay events (see p.269) such as a Masquerade where competitors perform skits in costume. There's always a Dealer's Room where vendors offer rare collectables and other merchandise, and an Artist's Alley where fans sell their own home-made anime-themed art.

Apart from the major cons listed below, there are many other smaller cons or events that feature anime as part of their programming. **AnimeCons.com** (www.animecons.com) has pretty comprehensive details of cons around the world with a focus on North America, as does **A Fan's View** (www.fansview.com).

USA and Canada

There's a con practically every week somewhere in North America. The major ten cons, in order of when they happen in the year are:

Sakura Con

www.sakuracon.org
Held in Seattle at the Washington State Convention and Trade Center in March, this con has been running since 1997 and attracts upwards of 15,000 fans over three days.

Anime Boston

www.animeboston.com
This three-day event occurs in April at the Hynes Convention Center in Boston, Massachusetts. Attracts around 11,500 attendees.

Anime Central

www.acen.org
Mid-May in Rosemont, Illinois. Around 12,800 attendees.

Anime North

www.animenorth.com
Mid-May in Toronto, Canada. Around 13,500 attendees.

FanimeCon

www.fanime.com
This one's held on Memorial Day weekend in May at San José McEnery Convention Center, San José, California.

A-Kon

www.a-kon.com
Held at end of May/beginning of June, this three-day event takes place in Dallas, Texas. Around 14,500 attendees.

Anime Expo

www.anime-expo.org

The big one, attracting in excess of forty thousand fans. Held at the Los Angeles Convention Center for four days over the 4th of July holiday weekend.

Otakon

www.otakon.com/default2.asp

A three-day event in Baltimore, at the Baltimore Convention Centre, every August. Close on twenty-three thousand attendees – thus the biggest East Coast con.

Anime Weekend Atlanta

www.awa-con.com

Around ten thousand fans head to this con held in Atlanta in mid-September.

New York Anime Festival

www.newyorkanimefestival.com

Making a splash with its debut in 2007 was this new con in the Big Apple at the Jacob Javits Center in Manhattan. Over fifteen thousand fans attended. In 2008 it was held in September and might also be in the future.

Do call me otaku

The stereotypical image of an otaku in Japan is of a person who is highly knowledgeable about their chosen field, be it a particular manga character, computer game, anime or toy, but also somewhat socially inept, i.e. a nerd. Mostly harmless, otaku were tarnished by the brutal child murders perpetrated in 1988 by Miyazaki Tsutomu, a young printer whose criminal behaviour had been fed by his vast collection of porn manga and videos.

Prior to this in the minds of most Japanese otaku was a word meaning "you" or "your home" and used as a polite but distant form of address. This formality had been taken up among hard-core anime and manga fans several years earlier when they met each other at conventions, then latched onto in the media by commentators writing about fandom.

Fast-forward two decades, and in Japan the term retains its nerdy credentials but has largely shed its pervy connotations and been supplanted by the term *moe* (see box p.223). "Ota-King" Toshio Okada, scriptwriter of the series *Gunbuster* (see Canon) has even taught a class in "otaku-ology" at the prestigious University of Tokyo. Even so you should still be cautious in referring to a Japanese fan directly as an otaku.

Meanwhile overseas anime and manga fans have enthusiastically taken to using otaku in a friendly, positive way to describe themselves and their friends. It's even adopted into the name of several magazines and websites devoted to anime and fandom.

International festivals

The cream of the year's anime often surfaces at the **Annecy International Animated Film Festival** (www.annecy.org), the granddaddy of animation jamborees held annually in the French town of Annecy. Other professional events held in high esteem at which you're likely to find subtitled screenings of anime include the **International Animation Festival Hiroshima** (www.urban.ne.jp/home/hiroanim) held in even-numbered years, the annual **Ottawa International Animation Festival** (ottawa.awn.com) and Zagreb's annual **World Festival of Animated Films** (www.animafest.hr).

For a full list of other animation festivals around the world, go to the website of the **Association Internationale du Film d'Animation** (asifa.net), the premier animation association founded in 1960 by such luminary animators as Norman McLaren and Lev Atamanov. The ASIFA organize the Annecy festival and also support **International Animation Day** on 28 October, celebrating the day in 1892 when Emile Reynaud first gave a public performance of animation in Paris.

The UK and Europe

Among fan-run cons in the UK, **Amecon** (www.amecon.org), held in mid-August on the campus of the University of Leicester, is the major event, with an attendance limit of around 1300. **Minami Con** (www.minamicon.org.uk) is the UK's longest running event, having being held since 1995. However its location at the Novotel Hotel in Southampton limits attendance to around three hundred people, making it one of the more intimate (and quickly sold-out) events of its kind.

The **London Movie Comic Media (MCM) Expo** (www.londonexpo.com) held in May and October is a professionally run event that has had an increasing focus on anime. The organizers also run a spin-off event, **Midlands MCM Expo**, at the Telford International Centre in September.

The biggest European convention, pulling in eighty-five thousand visitors over four days, is **Lucca Comics and Games** (www.luccacomicsandgames.com) held in Lucca, Italy, in early November. Its focus is comics, hence manga is included, but there are also anime screenings. Hot on its heels are **Japan Expo** (www.japan-expo.com) in Paris in July and **Salon del Manga de Barcelona** (www.salondelmangadebarcelona.com) in November.

Australia and New Zealand

The Melbourne Anime Festival or **Manifest** (www.manifest.org.au), held for three days in September, is Australia's major fan-run con. The **Armageddon Expo** (www.armageddonexpo.com) is a professionally organized science-fiction and fantasy media convention held in Sydney and Melbourne, Australia, and Auckland, Christchurch and Wellington in New Zealand. Similar is **Supernova** (www.supanova.com.au) held in Sydney, Melbourne, Brisbane and Perth.

© Simon Richmond

Just some of the fun to be had at the Tokyo International Anime Fair

Anime tourism in Japan

The world's largest anime expo, clocking up over one hundred thousand visitors during its four-day run at Tokyo Big Site, is the **Tokyo International Anime Fair** (www.tokyoanime.jp/ja/index.php). The latest anime works and character designs are unveiled here, awards presented to the best anime series and films of the past year, and past pioneers and innovators of the medium honoured. One of the most interesting sections is the **Creator's World**, showcasing a handful of up-and-coming animators – this is where you'll see interesting, cutting-edge animation unbludgeoned by commercialization.

The fair is huge fun and visually exhausting. If you come expecting all the hoopla of a regular anime con, though, you'll be disappointed: cosplay by attendees is banned,

Organized tours

Independent travel in Japan is easy but, if you don't speak the language, it can be daunting. Buying into an organized tour can make some sense, especially if you want to access some of the anime highlights outlined here without any hassles. The following companies all offer tours that zone in on Japanese popular culture:

Pop Japan Travel (www.popjapantravel.com) – they've run tours since 2003 with themes such as Neo-Tokyo, Comiket, samurai, gothic lolita or *yaoi*/boys' love.

Destination Japan by HIS (www.destination-tours.com) – one of Japan's biggest travel agencies offers the Tokyo Anime Freedom tour which includes admission to the Tokyo International Anime Fair.

Intermixi (www.intermixi.com) – a founder of Pop Japan Travel has branched off to create his own company, offering tours in Tokyo, Ōsaka and Kyoto that include visits to Akihabara, a manga drawing class at a Manga University and samurai sword fighting experience.

Japan Journeys (www.japanjourneys.co.uk) – this UK-based company's manga tour includes entry to the Ghibli Museum, visits to Akihabara and Nakano Broadway and a trip to an anime studio.

although many of the booths at the show are manned by staff in character costumes. While the fair's first two days, are strictly for business, it's open to the general public for the final two days, when the atmosphere turns more convention-like with plenty of giveaways and screenings of upcoming shows.

Also, see p.184 for details about **Comiket**, the massive twice-yearly dōjinshi manga convention also held at Tokyo Big Site.

Just as a trip to Disneyland is a rite of passage for lovers of Disney's animation, any self-respecting anime fan will crave a visit to Japan. As the cradle and eternal inspiration for all things anime, such a pilgrimage (for that's what it will feel like to many fans) offers the chance not only to visit the real locations that those in favourite shows are based on, but also to fully enter into anime, i.e. Japanese life – eating the food, travelling on the trains and buying all the latest fashions and technological gizmos. Below are listed the places you wouldn't want to miss, starting with Tokyo, anime's ground central. For in-depth information on travel to and around Japan read *The Rough Guide to Japan* and *The Rough Guide to Tokyo*.

Central Tokyo

First stop after touchdown at Narita airport for most fans will be the central Tokyo district of **Akihabara**. Known as Akiba to locals, Akihabara established its reputation during the boom years of Japan's economy as the capital's prime shopping area for electrical and electronic goods, everything from computers to "washlets" – electronically controlled combination toilets and bidets. Naturally it also attracted many computer-obsessed otaku and so has morphed in recent years into Tokyo's anime and manga showcase, with shops selling all kinds of merchandise associated with both mediums.

The Akiba district caters to an otaku's every need

For an English map of many places of interest in Akiba go to the Akihabara Channel (www.akiba-ch.com/?p=416). Head first to the **Tokyo Anime Center** (open daily 11am-7pm; see www.animecenter.jp) on the fourth floor of the UDX Building. Apart from a shop selling memorabilia and souvenirs, it also has life-size *figua* of famous anime characters, information and screenings of the latest anime, a recording studio where you can watch voice actors take part in radio shows and the Akiba 3D Theater which hosts special previews.

While you're hanging out in Akiba check out the phenomena known as **maid cafés** which tap into the cosplay scene (see box above) with young women dressed in Victorian and French maid-type costumes. Friendly places used to *gaijin* (foreign) visitors include Mai:lish (second floor, FH Kowa Square, 3-6-2 Soto-Kanda, Chiyoda-ku; daily 11am–10pm; www.mailish.jp) and @home café (Mitsuwa Bldg, 1-11-4 Soto-Kanda, Chiyoda-ku; daily

© Simon Richmond

The Tokyo Anime Centre, Akihabara: packed with absolutely everything anime

11.30am–10pm, closed third Tues of the month; www.cafe-athome.com) , which also includes a wacky *sabo* (traditional teahouse) where the maids accessorize their kimono with fluffy rabbit ears and other contemporary accoutrements.

Tokyo locations are used in anime all the time, the most iconic being **Tokyo Tower** (daily 9am–10pm; main observatory ¥820, top observatory ¥1420; www.tokyo-tower.co.jp). This 333-metre red-and-white communications tower, a copy of the Eiffel Tower and opened in 1958, has an observation deck at 250metres and more negligible attractions (most incurring additional fees) at its base.

A very familiar sight to most anime fans will be the crossing in front of **Shibuya station**, surrounded by neon-festooned towers and always thronged by milling crowds. Shibuya and the nearby district of Harajuku are the epicentre of Tokyo teen culture and should be high on your list of places to visit. **Shinjuku**, with its gaggle of giant skyscrapers dominated by the massive edifice of the Tokyo Metropolitan Government Building, is another area that's frequently been featured in anime, including *X: The Movie* and *Demon City Shinjuku*.

Western Tokyo

Strung out along the Chūō railway line from Shinjuku station are a series of suburbs long associated with the anime industry. Here you'll find the headquarters of major studios such as Sunrise and Studio Ghibli. First stop should be Nakano, for the premier anime and manga memorabilia store **Mandarake** (5-52-15 Nakano, Nakano-ku, www.mandarake.co.jp), with sections on three levels of the Nakano Broadway shopping mall. It sells everything from anime cels and original drawings to trading cards and cosplay outfits. There are other branches around Tokyo (in Shibuya and Ikebukuro) but this is the main one.

Further west along the Chūō line, a short bus ride from Ogikubo station, is the **Suginami Animation Museum** (Tues–Sun 10am–5.30pm; free; www.sam.or.jp), reached by a five-minute bus journey from either platform 0 or 1 outside Ogikubo station. Colourful displays trace anime's history, from the simple black-and-white 1917 feature *Genkanban-no-maki* (*The Gatekeepers*) to the digital technology used in recent features such as *Blood: The Last Vampire*. Videos with English subtitles explain how anime are made, while interactive computer games allow you to create your own animations. You can watch anime screenings in the small theatre, and there's also a library packed with manga and DVDs

A watchful Doraemon welcomes you to the Suginami Animation Museum

A Rough Guide to anime slang

Ada Palmer is a Harvard research graduate and author of the Tezuka in English website. As a frequent attendee at anime conventions, she provides a helpful guide to some of the specialized slang you may hear:

Fanart/fanfic are fan-created art or stories which borrow characters from published fiction. They're common in the anime world and other fandoms. **Slash** is a popular genre of fanart and fanfic which depicts sexual relationships, usually between same-sex couples who do not have such relationships in the original story. Of the thousands of *dōjinshi* fan comics produced every year, the majority are slash.

A **fanboy** or **fangirl** is an obsessive fan, usually of something specific, such as a particular genre, series, character, seiyū, author or director. Miyazaki fanboy or Gundam fangirl are typical examples, but *dōjinshi* authors, fan artists, columnists, even panellists and con staff can have "fangirls."

Fanboy/fangirl Japanese refers to the odd, usually useless selection of Japanese words and phrases which fans pick up from watching anime. Among the first words learned are often *hai* (yes), *kawaii* (cute), *sugoi* (awesome), *bakka* (idiot), and *shine!* (pronounced shi-ne and meaning *die!*). Many fans enjoy throwing such words into conversation, especially at cons.

Anime characters often speak in strange ways which would never be used on the street, so the phrases fans learn usually bear minimal relation to real Japanese, even though after years of watching one can acquire an extensive, if useless, vocabulary. For

(some with English subtitles).

Located at the southwest corner of leafy Inokashira Park in the western Tokyo suburb of Mitaka, is the captivating **Ghibli Museum, Mitaka** (daily except Tues 10am–6pm; ¥1000, reductions for children; www.ghibli-museum.jp/en), a must-see location for all Studio Ghibli fans. This inventively designed facility, with a giant cuddly cat bus and the huge robot from *Castle in the Sky* on its roof, not only brings to life the wonderful art of Ghibli's films but also illuminates the animator's craft in general. A child-sized movie theatre here screens original short animated features that you won't see anywhere else.

In order to keep the museum free of crowds, only 2400 tickets are example, I learned seven ways to say "That man is a vampire!" before I learned how to ask "Where is the bathroom?"

Sometimes Japanese words are modified to become fan slang, such as the term **bishie**, short for *bishōnen* (pretty boy), referring to the highly feminized males common in anime. Bishie is used by English-speaking fans either as a noun ("Look at the hot bishie!") or an adjective ("Shigure is so bishie!").

Engrish or **Japlish** refers to the gibberish English which frequently appears on Japanese products or in Japanese song lyrics. Japanese pop culture has a fascination with foreign words from many languages, and if you listen to enough anime themes you will hear phrases in "Spanglish," "Itarian," "Flench," even "Ratin".

Fan slang is not all fun and solidarity. There are also negative terms such as **Narutard**, a mocking name for a Naruto fan, or **dub-dressed**, an elitist term which insults cosplayers who buy pre-made costumes instead of making them at home, associating them with fans who only watch dubbed anime, looked down on by some who consider subtitles the only "pure" way to watch. Some fans even insist on watching anime **raw**, that is in Japanese with no subtitles whether they understand the language or not.

Glomping refers to the peculiar phenomenon of fans who wander through conventions trying to **glomp** (hug) people cosplaying their favourite characters, or stand around inviting hugs with signs reading "Glomp me!" This phenomenon makes some fans uncomfortable and many cons discourage it, but the fad shows no signs of going away.

available daily; all must be purchased in advance and are for a specified time. The museum's website lists details in English of how to apply for tickets overseas. Given the massive popularity of Ghibli's movies, the museum can be booked out for weeks at a time, particularly during school holidays and over weekends.

Northern Tokyo

The contrast between the imaginative Ghibli Museum and the dowdy **Tōei Animation Gallery** (2-10-5 Higashi-Oizumi, Nerima-ku; Tues–Sun 9.30am–5pm; free; www.toei-anim.co.jp/tag), displaying mainly posters and images from some of anime's most historic films and series couldn't be more acute. Nevertheless,

© Simon Richmond

anime fans should consider making the trip out to the northern Tokyo suburb where the major animation studio is based.

Nothing more than a handful of rooms scattered around the ground floor of Tōei's ageing production facilities, linked by corridors lined with framed scenes from practically all of the studio's past productions, the gallery provides a thorough overview of the company's creative history, albeit one that largely ceases in 2003, the date the gallery was opened. There's always a special exhibition devoted to one of Tōei's anime, as well as a fine art section and a room where you can inspect a couple of antique rostrum cameras used to make anime before computerization became the norm. There's a tiny shop selling character goods and all visitors get to pick a strip of anime film to take as a free souvenir.

The gallery is reached on the Seibu-Ikebukuro line out of Ikebukuro station to Oizumi-Gakuen station, from where the gallery is a ten-minute walk. It's easy to combine a trip to the gallery with a visit to **Animate** (3-2-1, Higashi-Ikebukuro, www.animate.co.jp), the flagship store of Japan's leading purveyor of anime, games and manga. The store is located a short walk east of Ikebukuro station, near the towering Sunshine 60 building.

The Bandai museum

Only die-hard *Gundam* fans or toy otaku will want to drag out to the Bandai Museum (Sat, Sun and public holidays 10am–4.30pm; ¥400; www.bandai-museum.jp).

Bandai (www.bandai.co.jp), established in 1950, is one of Japan's leading toy manufacturers. In the 1960s it produced *Astro Boy* tie-in toys, in the 1970s models of Mazinger-Z and in the 1980s it really hit pay dirt with its Gundam plastic model kits. A little bit of this history is related at the museum, which primarily houses an impressive collection of toys.

The head, torso and one arm of a huge Gundam stands in the foyer. The museum is a ten-minute walk from Omochano-machi station on the Tobu Utsunomiya line, or a fifteen-minute cab ride from Ishibashi Station on the JR Utsunomiya station. The fastest journey time from central Tokyo is one and a half hours.

For most fans, posing for photos with the models of Bandai character goods, including Doraemon, outside of the company's Tokyo HQ (1-4-8 Komagata, Taito-ku) near Asakusa will be sufficient a thrill.

Ishinomaki

The northern Honshū port of Ishinomaki is home to the **Ishinomaki Mangattan Museum** (Wed–Mon 9am–6pm; ¥800; www.man-bow.com/manga) dedicated to the works of manga artist Shōtarō Ishinomori (see p.193), creator of *Cyborg 009* and the live-action *tokusatsu* series *Kamen Rider* (*Masked Rider*). Inside the UFO-like building are exhibitions on Ishinomori's work and that of other manga and anime artists. The one-kilometre route from the town's train station to the museum is lined with statues of Ishinomori's famous characters, and on weekends and national holidays the Mangattan Liner train, decorated with manga characters, inside and out, runs between here and the nearby city of Sendai, on the main Shinkansen (high-speed train) line from Tokyo.

Nagoya

For the Nagoya EXPO in 2005 a life-size replica of **Satsuki and Mei's House** (Tues–Sun 9.30am–4.30pm; ¥500) from *My Neigbour Totoro* was constructed in the EXPO 2005 Aichi Commemorative Park west of the city centre.

© Simon Richmond

No trip to Kyoto is complete without a visit to the International Manga Museum

You're unlikely to encounter the soot sprites or Totoro here but this charming structure, a meticulous re-creation of a traditional 1950s rural home, is authentic down to the Wellington boots and umbrellas in the *genkan* (entrance hall) and the clothes hanging in the closets – all of which you're allowed to peer into.

A maximum of fifty people a time over seven sessions a day (fourteen at weekends) are allowed into the house. Like the Ghibli Museum, Mitaka, it's so popular that visitors are advised to make a postal application two months in advance – you may luck out and be able to visit on the day, but it's a long way to go on the off chance. There's an application form (in Japanese only) that you can download from www.pref.aichi.jp/koen/AI_CHIKYU/ouboyouryou0501.pdf. Otherwise, write a letter stating: your name, address and country of residence; the desired date and whether you'd prefer a morning or afternoon visit; the number of people in your group (up to a maximum of six people per application); and whether anyone in your party will be in a wheelchair.

Kyoto

Japan's ancient capital is usually associated with traditional aspects of its culture such as temples and shrines, beautiful gardens, tea ceremonies and geisha. But recently Kyoto has gained a few places to engage those interested in contemporary anime culture, too. The excellent **Kyoto International Manga Museum** (daily except Wed 10am–7.30pm; ¥500; www.kyotomm.com), a joint project between the city and Kyoto Seika University, is based in the handsomely restored building of a former primary school. As well as having one of Japan's best-stocked libraries of manga, the museum hosts various exhibitions and talks.

© Simon Richmond

When you alight at Kyoto's train station, be sure to check out Tezuka Osamu World

Within Kyoto's futuristic train station complex you'll find **Tezuka Osamu World** (daily 10am–5pm; ¥600). The small cinema here screens original anime, including ones starring Astro Boy and Black Jack, that you won't see anywhere else. It also has a shop selling a wide range of Tezuka character merchandise.

Takarazuka

In the town that Tezuka grew up in is the **Tezuka Osamu Manga Museum** (daily except Wed 9.30am–5pm; ¥500; en.tezuka.co.jp). This colourful and well-designed memorial to the artist displays art from his books, comics and animated films, charts his career,

© Simon Richmond

The Manga Museum dedicated to Osamu Tezuka is a fascinating testament to his life and work

screens cartoons and gives you the chance to become an animator in the basement workshop (40-min session; 10am–4pm). There's always a special exhibition on some aspect of Tezuka's manga on display and you can view many clips and even full features of his anime.

While in town you might also want to see what's playing at the famous **Takarazuka Grand Theatre**, home to the all-female musical drama troupe the Takarazuka Revue (see p.249). Several of Takarazuka's most famous shows have both inspired and been inspired by manga.

Glossary

Note: Japanese does not have plurals, so words are either singular or collective. The noun anime can therefore either refer to an anime or to anime in general – and mangaka can refer to either one or several manga artists.

akabon literally meaning "red book", this was a type of cheaply produced comic book in the post-World War II period. The name comes from the books' typically red covers. Osamu Tezuka's earliest works, including *Shin Takajima* ("New Treasure Island"), were published in akabon format.

AMV anime music video: a fan-produced video clip set to music, using images from one, or a variety of, anime.

Animage the first Japanese magazine devoted to anime, published since 1978.

animanga a manga/graphic novel created using cels from an anime laid out and printed with speech bubbles. Unlike regular manga, all the pages are coloured.

anime in Japan, this term covers all types of animation, whether produced locally or overseas. Outside of Japan it refers exclusively to animation made in Japan.

bishōjo a beautiful girl character.

bishōnen a beautiful boy character.

BitTorrent an online protocol enabling users to connect to each other directly in order to send and receive digital files.

CB child body: a pun on the Japanese word *chibi* ("little"), referring to childlike or squashed-down characters. See also **super deformed**.

cel a translucent sheet of celluloid (nitrocellulose) on which the moving parts of an animated scene are painted.

CGI computer-generated images, sometimes shortened to CG.

chara short for character.

Comiket twice-yearly convention, mainly for dōjinshi works, held in Tokyo.

compositing combining the backgrounds and moving parts of an anime to be filmed for the final image.

con short for convention.

cosplay short for costume play – fans dressing up to look like their favourite characters.

dōga Japanese for "moving pictures". Often used in an anime studio's title, as in Tōei Dōga or Nippon Dōga.

dōjinshi self-published manga by fans. Can be either original or works using fans' favourite characters. See also **ero-dōjinshi**.

dōjinshika a dōjinshi artist.

dōjinshi circle a group of artists creating a dōjinshi; can also be a single artist.

DRM stands for **digital rights management** and refers to access control mechanisms used by publishers and copyright holders to limit usage of digital media, such as downloads of anime.

dub/dubbing recording of the voices for an anime; usually refers to the replacement of the original Japanese soundtrack voices with those of actors speaking in another language.

dubtitling the use of a dubbing script as the source for subtitling.

e-conté anime storyboards. Formed by amalgamating the Japanese word for picture ("e") with the word conté, a shortening of the English word continuity.

Edo pre-1868 name for Tokyo. The Edo period refers to the time before Edo became Tokyo.

eiga Japanese for movies. See also **manga eiga**.

ero-dōjinshi self-published manga by fans with an erotic theme.

etchi another word for pornographic videos; short for **hentai**.

fan service when animators dwell on, or insert, a particular scene or image tokenistically to please certain fans. This usually involves female characters appearing in provocative poses or nude, but can also be of particularly cool mecha designs.

fansub video/DVD subtitled by fans.

fifteening the insertion of more "adult" material, such as the use of swearing in the English dub, to help an anime receive a more credible rating among certain fans – receiving, for example, the 15-plus category of film classification in the UK.

figua a plastic model of an anime or manga character.

filler anime episodes not based on the original manga source, usually created to allow time for the manga to catch up with the on-screen action, or to fully develop a new story arc.

furigana the transliteration of kanji into phonetic hiragana and katakana in manga. Often seen in manga aimed at children who may not be able to read all the kanji yet. See also **hiragana**, **kanji** and **katakana**.

gachapon small toy models, often of anime characters, encased in plastic capsules and sold from vending machines. The name refers to the sounds of the machine's handle being cranked (*gacha*) and the capsule dropping (*pon*).

gaijin Japanese for "foreigner".

Garo avant garde manga magazine that began in the 1960s.

geisha traditional female entertainer accomplished in the performing arts.

gekiga "dramatic pictures"; refers to manga aimed at adults and is usually drawn in a more realistic style. The term dates from the 1960s and is rarely used today.

gothic lolita often shortened to goth loli, this is a street fashion style that has infused the look of a sub-genre of anime, one that usually has a horror theme.

hanami Japanese for "cherry blossom". In spring there are parties beneath cherry trees to admire the fleeting beauty of the flowers. Flurries of falling cherry blossom petals are often used as a decorative and symbolic device in anime.

hentai erotic and pornographic anime (the literal meaning is "perverse"). Sometimes contracted to the letter "H", pronounced *etchi* in Japanese.

hiragana one of the two phonetic scripts of Japanese. See also **katakana**.

in-betweening the process of generating intermediate frames between two images to give the appearance that the first image evolves smoothly into the second image.

Japanimation a term, generally out of favour, for animation from Japan, coined by US fans in the 1970s.

Japlish a mixture of English and Japanese, often grammatically incorrect or wrongly spelled. Also sometimes known as Engrish.

josei Japanese for "young woman" and hence a category of anime/manga aimed at women.

kami Shinto deities residing in both animate and inanimate objects, including animals, trees, rocks and rivers, as well as in natural forces such as the wind.

kanji ideograms used as the basis of written Japanese, originally derived from Chinese characters. See also **hiragana** and **katakana**.

kantoku Japanese word for director.

katakana one of the two phonetic scripts of Japanese. Used mainly for writing names and foreign words in Japanese. See also **hiragana** and **kanji**.

kawaii Japanese for cute, pronounced *kawai-ee*. An example of a kawaii anime character would be Hello Kitty.

keitai anime/manga anime or manga distributed via mobile phone (keitai).

kibyōshi "yellow covers"; illustrated picture books produced from woodblock prints around the 18th and early 19th centuries. They often had satirical or political themes.

kodomo children and, by extension, anime for children.

lolicon stands for Lolita complex; pornography or erotic material that has underage girls as its focus.

magical girl a genre of anime/manga, in which the lead character is a girl with magical powers.

mahō shōjo Japanese for magical girl.

manga Japanese for cartoon images. Covers single drawn images, as well as strips or stories published in a newspaper, magazine or book.

manga eiga animated films.

mangaka a manga artist or artists.

matsuri Japanese festival. It may have a religious basis or could be a fair at a school.

mecha referring to machines and mechanical items in general, but more popularly used to describe robot and spacecraft-themed science fiction anime.

moe a type of character, usually young and female, that appeals to, and is fetishized by mainly male fans but (supposedly) not in a sexual way (see also **lolicon**). Can also mean an obsession with any particular given style of anime, topic or hobby, in much the same way as **otaku**.

Newtype A Japanese animation magazine. The name derives from the concept of the next stage of human evolution in the *Mobile Suit Gundam* series.

NHK stands for Nippon Hōsō Kyōka; Japan's public broadcasting corporation.

ninja a warrior who studies and practices the ancient Japanese fighting arts of ninjitsu.

OAV/OVA original anime video/original video anime: an anime film or series not screened previously on TV or in cinema but released straight to video/DVD.

OEL manga original English language manga, meaning a non-Japanese comic book or strip drawn to imitate the typical style of Japanese manga.

ONA original net animation; an anime that premieres on the Internet.

OP/ED stands for opening theme/ending theme, the musical introduction and closing sequences for anime.

otaku means a geek or nerd who is usually, but not always, an obsessive fan of anime and manga. Outside of Japan it has shed its negative connotations to be embraced by the fan community as a general term for anyone who is into anime and/or manga.

P2P stands for peer-to-peer and refers to a computer network made up of ad-hoc participants for the purpose of sharing data files.

ponchi-e an early form of manga from the late 19th century, named after British magazine *Punch*, which carried cartoons.

Pro short for Productions, as in Mushi Pro or Tezuka Pro.

rōmaji system of transliterating Japanese words using the Latin alphabet.

rōnin a masterless samurai (see below). Can also refer to a student retaking college entrance exams, like the character of Godai in *Maison Ikkoku.*

RPG role-playing game.

salaryman the suited office worker who keeps Japan's companies and bureaucracies ticking over. The father in *My Neighbours the Yamadas* is a typically comic salaryman character.

samurai a Japanese warrior of old Japan (prior to 1868, the start of the Meiji Era). Retainers to *daimyo* (feudal lords). See also rōnin.

seinen Japanese for "young man". A type of anime/manga aimed at young men, usually of college age, the themes of which are more mature than for **shōnen** works.

seiyū Japanese voice actor.

sensei teacher or respected elder.

Shinto Japan's indigenous religion.

shōjo Japanese for "girl". A type of anime/manga aimed at girls.

shōnen Japanese for "boy". A type of anime/manga aimed at boys.

shōnen-ai Japanese for "boy's love", it's another term for homosexual romance anime/manga. See also **yaoi**.

shotacon anime that is fixated (usually sexually) upon young boys. A contraction of "Shotarō complex", after the character of Shotarō Kaneda in *Tetsugin 28-go* (*Gigantor*).

shunga erotically themed woodblock prints. See also **ukiyo-e**.

Steampunk a style of anime/manga featuring fantastic steam-driven technology in an anachronistic setting. Examples include *Castle in the Sky* and *Steamboy*.

super deformed (SD) the squashed down, comically deformed variants of characters in an anime. Normally used in comedy or parody sequences.

superflat modern style of art, influenced and inspired by manga/anime images.

Takarazuka an all-female theatre troupe from the town of the same name near Ōsaka, which was also the hometown of Osamu Tezuka. The cross-dressing of the performers inspired similar characters in the work of Tezuka and other manga/anime artists.

tankōbon a book made up of the manga strips of a single story originally published over many editions of a magazine comic book – like a graphic novel. Manga tankōbon often come in several volumes depending on the length of the story.

toba-e humorous caricature sketches from the 18th century, named after the artist and priest Toba Sōjō.

tokusatsu meaning special effects, it refers to live-action TV series and movies – usually in the sci-fi, fantasy and horror genres – which rely heavily on such effects, for example the movie *Godzilla*. Some tokusatsu productions use animation as part of their effects.

tweening the process of generating intermediate frames between two images to give the appearance that the first image evolves smoothly into the second image.

ukiyo-e colourful woodblock prints; highly popular in the 18th and 19th centuries.

utsushi-e magic lantern light shows. A form of entertainment in Japan that preceded the movie-projector.

VOD stands for **video on demand**: anime that can be downloaded from the Internet to your computer or TV at will.

yakuza Japan's version of the Mafia; professional criminal gangs.

yaoi homosexual-themed anime. Stands for "yamanashi, ochinashi, iminashi" – "no climax, no punchline, no meaning". See also **shōnen-ai**.

yōkai Japanese mythical monsters and ghosts.

yuri lesbian-themed anime. The word derives from *yurizoku*, meaning "lily tribe", a Japanese term for lesbians.

Index

7-09 do